Waters, John M.

Rescue at sea

	DATE DUE		

Rescue at Sea

Rescue at Sea

John M. Waters, Jr.
Captain, U.S. Coast Guard (Retired)

Second Edition

Naval Institute Press
Annapolis, Maryland

First edition published by D. Van Nostrand Company, Inc., 1966

Copyright © 1989 second edition
by the United States Naval Institute
Annapolis, Maryland

Library of Congress Cataloging-in-Publication Data

Waters, John M.
    Rescue at sea / by John M. Waters, Jr.—Rev. ed.
      p. cm.
    ISBN 0-87021-542-6
    1. United States.   Coast Guard—Search and rescue operations.
  I. Title.
  VK1323.W3   1989
  623.88′87—dc20   89-36979
                                                    CIP

Printed in the United States of America

9 8 7 6 5 4 3 2 1

There is a time-honored saying in
the Coast Guard, *"You have to go
out, but you don't have to come back."*

TO THOSE GALLANT MEN AND WOMEN
who went out when others were in danger,
but did not return,
this book is respectfully dedicated.

Contents

Foreword to the First Edition ix

Foreword to the Second Edition xi

Preface xiii

1 That Others May Live. 1

2 Medico 17

3 Lost and Crippled Sheep 41

4 Needle in a Haystack 71

5 Rescue the Hard Way 111

6 Choppers and Rotorheads 131

7 The Lonely Vigil 167

8 Variety Unlimited 191

9 For Whom the Bell Tolls 209

10 The Chamber of Horrors 237

11 Lawmen of the Seas   259

12 The Drug War   275

13 The Caribbean Connection   289

14 The Changing Picture   313

       Index   317

Foreword to the First Edition

THIS BOOK ON SEARCH AND RESCUE has the authenticity that only a seasoned professional, such as Captain John M. Waters, Jr., USCG, can provide. As a combat officer, ship captain, and rescue aircraft commander, he has taken part in the events described. This firsthand experience, combined with his unusual ability as a writer, has resulted in an outstanding book on maritime rescue. The excitement, the triumphs, the humor, and the not-infrequent heartbreaks of a hazardous profession have been captured and woven into a story of high adventure. It is a story not only of the Coast Guard but of dedicated and selfless men of many services and nationalities ashore, afloat, and aloft, maintaining their ceaseless and often lonely vigil that others may pass in safety on and over the seas.

Captain Waters tells clearly of the workings of the worldwide search-and-rescue organization and how it carries out its mission. But, this is also a story of men and their reactions to stress and danger. The reader lives the story with the men of a cutter battling her way through mountainous seas, with the flight crew of a rescue aircraft on an intercept-and-escort mission, and with the men of a shore station heading out into a stormy night in their small boat.

From large vessels and airliners in distress to a small boatman lost on a weekend outing, the entire spectrum of search and rescue is covered. In giving the reader a lucid and exciting account of rescue as it is practiced in the Coast Guard today, "Muddy" Waters has provided a uniquely human document, reflecting his deep personal involvement in the intense drama of rescue at sea and the pride that he and every Coast Guardsman feels in the service and its mission. This is an operational officer's view as seen from the Rescue Coordination Center, the cockpit, and the bridge. To read this book is to share his experiences.

E. J. ROLAND
Admiral, U.S. Coast Guard
Commandant, 1962–1966

Foreword to the Second Edition

CAPTAIN JOHN "MUDDY" WATERS stands out amongst a handful, at most, of individuals who best combine the two attributes necessary to describe the performance of the world's premier sea-rescue organization, the United States Coast Guard. He has experienced much of what he has written, and he writes in the same fashion he speaks—with sufficient, not overwhelming, background and detail—with the authority of an expert, but the conciseness of a reporter, and with, above all, the sincerity of one who truly has "been there."

Although Coast Guardsmen properly remind anyone within listening range that they are proud members of one of the five armed forces—in fact, the "oldest continuous sea service" of the United States—our peacetime forte has traditionally been assistance to those in peril on the sea. During the past two decades, however, the Coast Guard has been readdressing the same threat that triggered Alexander Hamilton to insist upon its formation nearly two centuries earlier—smuggling.

This time, however, the cargo is not legitimate goods, and the shippers are not simply attempting to evade the payment of import fees. The commodity is marijuana and, increasingly, cocaine, both illegal, so that the only issue normally raised in the courts concerns the legal procedures followed by the Coast Guard boarding parties.

Empowered with unique authority (Coast Guard commissioned and petty officers can require any U.S. registered vessel to "heave to" for boarding and inspection anywhere in U.S. waters or on the high seas), only strict adherence to proven law-enforcement procedures, coupled with the self-discipline of boarding party petty officers and seamen often too young to vote, have kept the complaints of inconvenienced (and honest) boaters to a mere trickle while the annual number of boardings has reached 30,000 plus.

In 1981, the Coast Guard was ordered to stop anyone attempting to illegally enter the U.S. from the high seas. What began as a minor task has become a major mission, with the rate of illegal immigrants being stopped now exceeding 4,000 per year. The vast majority come from Haiti, and they are seeking only a better economic opportunity; while the cold "immigration aspects" will never generate a feeling of satisfaction to the cutter crews, there is no doubt that interdiction of so many grossly overloaded, basically unseaworthy boats has saved hundreds of poor migrants from a watery grave.

There have been, and will be, changes in *what* the Coast Guard does. Equipment and procedures will continue to be improved and fine-tuned; so long as even one life is lost in circumstances that *should* have allowed us to make a "save," the quest for improvement will continue. Ultimately, however, hardware and doctrine take a distant back seat to the most critical factor in all rescues, people. Today, as in the past, the Coast Guard is blessed with the finest men and women to ever mount a rescue effort. I salute each and every one, and thank my friend, the author, for this tribute to all those professionals who so proudly and unselfishly serve.

Howard B. Thorsen, Vice
Admiral, U.S. Coast Guard

SEMPER PARATUS!

*P*reface

The original edition of *Rescue at Sea*, published in 1966, was a story of Search and Rescue (SAR) over a twenty-five-year period beginning with World War II. Though maritime rescue developed slowly by trial and error over hundreds of years, not until 1942 was a sophisticated communications, command, and control system begun to better direct the efforts of ships, boats, and rapidly improving aircraft to help rescue the thousands of airmen and seamen endangered by the hazards of war and combat training. The original edition, about my generation of sailors and airmen, was largely autobiographical or derived from firsthand knowledge of the events and participants.

As the 200th anniversary of the U.S. Coast Guard approached, I was asked to update *Rescue at Sea* to reflect the changes and technical advances in SAR from 1966 to the present. After my retirement from the Coast Guard, I remained active in emergency and rescue work as Public Safety Director of a major city and as a consultant. I also continued to fly, and sailed a series of racing and cruising yachts offshore, during which time I closely followed SAR activities. Nevertheless, to paint an accurate picture of SAR today, I felt it necessary to visit a number of SAR units and observe their operations firsthand. Comparing the new generation of rescuers and their facilities with their predecessors showed that many things have changed, an obvious one being the presence of women in the cockpit and on the bridge in key operational slots. Many things have remained essentially the same, while other rescue methods have ceased to exist. Just as the oar-powered surfboats of the nineteenth century disappeared with the advent of fast motor craft and helicopters, the seaplanes and the ocean station vessels gave way to long-range helicopters, jet aircraft, and improved navigation and safety techniques. The amphibious helicopter, just coming into its own in 1966, will soon be completely replaced with helicopters unable to land on the water—a perhaps regressive change dictated largely by high aircraft development costs. But in the professionalism and courage of the men and women who guard those passing on and over the sea, there has been no letdown. Like their antecedents, they continue to uphold a proud tradition, while continually upgrading the performance of a great humanitarian profession.

I am most grateful for the assistance and help of numerous Coast Guard people in briefing and updating me on how things are done today. I am especially grateful to Vice Admiral Howard B. Thorsen, then Commander Seventh Coast Guard District, and the people of his widespread command for taking time from a busy operating load to help me. Special thanks are also due Captain Kent Ballantyne, commanding officer, Coast Guard Air Station, Miami, Florida, and his officers and crew for their help and hospitality. Captain James C. Rahman, the station flight surgeon, and his medics were most helpful in sharing with me many experiences with the thousands of refugees fleeing from the Caribbean and seeking shelter in the United States. Lieutenant Michael McCoy, the Seventh District staff Haitian Project/Intelligence officer, also provided valuable data and insights into the problem.

I also extend my thanks to the many staff experts in U.S. Coast Guard Headquarters, Washington, D.C., for technical help and advice. These include Captain R. D. Peterson of Public Affairs, Captain Anthony Pettit and Captain Kenneth Holleman of the Search-and-Rescue Division, Commanders Jonathan Embler and Gary Dehnel, who headed key technical projects, Mr. Wayne Paugh, who assisted greatly in my obtaining key photographs, and Dr. Robert Scheina, the Coast Guard Historian, who was of such great help in locating historical files and pictures, and who encouraged the development of this extensive book revision. I am also grateful for assistance from personnel at many Coast Guard Air Stations and ships too numerous to list here, but whose stories are contained in this book.

I am most appreciative of the assistance of Paul Wilderson, Carol Swartz, and Linda Cullen of the Naval Institute Press, always knowledgeable, helpful, and pleasant to work with.

Blending this massive amount of new information with my own earlier recorded experiences, I have attempted to provide a picture of modern SAR as it has developed over the last half century into the highly efficient system we have today. It is an inspiring story of the courage of both rescuers and victims in often hazardous situations. Observing the men and women of the Coast Guard today makes me even more proud to have been a part of its great tradition.

Rescue at Sea

1

That Others May Live

On 10 October 1965, ten long-range patrol aircraft of the Japanese Navy departed Japan and set course for Guam. Shortly afterward, four destroyers and an oiler under command of Rear Admiral Momoji Hashiguchi cleared the Bungo Suido and headed southeast. In Hawaii, 3,500 miles to the east, a big Coast Guard turboprop Hercules lifted into the air and winged westward. In Guam, Navy, Coast Guard, and Air Force flight crews hurried preparations for takeoff. Captain R. C. Giffen, Commander Submarine Squadron Fifteen, sailed from Guam in the USS *Conserver*. From widely scattered spots covering much of the western Pacific, the tracks of the moving aircraft and ships converged toward a spot 300 miles north of Guam. The thoughts of many of the older officers and men wandered back to 1944 and the bloody battles fought in this same area. Now, for the first time in twenty years, the Japanese Navy was returning, but for a far different purpose.

In early October, Typhoon Carmen smashed into the Marianas, catching a large fleet of Japanese fishing vessels off Agrihan Island. When it passed, seven trawlers were missing. American forces on Guam promptly started search-and-rescue (SAR) operations, but additional help was needed. The Japanese, reversing a policy in existence since the end of World War II, promptly dispatched fleet units outside of home waters. Under overall command of the U.S. Navy, with a Coast Guard aircraft directing on-scene air operations and Japanese interpreters riding in the American aircraft, the four services operated as a smooth running team. Three of the missing vessels were accounted for in the following week, and a number of survivors were recovered. Relations were cordial, reported the senior American officer on the scene, ". . . as would be expected of sailors engaged in a common purpose."

SAR over the years has provided a common purpose in which men, regardless of nationality, have responded to help other men in trouble. In a world in which nations are usually at odds, men often give up their lives to save men they have never seen and whose language they don't speak. It may be a rescue aircraft escorting a crippled Italian airliner into a safe landing or a Coast Guard cutter fighting an Atlantic storm to save the crew of a Greek freighter. It can involve five merchant vessels of three different nationalities going to the aid of a sinking ship of a fourth nation, a large French ocean liner racing to remove a sick seaman from an American naval vessel, or a search by nearly one hundred aircraft to find five Military Airlift Command (MAC) crewmen missing at sea. The crew of an ocean-station vessel, on her lonely vigil protecting those whose business takes them on and over the sea, had a common bond with a volunteer crew on the bleak Scottish coast launching their lifeboat to rescue men from a grounded trawler.

The first government lifesaving stations were organized by the Chinese as early as 1737. The Netherlands and Britain followed soon after, but their lifeboats and equipment were purchased and maintained by private benevolent societies. When a vessel went aground, the alarm was spread, and all able-bodied men in the town who were qualified to help ran for the boathouse, where the lifeboat was kept in readiness. A crew was selected and the boat launched through the surf. Many of these volunteer crewmen were lost when their boats capsized or were swamped in the heavy breakers, but there was never a shortage of replacements. The same type of lifeboat service still exists today in Britain, organized under the auspices of the Royal National Lifeboat Institution, a private benevolent society.

In 1786, the Massachusetts Humane Society was formed to render aid to shipwrecked mariners. It built refuge huts along the beaches. If a wreck survivor could reach one of these, he would find food, clothing, and firewood. Too often, however, a mariner would stagger into one of the huts only to find bare walls. It had been stripped by looters. In addition to the huts, the society equipped lifeboats at points along the coast, relying on the volunteer manning system used by the European societies.

In 1831, the federal government entered the rescue picture when the Secretary of the Treasury ordered the Revenue Cutter Service—the predecessor of the Coast Guard—to patrol off the Atlantic Coast during the winter storm season to provide assistance to distressed mariners.

Following the heavy winter storms of 1847, Congress finally took note of the work of the Massachusetts Humane Society and voted a modest appropriation to aid them in their work. A small amount was also voted to set up unmanned stations along the New Jersey coast, but they were not successful. Thieves stripped the unmanned boathouses, and the upkeep of the boats that were left was poor. Finally in 1854, a paid keeper was provided at each station to maintain the equipment. Shortly after the Civil War, the U. S. Life-saving Service was established under the Treasury Department, with full-time station crews. It expanded rapidly and, by 1900, had 269 lifeboat sta-

Hatteras Inlet Lifeboat Station, typical of many built along isolated beaches in the late nineteenth century.

tions in operation along the coasts. In 1915, it was combined with the Revenue Cutter Service to form the Coast Guard. The nation's primary rescue agencies had at last been combined into one service.

The takeover of rescue responsibility by the government was an inevitable outcome of the country's growth. When vessels were few in number, and most accidents occurred in coastal waters, the volunteer system was adequate. But as the number of incidents increased, and the demands for services rose, the volunteer system was unable to provide the continuity required, or the equipment and skills necessary for offshore operations. A professional force was in order, and the Coast Guard provided it.

The demands on the nation's SAR system are constantly changing. Prior to the coming of radio at the turn of the century, a ship in trouble beyond the sight of land was dependent on its own resources or assistance from another ship within visual range of its distress signals. Fortunately, many of the smaller vessels operated along the coastal routes and were frequently within sight of the lookouts at the numerous lifeboat stations. Most rescue alerts originated with reports from these lookouts or from chance observers along the shore. Radio was developed by Marconi in 1895, and by 1905 most of the larger transoceanic vessels carried radiotelegraph (C-W) for communications with

Coast Guardsmen launch a pulling boat through light surf to aid the steamer *Northern Pacific*, aground on Fire Island, N.Y., in 1919.

shore stations; but not until after the *Titanic* disaster were international agreements reached on the regulation and use of this new communications mode. The early radio equipment was bulky, expensive, and required skilled Morse code operators, so only a few among the smaller vessels carried radio until World War II, when military needs led to the development and massive use of voice radio (radiotelephone). The immediate postwar years saw greatly increased use of such medium-frequency voice radio by small fishing and pleasure craft, though it was often noisy and unreliable. Not until the coming of single-sideband radio in the 50s and short-range VHF/FM radio in the early 1970s did seafarers, large and small, have a highly reliable and affordable means of communicating with each other and with rescuers in an emergency. This "insurance" has played no small part in the dramatic increase in pleasure boating in recent years, as well as in the marked decrease in the death rate from boating mishaps, which has dropped dramatically from 21.4 per 100,000 boats in 1965 to only 6.1 in 1987.

The years following World War II also saw a major change in coastal traffic patterns as commercial coastal shipping was largely replaced by trucks, trains, aircraft, and large container ships. Shipwrecks along the remote beaches decreased with this drop in traffic and with improved navigation methods. At the same time, there was a rapid increase in numbers of pleasure boats.

As these trends became evident, many of the old lifeboat stations along the beaches were closed, while new rescue stations were established at the ocean inlets and ports where pleasure boats gathered. With the advent of more reliable radio communications, faster small boats, and helicopters able to rapidly respond to incidents anywhere along the coast, more of the remote beach stations were closed in the 1960s. Today, less than a third of the number of shore stations existing in 1900 handle twenty times the number of cases. The distressed craft are largely yachts and small fishing boats rather than commercial coastal vessels. That this work load can be handled by an overworked service also engaged in other high-priority missions such as drug interdiction, aids to navigation, and military duties can be largely attributed to the Coast Guard's great versatility, as well as its ability to divert units from other jobs to assist those in distress, such urgent rescue missions always carrying top priority. There is also help from other sources such as the Coast Guard Auxiliary, a 35,000-member

Newer Coast Guard station near an inlet showing two small heavy-duty motor life-boats with a larger 82-foot patrol boat.

civilian volunteer organization, whose members use their own boats and aircraft to assist the service in its missions.

The United States had another professional SAR service, the Army Air Force's Aerospace Rescue and Recovery service (ARRS). During World War II, Coast Guard and Navy units, heavily engaged in antisubmarine operations, were unable to provide search-and-rescue services to the Army Air Forces in all theaters. The Army, therefore, organized a number of independent units throughout the world to rescue downed Army Air Force pilots. These were combined in 1946 into a formally organized service. In 1988, however, the service was phased out, and men and equipment transferred for use in special operations. In 1956, the National SAR Plan was drafted, charging the Coast Guard with SAR on and over the water, and the Air Force with such assignments over the continental land areas. It has proven to be a logical and smooth working arrangement, and the two services work in a spirit of close cooperation.

In addition to USCG/USAF involvement, the "volunteer professionals" are available. These consist of the other armed services, the state and local public-safety agencies, and the merchant marine. The public-safety agencies are especially valuable in land rescue, where they have the advantages of proximity and local knowledge, and demands on rescuers are less rigorous than at sea. At sea Navy vessels and aircraft are used frequently to supplement Coast Guard forces, but the primary source of help is from the merchant marine.

For hundreds of years, merchant vessels have rendered aid to other vessels when distress was encountered on the high seas. With the coming of radio, a distressed vessel could broadcast SOS signals to summon aid from other ships in the vicinity, which were often much closer than the rescue cutters. However, there was no positive system for alerting other vessels, as few ships guarded the radio frequency around the clock. When the RMS *Titanic* went down in 1912, several vessels were close by but did not hear the SOS call. An international convention was called as a result of this catastrophe, and a common distress frequency and uniform safety procedures were adopted. Later, an auto-alarm system was developed to alert other vessels that might not have radio operators on watch. This system uses a "black box" designed to receive a special alerting signal on the distress frequency of 500 kilocycles. When the signal is received, the auto-alarm triggers off loud bells on both the bridge and in the radio operator's cabin. It can only be silenced by the radio operator coming to the radio room and turning a switch, at which time it has accomplished its purpose of getting him there. Since this is a "general alarm" type of signal, it has drawbacks, for it alerts all vessels in a large area of the ocean, and many respond when perhaps only one is needed.

In 1958, the Coast Guard developed the AMVER system. AMVER, an acronym for Automated Mutual-Assistance Vessel Rescue System, uses a powerful computer to monitor and keep track of participating merchant vessels at sea. A merchant vessel, departing on a voyage, radios its departure and intended routing to the Coast Guard. This information is fed into the computer, which computes an up-to-date position of each vessel on its memory discs, together with complete information on the vessel's characteristics, including whether or not a doctor is aboard. If an emergency arises, the computer is interrogated and within minutes prints out a Surface Picture (SURPIC) showing the positions of all vessels within a designated area. The Coast Guard can then select the nearest suitable vessel and request that it proceed to the aid of the distressed vessel. AMVER not

Handling the big liner like a destroyer, the skipper of the Furness liner *Queen of Bermuda* prepares to create a lee for his lifeboat (lower left) to take the crew of ten off the sinking *Student Prince*, located by Coast Guard aircraft 200 miles north of Bermuda. The liner was an AMVER participant.

only provides the means of rapidly locating and diverting aid to a distress scene, but saves hundreds of thousands of dollars yearly by avoiding needless diversions.

The memory discs of the AMVER computer carry the characteristics of over 10,000 vessels, representing 124 countries. On 23 April 1987, the 150-foot tug *Marine Constructor* with a tow suffered an engine-room explosion and fire 1,100 miles west of San Francisco. Three crewmen suffered first- and second-degree burns, and a fourth suffered from smoke and halon extinguisher inhalation. A 120th Air Rescue and Recovery Service HC-130 aircraft with a flight surgeon on board dropped five paramedics to the tug. The next day a Coast Guard HC-130 aircraft dropped additional medical supplies, and within hours, the Japanese motor vessel *Jinyu Maru*, participating in the AMVER system, rendezvoused with the *Marine Constructor*. The patients, now stabilized, and the paramedics were placed aboard the

Jinyu Maru, and the ship proceeded to a rendezvous with the USS *Ranger* (CV 61), to which the paramedics and their patients transferred. The following day a *Ranger* aircraft flew the patients to medical facilities in San Francisco.

Effective as the AMVER system is, it is not a panacea. In high winds and seas, most merchant vessels have limited maneuverability, and the newer and highly automated vessels have limited manpower. Under such conditions, the specially equipped and highly maneuverable Coast Guard cutters still must effect many of the difficult rescues.

Though rescue units from many sources are used, the control and coordination of these ships and planes in our sea areas is the responsibility of the Coast Guard. To do this effectively, Rescue Coordination Centers (RCC) are maintained at strategic locations, connected by an intricate communications network. At San Francisco and New York, master centers coordinate operations that involve two or more of the smaller centers. The RCCs are manned twenty-four hours a day by officers and enlisted personnel who dispatch aircraft and vessels to the scenes of distress. Often, as many as a dozen cases will be in progress simultaneously at one RCC. After assigning units to each case, the RCC receives from them frequent situation reports (SITREPS) on their progress. On large cases, an on-scene commander (OSC) is assigned to control and coordinate efforts of units at the scene of action.

Day in and day out, most of the distress cases in the western Atlantic and eastern Pacific are handled by Coast Guard cutters, aircraft, and shore stations. The Coast Guard is a wide-ranging service, however, and is authorized by U.S. statutes to render aid at any place where Coast Guard facilities may be. This has included aid to vessels off the South American coast by drug-interdiction units; on the other side of the world, a fast Coast Guard cutter diverted from North Pacific fisheries patrol was one of the first to arrive at the crash scene of a South Korean jumbo jet shot down by a Soviet fighter. In late 1987 a Coast Guard C-130, investigating a flare sighting, discovered the distressed sailboat *Saci,* 400 miles west-southwest of the Cape Verde Islands. The boat had lost its rudder, rigging, and sails. The Liberian SS *Harbel Tapper* was diverted to the scene by AMVER, and was assisted in the rendezvous by a Senegal rescue plane from Dakar. When sea conditions prevented the merchantman from picking up

A long-range C-130 turboprop Hercules, a mainstay of the Coast Guard air arm.

An HH-52 helicopter flown by the author hovers over a Russian vessel 100 miles off Cape Cod to hoist up an Air Force fighter pilot who had been picked up by the Soviet vessel after bailing out. Such cooperation in SAR has long prevailed at sea.

the crippled boat, the sole occupant was taken on board and carried to Newport News, VA.

This cooperative international nature of SAR is made possible by interlocking agreements and treaties, a constantly improving communications capability between SAR forces of different nations, and common operating procedures. During President Reagan's 1988 visit to Moscow, an SAR treaty between the USSR and USA was signed providing for cooperation, joint exercises, and logistic support between the two nations. Only a few days later, Soviet and American forces were working together in a search for seven missing walrus hunters near St. Lawrence Island in the Bering Sea. They were found nineteen days after being reported overdue. Both nations used procedures prescribed by the National Search and Rescue Manual, first issued by the Coast Guard in 1957 for U.S. use, and now the world authority and guide for SAR operations. The most recent revision of the manual was described by the U.S. Government Printing Office as the "best-selling publication since the Watergate papers." The Soviet Union placed an initial order for 1,000 copies, while the French ordered 500.

In 1966, the Coast Guard and Air Force established the National

Help is a two-way street. Soviet crewmen on a fishing factory ship crowd around a helicopter for a rare view of Americans. The chopper had landed to pick up an injured Russian crewman.

A helicopter from the British carrier HMS *Eagle* hoists a crewman from the American SS *Steel Vendor*, which had lost power and drifted onto the Loaita Banks Shoal. All hands were removed, and only one person was injured.

SAR School at Governors Island, NY, for the training of personnel of the U.S. armed forces in search and rescue. The mission was soon expanded to include foreign nationals, and by 1988 students from eighty nations, ranging alphabetically from Afghanistan to Zaire, had completed the school. Over 8,500 U.S. military and 1,500 civilian personnel have completed the course. Extension courses are also conducted by the school in foreign countries.

As a result of the common doctrine and training, international cooperation in SAR has achieved new heights of efficiency. The Soviet Union and a number of Eastern Bloc countries have evidenced an increasingly cooperative attitude that includes AMVER participation, a joint SAR satellite venture (SARSAT/COSPAC), and hotline communications between U.S. and Soviet RCCs to expedite cooperation during distress cases. Though other military services and other nations are called on for help when needed, the first responder in most cases in U.S. waters is the Coast Guard. Assisting units may include ships, aircraft, or boats from shore stations.

The cutters range in size from the small 82-foot patrol boats up to large 29-knot high-endurance cutters, 378 feet long, and able to carry a helicopter.

A 210-foot cutter air-refuels an HH-3F helicopter while cruising in company with a larger high-endurance cutter.

Coast Guard air stations, extending from Puerto Rico to Alaska and Hawaii, provide SAR services and logistic support for a wide range of activities. Long-range C-130 turboprop Hercules, Hu-25 Falcon jets and the turbojet HH-3F and HH-65 helicopters make up

A fast and versatile 41-foot utility boat, the workhorse of the Coast Guard's small-boat fleet.

the backbone of the air fleet, with HH-60 helicopters due to enter service soon.

Numerous Coast Guard shore stations extend around the coasts of the United States and the Great Lakes. At each are high-speed utility boats or heavy-duty 44-foot motor rescue boats able to proceed in the heaviest sea and surf. On these small stations, aided by aircraft, fall the brunt of the routine SAR cases involving small boats and fishermen. It is a never-ceasing job. This is the SAR complex—ships, aircraft, and shore stations, tied together with fast communications circuits, and controlled by the RCCs.

In 1988, Coast Guard SAR units responded to calls for help twice as often as they had twenty years before. That same year witnessed dozens of large ships in distress at sea, and worldwide a vessel over 1,000 tons was lost (on the average) each day. But most of the cases were pleasure craft, which were involved in 77 percent of Coast Guard responses to emergencies. The reason is not hard to understand. In addition to the small size of most of the pleasure craft and the relative inexperience of their crews, their very numbers make losses inevitable. Since 1966, the number of pleasure boats in the U.S. has increased from 6.85 million to 16.5 million. Over 70 million Americans go out on the water yearly! Three of every four Americans will soon live within 100 miles of the coast, and by the year 2,000 there will be twenty million boat owners.

In 1988, with approximately the same size force it had twenty years before but with vastly increased responsibilities, the Coast Guard saved or assisted over 150,000 people and over two billion dollars in property. It is a highly satisfying economic return, for the Coast Guard spends only $408 million of its $1,815-million operating budget on SAR. The payoff in relief of human suffering is not measurable.

Medico

Outside, the cold wind of a late New England fall blew gustily, rattling the window, and an occasional splatter of rain hit the glass. It was late, and I wearily slipped off a shoe, thinking with anticipation of a hot shower and a good night's sleep. Suddenly, the Offshore Alarm gong outside my cabin erupted with a CLANG CLANG CLANG, and a shot of adrenalin hit my system at the bell's demanding clamor. The loudspeaker blared, "Now hear this! Put the ready helicopter on the line. Helicopter crew report to Operations for offshore medico!"

Quickly peeling off my clothes, I squirmed into the rubber exposure suit, cursing as I tried to get the rubber socks on. Over the rubber suit came an orange flight suit, and then sheepskin boots. Finally, after nearly ten minutes, I was suited up and already sweating in the cumbersome rig. Grumble he may, but no helicopter pilot willingly goes offshore without the rubber anti-exposure suit during a New England winter. Without it, life in the water is measured in minutes, and the night was cold and rough. With only that one turbojet engine powering a chopper, an engine failure over water, especially at night, is likely to prove fatal—unless everything is going for you, and the rubber suit is one of the big things.

Trotting into Operations, I saw Lieutenant Commander Bob Russell, my copilot, and the crewmen, Hospital Corpsman Don Jorgensen and Aviation Machinist Mate John Williams, all real helicopter pros. The Operations duty officer handed me the teletype slip with the case information. A crewman was badly injured on a Dutch vessel 110 miles southeast of Boston near Texas Tower No. 3. Seas were rough and 15 feet high, winds 20–25 knots, and visibility poor. Not pleasant, but flyable. Turning to the others, I said for the hundredth time without an answering laugh, "Well, as one wheel said to the other wheel, let's roll."

Now, only five minutes later, we are in another world, with dozens of dim red-lighted instruments glowing around us in the cockpit. We increase RPM and torque to 100 percent, climbing out over the lights of Marblehead, past Nahant, and head across Massachusetts Bay for the tip of Cape Cod. The lights of Boston quickly fade out, and we hear only the occasional radar advisories from Boston Departure Control Radar and the high whine of the jet turbine. Every fifteen minutes, Bob flips his mike-selector switch to high-freq radio, and reports to the station, "Operations normal," so they will know we are still alive and airborne. Every half hour, the "ops normal" report is followed by our position, allowing station ops to "flight follow" us.

Now we hear our escort calling. Coast Guard 1266, a Grumman *Albatross* several thousand feet above us, reports that he is being diverted to evacuate an Army man seriously injured in a car accident in Provincetown at the tip of Cape Cod. He will rejoin us as soon as he delivers the man to Boston. We plow on through the night, and through the darkness ahead, soon see the few lights on Nantucket. A short time later we take our departure from the southeastern point of the island. Ahead lies only blackness, and the stormy ocean. We occasionally glimpse the white foam of the breakers pounding the reefs off Nantucket. Radio contact with the base is poor, and we call the escort. No answer; he hasn't rejoined yet.

Frankly, I don't enjoy flying a single-engine aircraft over the water at night with no radio contact, but our only alternative is to return to Nantucket and wait. If we do, fuel may become a problem. I elect to keep going, and hope that the General Electric turbine does the same. Now we must find the vessel ahead.

Ten minutes pass, and we try radio contact with the vessel. No answer. We call the escort. No answer. We call Salem Air Station.

Then a faint reply, "Cogard 1266 was airborne from Logan at 55, estimating intercept at 0045 Zulu."

This is better. Ten minutes later, we try another call on UHF, and 1266 answers. He is coming hell bent for election, for he realizes that we may have trouble locating our Dutch friend; better yet, we now have radio contact in the event of trouble. Before long, we have the Dutch vessel in radio contact, and as he talks, we tune our radio direction finder to take a bearing on him. The needle swings ten degrees to starboard and stays there. We alter course to the new heading, then add another 20 degrees to compensate for the wind. The correction is about right, for the bearing remains steady each time he talks. Fifteen minutes later, we can see him through the light rain, and the view isn't pretty. He is rolling badly in the heavy seas and has unusually high masts, located well forward and well aft. We are going to have to take the injured man off the bow, or at the very stern, and will have to hover about 80 feet over the ship in darkness. I turn to Bob and remark, "Well, we've got another damn cliff hanger on our hands." He nods without smiling.

A night helicopter hoist over rough water is one of the most exciting and dangerous of aeronautical maneuvers, and the Coast Guard has lost a number of machines doing them. Although I have carried out a number of such operations and have practiced continually, I have never really been satisfied that I have it down cold.

To make a night hoist, a pilot comes to a hover, hopefully where he can see part of the ship's structure. If this structure is tossing and working heavily, he must never lose sight of it; for if the whirling blades strike the ship, the helicopter will explode. Death will be instantaneous for the helicopter crew and probably for many on the deck below.

While watching the ship, the pilot must avoid the temptation to go into a dance with it by trying to "fly formation." He instead tries to keep a stable and level hover by reference to his instruments, and most important, by the instructions relayed from his hoist operator, who controls the winch raising and lowering the basket. Only the hoist operator can see the basket as it is lowered to the deck directly below. He must put what he sees into words, which he relays to the pilot. The pilot must take what he hears, and translate it into control movements. It is a different kind of flying, and bears no resemblance to hovering over land, where a good pilot will not vary two feet in a

An HH-52 helicopter from the Salem Air Station hovers over a vessel to lower a Stokes litter to pick up an injured man. Only a few feet separate the mast from the whirling blades.

hover. Even a sudden inflection in a hoist operator's voice can affect the pilot's control movements.

While all this is going on, the pilot is glancing at his instruments, keeping an eye cocked warily at the mast flashing by in front of the whirling blades, and attempting to disregard other visual and middle ear stimuli that could start vertigo or spatial disorientation. It is a tense, busy, and often hair-raising experience when conditions are marginal. Tonight is marginal, and my shoulders tighten as I bring the chopper to a hover, and ease it into position just ahead of the ship. Cautioning Bob to keep an eye on the foremast, which is now on my quarter, I head into the stiff wind. He rogers, and I note his hand cocked just ahead of his stick. Now the hoist operator says, "Going onto hot mike. Come ahead ten feet. Your altitude is good. Now left five feet and ahead ten. You are sinking slowly, hold what you have. The basket is going down. Pick it up a little. Now you are drifting aft. Come ahead 20 feet, and 10 feet to the left. Your altitude is good. . . ."

As he relays the steady flow of directions, I make minute adjustments to the controls to do his bidding. My hands are gripping the controls hard, and as I realize it, I loosen my grip. A tight grip never produces precise flying, which is what we need now.

"You are fine. Now bring it down a bit. You are too high. The basket is swinging badly. Now come right ten feet. PICK IT UP!"

At the sudden sense of urgency in his voice, I pour on power, and the chopper leaps 25 feet in the air.

"You were getting a little too low over that mast. Now ease it down. . . ."

The sweat is pouring off me in the rubber suit, and a little trickles into my eyes and stings. Five minutes we have been holding in this hover, and I am already tired. The basket is swinging in a wide pendulum down below, and each movement I make is multiplied by the 80 feet of cable and the howling winds. I pull out to the side, order the basket pulled up and signal to Bob to take the controls for a moment. I flex my hands and arms.

"Let's try it from the stern," I suggest. "At least there I can see that damn mast. With it out of sight, it's like playing Russian roulette."

We call the ship, and ask them to bring the man back to the stern for another try. When the stretcher party reaches the stern, we start in again. This time, we can see the ship below, and I ease in until the mast is swaying madly in long arcs just 10 feet ahead of our blades, occasionally lurching at us when the vessel pitches. We can't get in any closer, but the basket is barely over the stern of the ship. I had stolen a quick look at the stern as we came in, illuminating it with our searchlight, and was appalled to see the fantail piled high with gear. There was one small cleared space, and in that space was a stretcher and an unconscious figure with bloody bandages around his head.

I say to Bob, "How in the heck are we going to get the basket into that small place without clobbering the man?"

Bob replies, "We'll need some luck."

Again the chant of the hoist operator as the basket is lowered, and knowing that I am tired, I realize I am in danger. A tired man will often reason, "Oh hell, let's get it over with," and so reasoning, will push too far, or overextend himself. Arlington Cemetery is full of pilots who took a short cut.

"Come left two feet. Hold it! The basket is just above the deck. Come left a little more. Now back four feet. The basket is swinging badly. . . ."

Fifteen minutes have gone by, and my arms are like lead. The sweat in my eyes is so bad that my vision blurs at times. Don't be proud, I think. Pulling back from the lurching mast, and turning to Bob, I say, "OK, you have a try at it. This is like trying to pin a tail on a hula dancer."

We back off slowly, Bob takes the controls, and then moves back in. I keep one hand poised just in front of the stick, and watch the mast dance closer to us. Bob is fresher and smoother than I was, but he still can't get the basket into the small spot. Finally, I glance at the fuel gauge, and say, "I know when we're whipped. Let's go in for fuel. While we are gone, we will ask him to get closer under Cape Cod and maybe we can do better with smoother seas."

As we departed, the ship was making preparations to head in for the heel of Cape Cod. Three hours later, we returned as first light was breaking, and with better light and smoother seas, picked up the patient in two minutes. Heading for Boston, with the helo on auto-pilot, I closed my eyes to rest them. I had been awake for twenty-five hours. Suddenly I snapped my head up, and looked over at Bob.

"You know, I think I dozed off there for about thirty seconds," I said, rubbing my eyes.

"To be exact, you were out four minutes," he said. Thank God for alert copilots.

I was tired and whipped; my professional pride was hurt at having to make two flights to get one man, and I was disgusted at the state of the art that should make night hovering such a risky chore. We

Other crewmen secure an injured man before he is hoisted.

are talking about going to the moon, we have already orbited the earth, and still, you have to break your neck to lower a basket and pick a man off a rolling ship at night. There had to be a better way.

Only two months later, we had part of the problem solved. The solution—a simple light steadying line, attached to the basket and hanging below it. As the basket is lowered, the men on deck grab the 50-foot steadying line and guide the basket to the exact spot they desire, at the same time dampening out the pendulum action. It was so simple, and so effective, that we could only blush at our failure to think of it before. But the helicopter is very young, and hasn't been doing the really tough night jobs offshore very long. When faced with the necessity, we came up with part of the answer. Things will be easier in the future.

An injured man being hoisted into a helicopter. Hoist cable leads up and right, while the steadying line leads left and down to the boat.

Easy is a relative matter, however, and when conditions are adverse, night offshore hoisting is still to be avoided except in life-and-death cases.

At sea, life and death are shipmates, and are seldom far apart. There are no large modern hospitals in mid-ocean, nor are doctors as close as the nearest telephone. Even if a doctor is on a ship (and only the largest vessels have adequate operating facilities), performing surgery on a table that rolls and bucks with the ship can be harrowing, and a ship's doctor might well have to paraphrase the old sailing-ship rule by saying, "One hand for the patient and one for myself."

Several things have changed the dismal prospects of the wounded

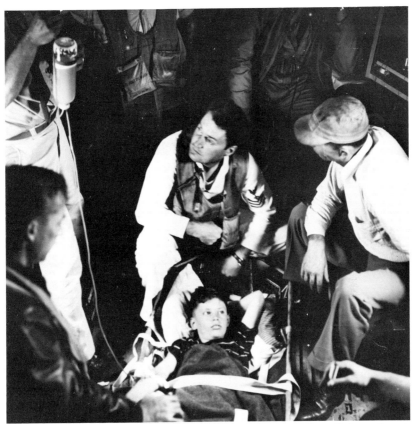

A young boy, lacerated by machinery in an accident 120 miles off Cape Cod, is given blood plasma in the after station of a PBM Mariner, while his father, skipper of a fishing boat (at right), looks on. The youngster was brought ashore after a hazardous open-sea landing by the rescue pilot.

or sick mariner. First was the coming of radio. Next came the seaplane, and later the helicopter. Then came antibiotics. In the fifties came a refinement based on radio—the Automated Merchant Vessel Reporting System (AMVER), which can in seconds not only select the nearest vessel, but also the ones having doctors and medical facilities. These things will never replace Massachusetts General Hospital, but medicine on the high seas has advanced as fast or faster in the last fifty years than has medicine ashore.

Before Marconi, a seaman's most likely fate was to be treated by

A seaman, partially paralyzed after an accident, is brought by ship's boat from the SS *Mormacport*, 400 miles off New York. The raft will be used to transfer him to the waiting seaplane and prevent the heavy lifeboat from damaging the plane in the moderate seas.

the captain from the ship's medicine chest. The same situation exists on many ships today, with the all-important exception that medical advice can be obtained by radio. Should things get beyond the scope of the ship's medical chest, help can be swiftly obtained. In much of the Northern Hemisphere, a ship can contact the nearest Coast Guard Radio Station for medical (MEDICO) advice. This can be done by a direct call, or through a commercial communications facility. There is never a charge for the Medico message.

In most of the rest of the world, medical advice can be obtained by requesting it from a unique organization known as CIRM (International Radio Medical Center), a private organization based in Rome and financed by the Italian government and private contributions. CIRM maintains a permanent medical staff to advise their worldwide maritime patients by radio and cable, the communication services being donated by the various large communications companies.

The flaw in this system comes from the fact that it is difficult to diagnose certain illnesses, and it is doubly hard to do so when the symptoms are distorted or inaccurately reported by an excitable layman, or even a calm layman without medical know-how. It is little wonder that a physician ashore will often refuse to commit himself, or will hedge his bet when the operational people who may have to remove the patient at sea press for a definite yes or no.

I remember with amusement a young flight surgeon, his confidence as unblemished as his new commission, diagnosing a case as scarlet fever from reports of an offshore lighthouse keeper. The three-man aircraft crew sent to evaluate the patient handled him like a hot isotope. All during the flight, I sat in the cockpit with a surgical mask across my face, while the pharmacist's mate huddled in the farthest corner aft, avoiding the patient. On landing, we managed with the help of the ground crew to get out the cockpit window, thus avoiding the contaminated cabin; but once out, the ground crew avoided us. The aircraft was hauled gingerly to a corner of the apron for decontamination, and the flight crew was ostracized. That afternoon after work, we were so shunned at the BOQ bar that I asked the doctor if the disease could be really that bad, and was assured it could be. We two "lepers" were cowering in growing fear at the end of the bar when the phone rang. It was the duty officer.

"Ask Dr. Thompson," he said, "if he is sure that this man has scarlet fever? We have the Marine Hospital on the phone."

Dr. Thompson said there was little doubt, though he had not personally seen him.

"Well," gleefully shouted the OOD, "tell him he is all wet. That man has the measles!"

According to my medical friends, such mistakes can occur any time that diagnoses must be made on symptoms that may be inaccurately reported. When one blends in the deception that can be introduced by a malingerer, or the exaggerations of a hypochondriac, medical advice can at times be little better than guesswork.

Malingerers are fortunately rare. We landed at sea 500 miles out of Bermuda to pick up an appendectomy case, only to have the "patient" help row the boat over from the ship and climb aboard the plane with his suitcase. He appeared to be completely free of pain, and all the way back in, I was in a slow burn. After landing, I grabbed the surgeon and said, "This is the second phony one we have had in a couple of months. When you get the bastard in the hospital, cut him open regardless!"

An HH-3F lifts an ill patient from a yacht off the New England coast.

The doctor did cut him open, but I had misjudged the seaman. He really had a hot appendix, but just before leaving the ship had been given a large shot of morphine by an overly solicitous captain, effectively masking the pain.

More common than the frauds are the noncritical cases that could really get by without evacuation to a hospital. There was the child who had eaten too much chocolate reported as an appendicitis case. There were two sailors who were removed by seaplane from a vessel 1,000 miles at sea, but the following morning were scrubbing decks in a naval hospital. Many "heart attack" patients suffer only from anxiety or hyperventilation.

In July 1965, the air station at Salem, Massachusetts, received a radio call for a medical evacuation from a yacht 90 miles offshore. A patient on board probably had appendicitis, and it had been diagnosed as such by a doctor who was aboard the boat. Although heavy fog prevailed over much of the area, a helicopter was dispatched with a fixed-wing aircraft as escort. They finally found the yacht, not 90 miles offshore as reported, but 140, a whopping error in position. The fog was so thick that the pilot was unable to see the yacht, though the boatmen could hear him overhead. Finally, he returned to shore because of a shortage of fuel, and was forced to land on an island with less than ten minutes reserve. Another helicopter was sent out and brought in the patient, but it had been a near thing.

The following morning, the patient walked out of the hospital in good health. He had not had appendicitis after all. The SAR people were a bit perturbed and asked why. It turned out that the patient was also the doctor, and he had diagnosed his own illness. As if that were not enough, the patient-doctor was also the navigator who had an error of 50 miles in his position.

Before we become too cynical or hardened, however, most of us who run the risks come to realize that most sailors have little expert medical knowledge and are only possessed of the usual human fears and pains, heightened by the loneliness of the seas. They often give in to the same impulses as do people who call up the family doctor in the middle of the night for a minor ailment. The difference is that Old Doc doesn't have to figure how to get his patient in from the middle of the pond.

Then there are always those unfortunates who are really sick, but will not recover even if they are evacuated to a hospital. Is it reasonable to risk a rescue crew in such a case? The true nature of the case often comes to light only after the evacuation, and it may be a good thing. I would not like to have to make the decision each time.

We landed 400 miles off Miami to pick up a seaman suffering from an internal hemorrhage. When we took him aboard, he was unconscious and had all the grey appearance of a man breathing his last. By the transfusion of two bottles of plasma, and a two-hour flight at maximum continuous power, we got him to an overseas naval hospital, awake and in much better shape than when we picked him up. We were congratulating ourselves that night on what appeared to be a really worthwhile save when the surgeon phoned and informed us that he was suffering not from bleeding ulcers, but cirrhosis of the liver in its terminal stage.

If we sometimes go out and bring in a "heart-attack" case that turns out to be indigestion, the error is honest. The man really thought he had a heart attack, and the symptoms sounded serious to the doctor ashore. There are the hypochondriacs who will expertly exaggerate their troubles, but no one has ever claimed that these troubled people stop their search for consolation at the water's edge. Most requests for Medico assistance involve people in real trouble and serious pain.

Unfortunately, one of the most frequent types of Medico, at sea as on shore, is the heart attack. Such cases are often dramatic, and there is a compelling sense of the need to do something about it. The result has been that over the years we have brought in quite a few coronary victims. Before the helicopter, we landed a seaplane in the open sea, loaded the patients aboard under considerable stress, finally bounced into the air, and delivered at least some of them to the hospital alive. For my money, if I ever have a heart attack, and the only means of evacuation is by a seaplane from rough water, leave me where I am.

The helicopter affords a fairly safe, smooth means of delivery. Usually it is not dangerous, but it may appear so to the patient hanging in a litter 30 feet beneath the helicopter. If it does, it will conceivably frighten him, and fright is not good for a new coronary victim, and each one must be carefully weighed by the medical officer.

Some cases are honest-to-God screaming-for-attention emergencies. These are usually the accident or injury victims, suffering from hemorrhage, shock, or excruciating pain, and a SAR pilot will risk a lot to bring them in.

The fisherman on a tuna clipper off Baja California was one. He had fallen overboard, and been run through by a swordfish. The fish's spear-like "sword" had gone completely through the man, and the doctors recommended immediate evacuation to a hospital. When I was first called and told I had the flight, it sounded suspiciously like a gag. I had never even heard of a swordfish spearing anything, much less a man. But it was real enough, and a half hour later, as we walked out to the big seaplane that the line crew was warming up, the case had caught the attention of the national press. As we winged our way south, the radioman tuned in the news broadcasts frequently to hear the latest news on how we were doing.

Four hours later, after an uneventful flight and landing, we had the man aboard, and I went aft and looked at the patient while the doctor worked over him.

"Lucky," said the doctor. "You know that the point of a sword-fish's sword is really a blunt point, up to an inch or so in radius?"

I didn't, but nodded understandingly.

"Well, it went in here," he said, pointing to a small blue hole about half an inch in diameter three inches to the right and below the navel, "and it came out in the back missing the spine and the nerves there by only an inch or two. Being fairly blunt, it probably penetrated no organs or gut, but pushed them aside without damage. If it had been a bullet or a sharp point, it would have been good bye, Joe."

I nodded in wonder. Then the doc said, "What did you do to get the fish mad?" The fisherman grinned, "Well, actually, I had just hooked him and I think he was trying to get away. In the excitement, I fell overboard, and I must have got in his way. He was probably more afraid than I was."

By the time I climbed back into the cockpit, and started the engines, it was dark outside, and we were going to have to make a night open-sea takeoff, not a pleasant prospect, even with the gentle swell. We taxied along the takeoff course, laying out five float lights to mark the path, and five minutes later roared effortlessly into the air as the four Jet Assisted Take Off (JATO) bottles lit up the dark night. The flight was easy, the patient recovered with no complications, and the press had a big day writing human interest stories about "Man speared by fish!" Yes, it was easy, but we had to sweat a bit beforehand thinking about it. The worry came before we started to work. That's the way most things turn out.

In 1957, Lieutenant Vic Sutton picked up two electric-power-company linemen in the southern California mountains who had been electrocuted and burned by contact with a 5,000-volt line. Rushing them back while his crewman gave artificial resuscitation to first one, then the other, Vic delivered them to the air station only to find the road between the station and the hospital clogged with afternoon traffic that even the sirens and lights of the ambulance and a police car could not clear. Both men survived, but it was touch and go. As a result of that episode, we made arrangements with Sharp Hospital, near the outskirts of town, to mark off a heliport by the emergency room. The bachelor pilots had quite a ball landing on the heliport for the numerous drills that were required to check out the emergency-room nurses and doctors. Pilot morale went up considerably, as did requests by nurses at Sharp to participate in the drills. The new heliport was soon put to use.

I was in operations having my ten o'clock cup of coffee when a radio message came in advising us of a heart attack on a party fishing boat about ten miles off Oceanside, CA. We ran for the ready helicopter, and the medical officer piled aboard with his bag just before we lifted off. Arriving over the boat, we lowered a basket to the vessel, and while some thirty fishermen watched with jaws agape, the boat crew loaded the patient into the basket, and the hoist operator started the basket back up toward the helicopter hovering 40 feet over the boat.

As the basket came up, I had a strong olefactory impression that I was outside a Scollay Square barroom. The wine smell was strong and unmistakable. As the air was drawn from the surface first out, up, and then down through the rotor blades, it was loaded with alcoholic vapors. As we left the boat and headed for the hospital, the fumes were, if anything, stronger.

Landing at the hospital, the patient was off-loaded onto a stretcher by the well-trained emergency-room shift and wheeled into the building. Our doc climbed into the cockpit with me, and we started back home.

"How was he, Doc?" I asked.

"I think he was dead when we got him. Anyway, he was DOA," he said, lighting a cigar.

"That's too bad. What was it, a heart attack?"

"Well, it could have been. I'd bet acute alcoholism, though," he said.

"That's a hell of a way to go," I answered.

"Oh, I don't know," said the Doc, puffing on his cigar, "I can think of worse ways. I think he went happy. He sure had enough in him, and he had probably been fishing and drinking to his heart's content. There was a rather contented look on his face. Can you think of any better way to go?"

I had heard of a couple, but I didn't have time to discuss their merits. We were approaching the field, and they were giving us landing instructions.

The Coast Guard is charged with responsibility for medical rescue on and over the seas. In recent years, this has been extended to include some of the cases occurring under water, because of the increasing popularity of Scuba diving. Most of these involve amateur divers suffering from the "bends," a painful and serious condition caused by improper decompression after lengthy dives at excessive depths. The most effective treatment is to place the victim in a pressure chamber, then slowly decompress him. These chambers are located on submarine tenders and at certain Navy Yards and hospitals. Each Rescue Coordination Center has a list of them, and arrangements have been made to bring in victims of the bends by air, flying as low as possible. The procedure has proven successful on a number of occasions.

On 20 May 1962, the Coast Guard Rescue Coordination Center at Cleveland received a call for help for a fifteen-year-old victim of bends at Toledo, Ohio, but the nearest pressure chamber was too far to risk the delay involved. However, the Navy submarine *Cero* was at Detroit for an Armed Forces Day exhibition. The victim was rushed there by Coast Guard helicopter and placed in the forward torpedo room, which was first pressurized to relieve the pain of the bends, then slowly depressurized over a period of hours. The patient recovered completely, thanks to the Navy, the Coast Guard, and some quick thinking by an RCC controller.

It is difficult to find a physician who will make a house call, and it is nearly impossible to find one who wants to go out to sea to practice his profession. So it was refreshing to see the speed with which one young doctor had responded to the call for medical help. As soon as he had parked his car, he was grabbed by the arm by a waiting air crewman and hustled toward the PBM at the head of the ramp. Though he didn't know it, Dr. Henry Terry was about to start out on what a medical journal would describe as probably the "longest house call in medical history."

Only two hours before, a radio call had been received from a tuna boat, 800 miles to the south. A crew member had been caught in the eye by a large fishhook that could not be removed. We had no doctor aboard the station, and a call to North Island revealed that they also were extremely shorthanded. The duty officer called the San Diego County Medical Society and explained the circumstances. Yes, they did have a couple of doctors on call for cases where a stranger might not have a personal physician. These stand-by assignments rotated among the younger members of the Medical Society. They would be glad to call one of the standby physicians. Shortly afterwards, the call service rang the doctor and asked him if he would go to the Coast Guard Air Station, where they had a case of a fishhook in the eye. They neglected to say that the patient was 800 miles away, that the trip would be by air, and that it would involve an open-sea landing, for which the doctor wouldn't get any extra fee. Promising his wife to be back in a short while, he grabbed his bag and left the house.

Now, twenty minutes later, he climbed into the plane, the hatch was closed behind him, and not for another fifteen minutes, when we were climbing through 3,000 feet, would he know where we were going, what the circumstances were, and the fact that it could prove a little hairy. When halfway to our rendezvous point off Cabo San Lucas, another fisherman reported he had an appendicitis case aboard and was told that if he could get to the rendezvous, we would take his patient aboard also.

At dawn, we landed, loaded the two patients aboard, and took off. The takeoff was routine. After leveling off, I went aft to see how the patients were getting along. The fisherman's friends had managed to get the fishhook out of the eye, but as the doctor lifted off the bandage, the eye appeared to be destroyed. The appendicitis case was in good shape, and would be OK. Five hours later, we pulled up the ramp, and the patients were off-loaded into an ambulance. A young woman came running up and threw her arms around the doctor and on learning I was the pilot, thanked me fervently for bringing her husband back safely. After assuring her that we always expected to return, and wouldn't take off if we thought otherwise, I learned that she had called the Air Station after midnight to ascertain her husband's whereabouts, and had then for the first time found out the true nature of his case. She had spent a sleepless night, and was only now slowly unwinding from the last twelve hours.

Several months later, I received a copy of a medical journal that described the "longest call." Nearly a year later, I saw a small item in the local paper reporting that the fisherman was suing the doctor, claiming the loss of an eye. Thoroughly upset, I called the doctor, who we had practically shanghaied into the case, and offered to testify if needed. Though I am a layman, the eye appeared to me to be wrecked when he came aboard. He thanked me and promised to call if I were needed, but explained that the suit was a routine legal maneuver in collecting injury compensation. "By the way," he said, "if you need me again, don't hesitate to call. I might have made a good flight surgeon."

I like gung ho people, be they pilots or doctors!

SAR pilots are typically tiger types, and sometimes you have to fight off the volunteers. A hot Tuesday afternoon in 1961 in Miami was one of those times. A message had been received from the American counsel at Belize, British Honduras, that the four-year-old child of an American missionary had been stricken by polio in the jungle and urgently required evacuation to the States for treatment. The aircraft was being fueled for the mission, and an iron lung was en route to the air station from the hospital. A dozen pilots were in Operations and they were all eager to go. So was I, but I didn't want to pull rank to get the job.

"How many of you have completed all four polio shots?" I asked.

No one had, in fact only five of us had completed two. Of the five, two of us were in our thirties, the other three were in their twenties.

"Well, Bill and I both have two shots each, and we are older. You younger bucks are more susceptible, and the disease at this stage is likely to be highly contagious, so you can't run the risk. Guillou and I will take the flight."

Winking at Bill, I said, "Let's walk by sick bay, and get the third shot anyway for whatever good it will do."

It was dirty pool, but who can argue with logic and a concern for safety?

We landed at Homestead Air Force Base at 1600 to take aboard an Air Force doctor and a technician to work the iron lung. Time was pressing, but we ran into a frustrating delay. Strategic Air Command regulations would not allow the flight surgeon to leave the continental limits on non-Air Force business without a clearance from Eighth Air Force Headquarters. Finally, after 45 minutes, and several digs at the tower to expedite things, the flight surgeon arrived. He had been ready to go for an hour, but no clearance had yet come through. I picked up the radio, and called the Coast Guard Air Station. Yes, they replied, they had already checked with Navy Key West, and a Navy flight surgeon and corpsman were available and waiting. Calling back to the Air Force tower, I informed them that if clearance was not through in five minutes, we were going to leave and pick up a Navy doctor instead. Predictably, service pride took over. The base commander authorized the doctor to go, provided he did not depart the continental limits until Headquarters approval came through. I assured the tower that this would be fine. Once we were in the air, Eighth Air Force could scream all they wanted, but we were going through to Honduras. I never doubted that the clearance would come through, especially with the Navy standing in the wings ready to take over. Before we departed the Florida Keys, we had the blessings of the Eighth Air Force.

Now another delay; we had to go all the way around the western end of Cuba; Havana Control would not grant clearance for a military mercy flight over the island, though they were still clearing commercial airliners.

Near midnight, approaching British Honduras (now Belize), we were racing some approaching thunderstorms brewing back over the jungles. The only navigation aid was a nondirectional radiobeacon, and I had no desire to make an approach to a poorly lighted strip with thunderstorms around to play tricks with the radio compass needle. I could only hope that the beacon, which only operated at night on special request, had been turned on. The jungle slid by below, lit occasionally by lightning flashes. Everything fell into place, the beacon was turned on, and we executed an abbreviated approach, touching down on the wet runway in moderate rain just ahead of the thunderstorm. While the doctor and corpsman took the portable lung and went after the sick child, Bill and I went to the officer's mess of a small detachment of the Duke of Cornwall's Light Infantry. We were kindly received and fed a midnight snack, reluctantly refusing the offer of some fine Scotch with the wry comment that we had enough trouble flying sober, much less with a drink under our belts. It was a brief but pleasant interlude, both for us and the British officers stationed at this isolated spot to guard against the use of the strip by dissident elements in nearby Honduras.

The return trip was uneventful until we were 100 miles from Key West. The doctor stuck his head into the cockpit and asked that we radio ahead and make arrangements for an ambulance at Key West, for the patient was sinking. Also, could I fly any lower. Due to breathing difficulties, the child should be kept at as low an altitude as possible. I glanced at my radar altimeter, which was working fine, and eased down to 300 feet over the ocean. That was low enough for me, and I hoped for the child, now fighting for life in the iron lung.

We boosted the engines up to maximum continuous power, and homed for Key West, where the tower was alerting the Naval Hospital. When we came in sight of Key West, the doctor advised continuing on to Miami. The little girl was still holding on. The sun rose as we sat down at Miami, and our patient was delivered to a waiting ambulance. Despite her serious condition, and several subsequent operations, she lived.

While international relations are touchy on most things, nearly all nationalities seem to get along when someone is in distress and a joint effort is needed to help him. Even the rank and file Castro Cubans were, at our last contact, sympathetic to the requirements for search and rescue. Only a few weeks before the Bay of Pigs landings, one of our planes was granted clearance to land at a small field on the western end of Cuba to pick up a Scandinavian sailor who was being put ashore after being badly hurt in a shipboard accident. After landing, and while waiting for the patient to be brought from the boat-landing site to the plane, the crew was surrounded by bearded militiamen, loaded with Russian burp guns and rifles. Professing great love for "Americanos," the militia leader offered to prove it in deed as well as words.

"Food?" he asked. "Vino? Cerveza?"

The crew declined with mucho graciases.

"Ah, women! You like women? Si?" he winked, indicating several militia women standing nearby, each cuddling a Russian submachine gun.

The crew averred that they did like women, Si! They regretted that they would have to leave shortly. Perhaps mañana.

Shortly after, with many adioses, handshakes, and hasta mañanas, the crew climbed into the plane, little knowing that as they departed, a curtain was being closed behind them. They were the last American military crew off a Cuban-controlled field.

The long-range medicos were interesting, and as they involved open-sea landings in many cases, they were often tough ones. In numbers, however, they did not compare with the many shorter range helicopter evacuations that we carried out each year. With the new turbine-powered helicopters able to go 350 miles offshore, and even farther with in-flight refueling or from helicopter-carrying cutters, open-sea landings by seaplanes ceased in the mid-sixties.

The helicopter is a fairly smooth way of switching from afloat to airborne transportation, and it is far safer for all concerned. Without a doubt, next to antibiotics, the helicopter has saved more sick and injured men at sea than any other device in recent years.

The modus operandi is fairly simple. After a vessel calls for medical evacuation and RCC orders it carried out, a fixed-wing aircraft may locate the vessel and verify its position. The helicopter and its escort then home in to the ship by electronic gadgetry. When over the ship, the helicopter hovers and lowers a metal basket, or a litter if the patient is not ambulatory.

When the patient is strapped in, he is hoisted into the helicopter and flown to a hospital. A hospital corpsman usually goes along on these evacuations and since the helicopter cannot afford to carry excess weight, often serves as the hoist operator. Such simple uncomplicated hoists at intermediate distances offshore present no great operational problem, and hundreds have been carried out. However, when the weather gets bad, or night descends, complications set in, and they can try a pilot's soul.

Sometimes even a routine job can turn to worms. One was a flight 80 miles offshore to take aboard an unconscious patient. Before lowering the litter down through the maze of rigging to the deck, we had carefully instructed the fishing boat to detach the litter, strap the helpless patient in securely, then reattach the litter to the snap hook of the hoist cable. They acknowledged that they understood thoroughly. When the litter was on deck, they did none of these things. Instead, four men hustled the patient to the litter, laid him in it, and without making any effort to fasten him in, retired to the bow to await the hoist. There was an extreme risk that the litter could snag on the rigging coming up and dump the patient out, so we called frantically by radio for them to lash him in. No one was in the pilothouse listening to the radio; they were all in the bow watching. Frantic hand signaling, fist shaking, and futile cussing produced no results. They only waved gaily back. It was take a chance on a risky hoist or cut the cable and leave the man. Finally, after ten minutes of hovering like a caught fish, I decided to chance a hoist due to the critical condition of the patient.

As the fishing boat rolled to starboard, the hoist operator yelled,

"Now!", and I added power, jumping the helicopter and the attached basket through the rigging and into the air. We were lucky, and soon had the man in the cabin. It could have been otherwise, and a simple hoist could have ended in tragedy. The line between being a hero and a scapegoat is often awfully thin.

At sea as on land, birth is the only "illness" that seems to bring happiness. Most pilots who have been in the rescue business a long time have had their race with the stork. Lieutenant Joe Tanguay made a midnight run from an offshore island to a naval hospital with the wife of the lighthouse keeper, only to read in the morning paper a statement by a doctor at the hospital that labor had not begun and that only hysteria was involved. That afternoon, the lady had the last laugh, giving birth to an eight-pound infant, who was named after the helo pilot.

At Elizabeth City, NC, the station flight surgeon, Dr. Andy Horne, didn't win the race, but he did just as well, delivering a healthy six-pound baby 500 feet over Currituck Sound in the helicopter's cabin. Two counties had a heated dispute over which would register the birth.

An Albatross amphibian crew from Coast Guard Air Station Kodiak, Alaska, had one nearly as close in February 1965 when they were called upon to evacuate a woman, already in labor, from a remote fishing village. The weather was so terrible that a local bush pilot had refused to attempt the evacuation, but the woman was in grave danger, as both her previous children had been born by Caesarian section. She had to be taken to a hospital. Landing in an inlet with ceiling varying between 50 and 200 feet, the Coast Guard crew took the woman aboard, together with a small child believed suffering from pneumonia. Five minutes later, just as they were airborne, an engine quit, and they were forced to sit back down on the water. In the chill of winter, with a woman in difficult labor and a small child with pneumonia, they had a real full-blown crisis. Working with the speed of desperation, they repaired the engine, buttoned up, and took off again. This time the engine behaved, and they soon landed at Kodiak, where the woman gave normal birth to a healthy baby in the ambulance. I never saw the birth announcement, but this one should have been named for the mechanic who repaired the engine while working out on a cold slippery wing.

With the phaseout of the seaplane and amphibian, such opera-

An HH-52 helo lands after a mission, as flight-deck crew race to snap on hold-down ties.

tions are a thing of the past. Fortunately, vastly improved twin-engine helicopters have filled their shoes, except on the very long range jobs, where operational ingenuity usually finds a way.

In October 1970, a para-rescue team from the Air Force ARRS squadron in Hawaii was dropped by parachute to treat a critically ill patient on Fanning Island, a tiny atoll 1,000 miles south of Honolulu. When an attempt to evacuate the patient to Christmas Island, which had a suitable runway, failed due to high seas, Lieutenant Commander Albert Allison landed a big Coast Guard C-130 on the narrow and rough 2,500-foot landing strip at Fanning. The 30-foot-wide runway was too narrow to turn the big plane around, so Allison backed down the runway using reverse thrust on his four engines. After a jet-assisted takeoff (JATO), the patient was flown to a Honolulu hospital.

Sometimes the combined efforts of ships, aircraft, and helicopters are required. In June 1986, the 276-foot Soviet trawler *Lotos* reported that a critically injured crew member required evacuation. The Russian vessel was 510 miles west of Kodiak, Alaska, but only 130 miles from CGC *Resolute,* which launched her helicopter to transfer the patient. With the patient on board and stabilized by the ship's hospital corpsman, the cuttter raced for Cold Bay, Alaska, where a waiting C-130 took the patient for the flight to the base hospital at Kodiak.

Helicopters can be refueled in flight from a helicopter-carrying ship, and some from a tanker aircraft. When the tanker *Reunion* requested the evacuation of a young crewman with acute appendicitis, AMVER indicated no other vessels near the tanker, which was 1,200 miles from San Diego and 800 miles from the nearest port at Manzanillo, Mexico. The Air Force offered to provide para-rescue men, who would be flown to the tanker in a Coast Guard C-130, an H-3 helicopter capable of mid-air refueling, and a tanker aircraft to supply the fuel. Early the following morning, two para-rescue men parachuted into the water and were picked up by the *Reunion's* boat. The H-3 departed from the San Francisco area, refueled from the tanker aircraft in flight south of San Diego, and arrived at La Paz, Mexico, the following morning. After refueling and taking aboard a relief crew, the H-3 proceeded toward the *Reunion.* Just prior to arriving, it was again refueled from an aerial tanker. Hoisting the patient and para-rescue men, the helicopter proceeded to Acapulco, Mexico, where the sick man was hospitalized. It was a striking demonstration of the helicopter's long legs, interservice cooperation, and aircrew stamina. The courage of the para-rescue men is beyond mere praise.

Today, from anywhere in the world, medical advice can be obtained by seamen from CIRM or from the U.S. Public Health Service through the Coast Guard. Such traffic is also handled by the Commercial Coast Stations on high-frequency single-sideband (SSB) at no charge. Direct contact with one's own doctor can be made by yachtsmen in the coastal areas through the VHF marine operator, or advice can be requested from the Coast Guard. Should evacuation of a patient be required, the SAR organization has the ability to remove him quickly over most of the world's ocean area, and will do so without regard to nationality. It is an area of international cooperation that should be an example in other relationships.

Lost and Crippled Sheep

3

We were sitting around the table sipping brandy after the banquet, listening with respect to tales of blood and thunder being spun by some of the "grey eagles," pilots who had flown past more range stations than most pilots do by telephone poles.

"Used to fly the old boats out of Pensacola when I was in the Navy in the twenties," said the aging airline captain, lighting his cigar. "You may not believe it, but we carried homing pigeons in crates on the over-water flights. On one flight, a squall line moved in, and we had to dodge thunderstorms for a hundred miles. When we finally got clear of them, there was no land in sight. We didn't know where in the hell we were. So we just took out a pigeon, turned him loose, and followed him."

"You mean that the pigeon flew straight back to Pensacola?" I asked, sensing my leg being stretched a little.

"I don't really know," said the old-timer, taking another sip of brandy, "he was so fast, and the crate I was flying was so slow that he soon left us behind. It was one of the few times that I almost got lost. Never did though, in spite of what these cynics say."

"How about that time going into Lajes?" asked another pilot.

"I wasn't lost at all," said the veteran. "I just didn't know where I was for a couple of hours. There have been a few hundred times when I didn't know where I was, but lost, never! You aren't lost until you don't get there. I always got there."

"I'm with you, George," said the chief pilot of an international airline. "I've never been lost myself, but I've sure as hell been pretty ignorant of my whereabouts."

There was laughing agreement from the crowd. We all had been there.

Professional airmen almost habitually depreciate their ability, at least outwardly. It is really a form of negative bragging. A smooth, perfectly executed flight will be described as one in which the teller staggered into the air, groped his way across the pond, finally consulted a Ouija Board to get a fix, and closed his eyes and hauled back on the yoke at minimums to make a landing from which he was able to walk away. It is conscious self-depreciation that can only be indulged in by men who know their job so cold that their ego is not threatened by such affected self-ridicule. If, at a meeting of the local Hangar of the Quiet Birdmen, you run into a fellow lodge member who actually tells a straight story about the excellence of his flying, look out. You are talking with either a green copilot or a Cessna pilot with all of 100 hours under his belt.

The accuracy of aerial navigation is a relative thing. Over the North American continent, with its vast electronics navigation system, a professional pilot on an Instrument Flight Plan will call his fixes down to the minute. On a Miami-to-Boston flight, there is not one minute when the aircraft is not under radar surveillance by the FAA Air Traffic Control people. From the time the wheels lift off at Miami until the runway at Boston is sighted dead ahead at the conclusion of an instrument approach, there is seldom any doubt as to the aircraft's exact position. But over many vast stretches of ocean, navigation aids are few, and the aircraft can be 25 to 50 miles in error in its position without seriously endangering the flight, as long as the engines keep running. As it approaches its destination and begins to pick up the shore-based navigation aids, the position will become increasingly more accurate, and at the conclusion of the flight, the aircraft will be guided by the precision instrument landing system within a few feet of the runway.

A ship navigator, on the other hand, traveling at 1/40th of an aircraft's speed would be hopelessly inept to have a position error of

50 miles. Yet, occasionally ships do just that. But a ship's navigation is less complex than that of an aircraft, and its equipment is considerably less sophisticated. Small pleasure craft, sometimes combining lack of equipment with lack of experience, are a story unto themselves.

An aircraft is subject to so many potential sources of error that it is remarkable so few lose their way. A ship's navigator, or a motorist lost in Kansas, can always stop and think things out. A pilot must continue flying. As he does so, he may be increasing his error and, at the same time, rapidly depleting his fuel. On an ocean crossing, there are winds—often unpredicted—that unless compensated for can displace him as much as 100 miles in an hour. A compass error of a few degrees will affect a ship's position by only a few miles in a day's run, but it can upset an aircraft's navigation as much in thirty minutes of travel. Even over land, a pilot attempting to navigate by reference to terrain and visual objects is at the mercy of weather, for if he loses sight of the ground due to clouds, he is soon lost unless he shifts to instrument flight. The air and the sea are both terribly unforgiving of human error, but a ship can always drop its anchor or heave to; there is no holding ground in the sky.

Aircraft do get lost. Sometimes it is equipment failure; often, it is inexperience; at times, the weather and elements are overwhelming; occasionally, it is human stupidity or negligence. Regardless of how they get lost, there is usually a way out, and the smart pilot has a plan of action for such an occasion. Flying off the East Coast, for example, one has simply to turn west and he will eventually hit land. If the basic "way out" doesn't work promptly, it is time to call Search and Rescue for help.

Some pilots feel that to call for help is a humiliation or, at least, an admission that they don't know what they are doing; and out of a false sense of pride, embarrassment, or in an effort to cover up the mistake, they either refuse to call for assistance or wait until they are in extremis before doing so. Often, the result is another intriguing article in the *Accident Bulletin*; sometimes it is only a paragraph. The editors find it hard to write much about a plane and pilot who were never found. The hot, bold pilot who feels confident that he is the master of his own fate and always capable of solving his own problems could well heed the old adage, "There are old pilots, and there are bold pilots; but there are no old, bold pilots." There are some pretty notable exceptions, of course, but th adage has a lot of validity.

The smart pilots, once they have progressed beyond the stage of mere "ignorance of position," don't hesitate to announce their predicament, though some are a bit cunning about how they do it. Once an alert is received on a lost aircraft, the vast resources of the air traffic control system and the SAR network are quickly focused on it. Within seconds, radio direction finder (DF) and radar stations over a wide area are alerted. The alarm rings at the nearest SAR station, and SAR flight crews scramble. Their mission—find the lost aircraft or vessel and bring 'em back alive.

Disaster does not always arrive full blown. It may start as a minor difficulty, soon to be compounded by others. More often than not, the first failure is in equipment. Most humans function well when everything is going smoothly. Only after equipment fails do the human errors begin to accumulate. With Navy 59072, a twin-engine patrol bomber flying in heavy clouds from an overseas island base to Norfolk, it started with a small black box.

Shortly after takeoff, the Loran, an electronics device for fixing position, was found to be inoperative. The flight continued, and the navigator computed his assumed positions from the course and speed flown. The clouds prevented taking a sun line by sextant or observing the water below to determine wind drift. But with land only a few hundred miles ahead, there was no real worry. The aircraft was on automatic pilot, and the fluxgate compass was steady as a rock at 295 degrees. In retrospect, it was too steady. The dead-reckoning positions were passed periodically to New York Overseas Radio. Everything was satisfactory.

Late in the afternoon, at a position the navigator estimated to be only 150 miles off the North Carolina coast, the aircraft broke out of the clouds. Glancing up, the copilot looked at the setting sun and sat up straight in his seat. Turning to the pilot, he said, "Shouldn't the sun be setting about west-southwest?"

The pilot agreed that it should, then also took a long look. The sun, instead of being on their port bow as it should have been, was setting on their starboard quarter. Both pilots glanced at the compass, which still read 295 degrees. Something was wrong! Disengaging the autopilot, the pilot started to turn toward the sun. As the aircraft turned, the compass made no movement. It was stuck, and had been stuck for God only knew how long! With the compass stuck, the gyros of the autopilot had drifted off, and the aircraft had gradually changed course throughout the flight. They had flown in a wide circle! Quickly, they pressed the re-cycle button of the fluxgate compass, and it spun around, settling on a new heading. Now the compass was probably indicating correctly. But without Loran, and unable to obtain radio bearings, the navigator was unable to obtain a fix. Not knowing what course they had been steering, he couldn't even estimate a dead-reckoning position. They were lost, without a clue as to their whereabouts.

With more attention to their navigation, it could have been prevented, but there was no comfort in crying over spilled milk. Night was approaching, and the ocean stretched out endlessly below. There was only one answer—tell New York everything and get help from Search and Rescue.

The call was promptly acknowledged by the operator at New York Overseas Radio. He picked up the hot-line phone and passed the word to the Coast Guard's New York Rescue Coordination Center, known by the voice call of "Atlantic Rescue."

Atlantic Rescue took over. First the alert went out on high-speed teletype to the various rescue commands along the Atlantic seaboard. The most important addressee on the net, however, was the Net Control Station of the Federal Communications Commission (FCC) in Washington. The first order of business was to locate the position from which the lost aircraft was broadcasting its signal. FCC had the means to do it.

These high-frequency direction finder (HF/DF) stations are able to take a bearing on the source of a radio signal, accurate within a few degrees. The bearings from several HF/DF stations, when plotted on a chart, intersect near the position from which the signal is being transmitted.

From Net Control in Washington, a teletype message went out to HF/DF stations in Texas, Florida, Georgia, Maryland, New York, Maine, and Bermuda.

"Navy 59072 lost and broadcasting on 6595 kilocycles."

Throughout the net, radio direction finder operators swiftly tuned in the frequency. As they heard the pilot talking with New York Overseas Radio, they began to take bearings and transmitted them to the Net Control Station in Washington.

"The first fix is a rough one," the DF Net Control Watch Officer warned Atlantic Rescue, "but it shows him to be about 240 miles northeast of Bermuda. We are trying to get a better one."

The controller at Atlantic Rescue whistled as he looked at the huge wall chart of the Atlantic. Instead of being 550 miles west of Bermuda where the pilot had supposed himself to be, the HF/DF fix placed the lost plane 700 miles farther to the east-northeast. Picking up the hot line to New York Overseas Radio, he passed the information. New York Overseas Radio transmitted the unpleasant news to the Navy pilot, adding, "Bermuda is your closest point. Suggest you take steers from Bermuda DF."

Bermuda, listening on the frequency, chimed in and advised, "Navy 59072, your steer to Bermuda is 205 degrees magnetic."

The time was 1824 local. Only thirty-two minutes had elapsed since the lost aircraft had emerged from the clouds.

In Bermuda, a rarity was occurring. Bad weather is no novelty there, but fog is, and a thick fog was setting in, with low ceilings and less than a quarter of a mile visibility. It was no place to bring in an aircraft, for the island had no precision instrument approach. Due to the hills, the minimum ceiling allowed for aircraft instrument approaches was 700 feet. Now it was already below allowable minimums. But the lost pilot had no choice—there was only one place he could reach with the fuel available, and that was Bermuda.

At 1832, the phone rang. I was the duty SAR aircraft commander. The duty controller at the Coast Guard RCC at Bermuda was on the line.

"We've got a real weirdie here, sir. A Navy plane supposed to be en route for Norfolk is lost and has been located by the DF net 240 miles northeast of here. Kindley DF is homing him to Bermuda. We estimate he should be over the island by 2015."

I took a quick glance out the window and stepped back to the phone. "I don't see much purpose in scrambling an escort. We couldn't help much, and we probably won't be able to get back in here. He is going to have a real problem unless this weather lifts. Let's sail *Cook Inlet* and have her take station off the island to provide him with radar and radiobeacon services. Also tell Lieutenant Commander Solberg to get over to the ship and board it before she sails. They'll need an aviator aboard to help out."

The Coast Guard Cutter *Cook Inlet* was the standby rescue vessel at Bermuda, moored at St. George. When the call came from the RCC ordering them to proceed, guests were just arriving for a formal dinner party. Within minutes, word was piped for guests to lay ashore, and preparations were made to get underway. As the lines were singled up, Lieutenant Commander Solberg, the Coast Guard Air Detachment operation officer, ran up the gangplank. The ship's job was to find a way of assisting the aircraft into a landing in the prevailing weather or to try and rescue the plane's crew if they couldn't make it. They had a lot of leeway, for it had never been done before. There were no prescribed procedures to go by other than those used to assist ditching aircraft in mid-ocean. They had about two hours to adapt these to the present situation.

At 1850, the RCC controller called again and he spoke rapidly. "The DF Net has got another fix. It's a much better one than the first, a Class A, and he was 420 miles from the island on this fix. The pilot says he doesn't have enough fuel to reach the island and has declared a distress."

"Sound the scramble!" Before slamming down the receiver, I added, "and tell the *Cook Inlet* to proceed toward him at flank speed!"

Racing toward the big Martin Mariner seaplane, I could see lights and scurrying figures as the plane crew and line crew went about their well-practiced routine. As I strapped into the left seat and slipped on my headphones, the flight engineer chanted, "Starting Two!"

The Pratt and Whitney engine coughed, then burst into power.

"Oil pressure up. All readings normal. Starting One!"

"Roger."

Number one engine roared into life.

"All stations report ready to go over the side."

"Aft Station ready."

"Flight Engineer ready."

"Radio ready."

"Radar ready."

"Copilot ready. Starting takeoff checklist."

I leaned out the cockpit window, and gave a thumbs up to the Beach Master. At his signal, we added power, and the big plane eased down the ramp into the water, restrained by the tractor on its

Flight and line crews race for the ready P5M Marlin after sounding of the alarm. Normal airborne time after alert was usually less than ten minutes.

stern line. As soon as it was in the water, the detachable wheels were released and pulled clear by the beach crew, the nose and tail restraining lines were cast off, and the 30 tons of land-based aircraft had become a seaplane. We taxied out into the fog and darkness.

Quickly the flight engineer and copilot completed the pre-flight engine checks, and as we rounded the point leading to the open bay, the copilot sang out, "Takeoff checklist complete. Ready to go."

Up ahead there was only fog and darkness.

"How does it look up ahead, radar?"

"You have a mooring buoy at 020 degrees relative at 3,500 yards, sir. Ahead is good for 3,000 yards."

"OK. Copilot, get emergency clearance and climb instructions."

RCC had obtained the traffic clearance from Bermuda Control after sounding the alarm, and it came in promptly. We were cleared to the point of intercept, with an unrestricted climb to a flight level 1,000 feet above the distressed aircraft. No essential traffic. With this weather, no one else was flying in the Bermuda Control area.

Less than a minute later, we were airborne and climbing. Before the flaps could be retracted we had entered the soup. The ceiling was less than 200 feet.

As we turned to the northeast, RCC was giving us the dope and initial vector.

"Your vector 026 degrees magnetic. Your estimated time of intercept is 2010. Navy 59072 now at flight level 4,000 feet, course 205 degrees, speed 140 knots. His 1835 position was 38-05 North, 63-15 West. Working 6595 kilocycles, and guarding 121.5 megacycles. *Cook Inlet* underway at 1855 guarding standard SAR frequencies. Contact Kindley Control when reaching 5,000."

I glanced at the panel clock. Only eight minutes had elapsed since the scramble alarm rang. So far, so good. Now it was up to us, and to the Navy crew some 400 miles away.

Our navigator would have to put us 75 miles ahead of the distressed plane where we could establish Very High Frequency (VHF) radio contact. From that point, we would home in using our VHF direction finder to get within 15 miles. The last 15 miles, we would rely on radar, pyrotechnic signals, and visual sighting to effect the rendezvous. At a closing speed of 300 knots, there would be no time for mistakes.

We broke out on top of the lower cloud level at 3,000 feet and continued our climb to 5,000. The navigator handed the copilot a paper slip with a course adjustment, and a revised time of intercept.

Picking up his mike, the copilot called the distressed plane on high frequency radio, "Navy 59072, this is Coast Guard Rescue 4732. We estimate intercept at 2013. Guard 121.5 megacycles now, and stand by for a call on that frequency."

When the distressed plane acknowledged, the copilot shifted over to the VHF frequency and gave a call. Faintly, but clearly, the Navy pilot answered.

"OK, Navy, each time I tell you, hold down your mike key on this frequency for thirty seconds so that we can take a DF bearing. Start now."

As the Navy pilot transmitted a radio signal, the VHF direction finder needle on our instrument panel slowly swung and settled down, indicating 5 degrees to starboard.

We altered course to starboard, and the copilot said, "We have you bearing 033 degrees, almost dead ahead. Now what is your situation and fuel state?"

Everything was functioning except his Loran and radar. However, he did not have enough fuel to make the island, and believed he would have to ditch it. The worry hung in his voice.

After advising him that *Cook Inlet* was clear of the island and coming hard, I urged him to keep pushing. If he could reach the ship, half of our problem would be licked.

Every two minutes, we took a DF bearing. They remained steady, a good indication that our course to intercept was good. At 2002 the navigator advised that we should intercept in ten minutes. He should now be 50 miles ahead.

It was time to start firing flares at regular intervals. The flight engineer fitted the Very flare pistol into the overhead receptacle, inserted a cartridge, and fired it. The flare shot into the air several hundred feet above the aircraft, and lit off. Out to the side could be seen a faint reflection of light from the flare burning astern of us.

After the fourth flare went off, the Navy pilot reported that he had a flare in sight dead ahead. We lowered a landing light and flashed it on and off several times, and he confirmed that he had us in sight. Soon his flashing red navigation light could be seen ahead.

At 2005, I wrapped the plane into a steep turn, and settled down in escort position one mile behind and 1,000 feet above him. The intercept was a little late. He was farther from the island than we had thought.

The navigator handed up another slip, giving the course back to Bermuda and the estimated time of arrival. This information was passed to our distressed buddy. Part of the job was done, but the tough part lay ahead.

"How's your fuel now?" I asked. "Can you keep pushing for the island?"

With help at hand, he steadied down, and his voice was nearly jovial. "Well, I've been holding out on you a bit. I've got about an hour's more fuel than I told you. Yes, I can make it."

Well, I thought, do we tell the patient now? He obviously wasn't aware of the weather there.

"Well, Navy, I've been holding out on you too. The weather at Bermuda is 200 feet overcast, visibility one-half mile. That is 500 feet below minimum."

There was no answer. Nothing like knocking a man back down again just as his hopes start to rise. But the more time he had to prepare, the better off he would be.

Soon we were in contact with *Cook Inlet*, and talked things over with her. She was taking position five miles off the runway, had turned on her radiobeacon, and was ready to provide radar services to talk the Navy pilot down to the runway. It was no approved approach, but there was little choice now. If this failed, he would have to try a night ditching—an extreme measure in any pilot's book.

After explaining the plan to the Navy pilot, I added a final word of caution, "On final approach the ship will call out the distance to the island every half mile. If you don't have the runway in sight at one mile, climb to the left. There is a good sized hill to the right of your approach path!"

When the Navy plane arrived over the ship, he let down to 1,000 feet, made a procedure turn 10 miles out, then began letting down toward the ship for his final approach. We orbited five miles north.

As he passed over the ship, and homed on the Kindley radiobeacon, *Cook Inlet* was transmitting a steady flow of information. "You just passed over the ship." "You are on course. Four miles to go."

"On course. Three miles."

"Two miles."

"Standby to mark one mile. Mark! One mile."

I could take it no longer. "Pull up!" I yelled into the mike. "Runway in sight!" he answered.

After he was safely on the deck, we made an approach to the Naval Station seadrome on our own radar, establishing visual contact at 300 feet. After getting out of the plane, we walked slowly in and stood around Operations drinking coffee and letting the tension ooze out. The phone rang. It was the tower at Kindley Air Force Base, calling at our request.

"It was damn near like a miracle," said the voice at the other end of the line. "The ceiling was right on the runway. After he started his approach, it lifted to about 300 feet. A bit later, it was down again. Now, even the sea gulls are walking. Somebody must have been doing some praying."

"Yep, I imagine you're right." I said. "Thanks a lot for calling."

I hung up the phone and looked at the crew. They looked tired, and they didn't look like deacons. Still, when things turn to worms, and you are walking the edge, there are mighty few atheists on the flight deck. I would guess that there had been some powerful praying.

Unlike the crew of Navy 59072, some victims don't give enough warning to allow even a prayer. A fighter pilot, lost over North Carolina for nearly an hour, exhausted his fuel trying to work out his own salvation. His first call to anyone was a report of a flameout— due to fuel exhaustion. He ejected and was saved, but Uncle Sam was out a multi-million-dollar fighter. It was a pretty stiff price to pay for misplaced pride. A simple request for a DF fix twenty minutes earlier would have done the trick. He could have been saved without the DF Net even knowing he was lost. With a little cunning, he could have asked for a "practice steer." It's childish, but better than bashing up the taxpayer's airplanes.

The DF and radar Nets in that area include a number of stations between Washington, D.C., and Cherry Point, NC. A pilot, unsure of position among the thunderstorms and the vast swamplands, has only to make a call on UHF radio and ask for a fix and a steer to the nearest field. Bearings are immediately taken by the various stations, relayed to the Norfolk RCC, plotted, and the positions passed back to the pilot.

Often pilots will ask for and be given practice steers, which affords training for both the pilot and the DF Net. One hazy May morning, two Navy aircraft were being given practice steers by the Elizabeth City UHF/DF, when they were interrupted by a call from an Air Force jet. The conversation was recorded as follows:

"Elizabeth City DF, this is Air Force jet 5902. Request a practice DF steer."

"Air Force jet 5902, this is Elizabeth City DF. Give me a call in twenty minutes, and I'll try to work you in. We are already working two Navy aircraft on practices now."

Silence for thirty seconds.

"Elizabeth City DF, this is Air Force 5902. You'd better make that a real steer. I am lost."

"Roger Air Force 5902. Understand you are really lost. Steer 050 degrees magnetic to Elizabeth City. Standby to transmit for a fix. Are you declaring an emergency?"

"Do I have to?"

"That's up to you. If you have an emergency, you are supposed to."

"This is Air Force 5902. Roger. I am declaring an emergency."

After that, I always wondered how many real ones have been passed off as practices. Some of the boys are real sly.

The DF Net has pulled all types out of the sky. A very embarrassed and lost Marine colonel, flying an F6F out of Anacostia, was steered into Elizabeth City by the DF. He had taken the morning off from his Pentagon desk to get in four hours of monthly flight time. Planning to stay in the Washington area, he carried only a local area chart. Soon he was unable to recognize any landmarks, despite some frantic scanning. The answer soon became obvious—the high winds at altitude had blown him outside the area covered by the chart, and he was effectively lost. He wisely called for a DF steer, and was vectored into Elizabeth City, 150 miles south of Anacostia. After being refueled, he was provided with the necessary charts marked with a red track line direct to Anacostia. Though a few soothing and heartfelt remarks were then made about how smart it was to call right away when you are lost, he was still shaking his head in disgust when he climbed back into the cockpit; his pride was hurt—but he and his aircraft were intact.

A Beechcraft full of Marines was lost at night in an area of heavy thunderstorms. They frantically called for a steer, and the DF net located them over the ocean off Cape Hatteras! After being vectored in and turned over by the DF to GCA for a straight-in instrument approach, they landed safely. One engine cut out from lack of fuel while they were taxiing in. The other was running on fumes and memories of fuel. The pilot climbed out, and said to the duty officer, "I just got back from thirty-seven missions in Korea. There was more pucker factor out there tonight than all of Korea combined. Hairy, hairy! You have a bar here?"

A lot of lost aircraft have been saved by the Radio Direction Finder Net, by SAR interceptors, or by alert air traffic controllers, but far too many have been lost. The air navigation system in the decade following World War II was inadequate, the fighter aircraft and small planes had limited equipment, and the pilots often had very little weather experience. Today with Omni radio stations that give an instant course, DME and TACAN electronic navigation systems that give constant readings of the distance to the station, and nearly complete radar coverage of the busy continental and coastal areas, lost military and commercial aircraft have fortunately become less of a problem. When a pilot does become lost, it is either due to equipment failure, inexperience, or gross carelessness. With complex and sophisticated control systems, plus demanding training in bad weather flying, most of the uncertainty has been taken out of navigation. But these advances have also taken much of the fun out of flying. It is virtually impossible for a young buck to fly along looking at the girls on the beach, or take side excursions to places of interest. For years, buzzing a girlfriend's house was frowned upon, and now it is career suicide. The sky is just too crowded, and individualism is not tolerated. In military aviation, seat of the pants flying and navigation by landmarks and highways are mostly confined to the helicopter drivers. Even they are being regimented. But regimentation (or standardization in official circles) is safer, and individual freedom must bow in this, as in other things, to the common welfare and safety.

Electronics equipment and navigation aids continue to improve, and our commercial and military pilots are better trained than ever. The human being is subject to errors in decision making, however, and even the best-trained man has a breaking point if enough circumstances combine against him. The threshold of the breaking point is later for a trained man, but everyone has his point.

The two fighter pilots cruising on top of the thick overcast on a February afternoon were a long way from being at a proper state of training. Both were reservists on two weeks' annual active duty, and their flying time for the last two years had been limited. Neither had ever made a practice Ground Controlled Approach (GCA), though this is the primary precision instrument approach used by military pilots, and their proficiency in instrument and weather flying was low. At the time of takeoff, the weather had been good, and was expected to remain so. But any experienced pilot knows that good weather can be a fleeting thing. Unless he is well qualified to fly instruments, weather must be watched carefully.

The flight, which had started an hour or so before, had been uneventful. Both pilots were carrying out their scheduled training, and had become so engrossed that they failed to notice the steady deterioration of the weather between them and their base. When they finally saw the coastal fog moving in rapidly, the flight leader became concerned and attempted to pick up the radio navigation facility serving home plate. He had no luck, nor did his wingman. For a half hour, they flew various courses and attempted to establish their position. Sixty miles either side of them were large well-equipped air-fields ready to answer a request for help, but the pilots said nothing. Instead, they discussed their predicament in carefully guarded words on the tactical frequency. As their predicament worsened, their conversational anxiety heightened. Finally, nearly two hours after take-off, an alert controller at the Coast Guard Air Station at Elizabeth City overhead them and grew concerned. Cutting in on their radio frequency, he asked if they were lost, and if they wanted a steer. They were and did.

An initial steer of 035 degrees was given, and only six minutes later they were over Elizabeth City. Now they knew where they were, but there would be no landing there. The fog had settled in and visibility was less than 200 yards. A quick check showed that Norfolk had 600 feet and two miles. Plenty good for an instrument approach. Weather at Cherry Point, 40 miles farther away, was marginal. Norfolk was the best bet. The Elizabeth City controller passed the weather information to the two pilots circling overhead, recommended that they proceed to Norfolk, and concluded with the instructions, "Vector 006 degrees magnetic. We will alert Norfolk approach control and have Navy GCA stand by to pick you up."

Back came the answer, "Neither of us has ever done a GCA."

The controller thought fast, hit the scramble alarm, and piped the word over the loudspeaker to scramble a PB1G, a rescue version of the B-17 *Flying Fortress*. Things were getting a little tight, but the PB1G could intercept them, then lead both pilots to Norfolk. Once there, the experienced PB1G pilot could fly the GCA approach while the two fighter pilots flew formation on him. When in sight of the field, the SAR aircraft could circle while the two fighters landed. They had only to fly formation, and this should be duck soup for them.

Flipping his mike switch, the controller said to the two fighters, "Orbit overhead at 3,000 feet. Coast Guard Rescue 7255 is scrambling and will lead you to Norfolk. He will be airborne in five minutes."

Then came the shocker! They reported only fifteen minutes of fuel remaining. The controller swung around and looked at me. On hearing the alarm, I had run into the operations center. Now, as operations officer, I had to take the ball. The look on the controller's face spoke a lot of words ending with, "What now?"

It didn't require much soul searching to rule out Norfolk. Two
planes running out of fuel over that crowded city would have been
disastrous. What about a bailout near Elizabeth City? Possible, but
the area was largely water and swampland, and the water was near
freezing. Once they bailed out, there was little possibility we could
conduct an effective search for them until the weather cleared. That
could be twenty-four hours or more, and they could be long dead by
then. What about GCA? Possible but neither had done a GCA, and
the weather was below GCA minimums. I flicked the intercom to
GCA, and got Lieutenant Swede Hansen, the GCA Officer, on the
box. Explaining the situation, I asked. "Can you do it, Swede?"

"It's a tough one, but if they'll follow instructions, I think we can."

"OK. Stand by."

I threw off the switch. Few men like to play God, especially with
other men's lives. I looked at the clock, twelve minutes to go. No
time left. They pay you to make decisions, but there isn't enough
money for one like this.

"Swede, we are going to bring them in. Give them each one pass.
If they don't make it, vector them out east of the river and bail them
out. One pass! They've got only ten minutes' fuel."

Picking up the radio mike, I called the two circling fighters. "We
are going to bring you in on GCA. One pass each. If you don't make
it pull up to 2,000 feet, and GCA will position you for bailout. When
they say go, bail out. If you don't want to try a GCA, we will bail
you out now. Over."

Both pilots elected to have a go at it. Paratroopers may like to
jump, but pilots have a decided aversion to it. They shifted to the
GCA frequency. We huddled around the receiver in operations and
listened. Outside the crash trucks and ambulance were taking position, and the crash boat had shoved off into the fog. Now we could
only sit, pray, and sweat. GCA Unit No. 2 had the ball.

Swede Hansen's voice came over the air, deliberately bored and
calm, giving instructions. He turned Hamlet 12, the first plane, on
final approach; Hamlet 5, the other one, was held in a nearby orbit.

Swede, looking into his radar scope, started talking the pilot in.
The pilot had to fly the plane, correcting his heading and altitude to
follow Swede's bidding. For an experienced pilot, it is simple. This
boy wasn't experienced, but he was doing OK. Now he was two miles
out, and Swede was talking like a Dutch Uncle.

"You are two miles from touchdown point and one quarter mile left of course. Turn right to 150. You are coming down very nicely. On glidepath. Now steer 152, a slight correction to the right. You are correcting nicely to course. Now you are going 10, 20, 30 feet above the glidepath. Ease it down. You are on course and one mile from touchdown. Turn left to 135. You are coming down and on glide path. Add a little power. Now turn right to 137. You are coming in nicely. Approaching field minimums. On course. On glide path. You are now over touchdown. If you do not have the field in sight, make an emergency pullup and climb to 1,500 feet on this heading."

Hamlet 12 did have the field in sight. He was too far to the left of the runway to land, but he wasn't even about to lose sight of terra firma. With his wingtip nearly touching the ground, he wrapped up the plane to the left, and added power to circle and land. The control tower operator looked on, petrified with fright, as the fighter missed the tower by feet, and the line crews dived for shelter as it thundered a few feet over their heads.

As it disappeared over the river, still in a tight turn, the roar of the engine could still be heard. At least he was still flying. Soon, he completed his turn and the noise came closer. Suddenly the power was chopped. Agonizing seconds ticked by as we waited for the crash, then the welcome screech of tires on the runway! Hamlet 12 was on the deck; he had made it the hard way.

Hamlet 5 was on final. Down he came, but his control was erratic, and he wandered to the left and right of the course, above and below the glide path. GCA was coaxing him, easily but insistently. Now he was over the threshold and the GCA outside observer sighted him through the fog, over the runway, with 4,000 feet of good runway ahead. He had it made. But the pilot of Hamlet 5 didn't know it. With only a few hundred feet of ahead visibility, he may have believed he had little runway or he may have been concentrating on his instruments. His engine roared as he started an emergency climb.

"Bail him out Swede!" I yelled over the squawk box. It was redundant advice, for GCA had already started the vector to bailout position.

"Hamlet 5, this is GCA. Turn left to 100, climb to 1,500 feet. Stand by to bail out on my mark. Acknowledge."

There was no answer. The pilot had his mike key depressed, and only the hum of his mike could be heard. Unless he let up his mike he couldn't hear GCA give him instructions.

"Hamlet 5, this is GCA. Release your mike key. Release your mike key." Only the hum.

"Hamlet 5, this is GCA. Turn left to 100. Stand by to bail out. Release your mike key!"

No answer. Suddenly the humming stopped. There was only silence, punctuated by occasional static.

The controller was busy. State Police were alerted, then the County Sheriff's Office. The Field Crash Detail was called in to prepare to leave the base. The Crash and Rescue Team was dispatched to the main gate. Word was passed to the local radio stations to broadcast to listeners, asking for any information on the crash.

Ten minutes later, the phone rang. A farmer reported hearing an engine and a loud crash. Men and equipment were dispatched. They found a large hole in the ground, with fragmented wreckage. The pilot was 100 yards from the plane. He had bailed out too late, and his chute had not deployed. Only his legs stuck up from the soft mud.

An hour later, the ambulance stopped in front of the sick bay. I walked over in the cold swirling fog and drizzle and looked at the figure wrapped in blankets, lying on the ambulance floor. If he had only given us a few more minutes warning, we could have got him in somewhere. If I had had only a couple of minutes to think, perhaps I would have elected to bail him out sooner. One in safe; the other dead. Statistically, the decision was a standoff. I rationalized that when we first became aware of their plight, they were half dead already. But second guessing yourself is useless self-torture, and the most sleepless word in the language is "IF." If you know your business, you are usually right. Even dealing in vast uncertainties, you hope that most of the time you are right. But most of the time isn't good enough in this business. In SAR, when you fail, you die a little bit with the guy who didn't make it.

When one considers the youth of most fighter pilots at that time, their limited equipment, and the average experience level, the wonder is that they had as low an accident rate as they did. It wasn't low, but it could have been worse. But we multi-engine boys pulled some boo-boos too. We weren't limited in equipment, and on the average had spent a few thousand hours in the air. Most should have known better.

An airliner belonging to a leading international airline missed an island and was finally located by the SAR intercept aircraft 200 miles south of the island and led in. When he landed with fifty-seven passengers, less than one hour's fuel remained. A B-29 that departed on a 600-mile flight to an island base became lost, and ditched over 200 miles north of its destination. The survivors were picked up several days later. The navigator, in correcting his courses for magnetic variation, had subtracted rather than added—a simple mathematical mistake that cost an aircraft and several lives. A Navy transport pilot misjudged his winds, and instead of reaching Norfolk, landed at Patrick Air Force Base in Florida—600 miles south!

Equipment failure, weather, inexperience—all contribute to navigation errors. But some defy such prosaic causes. A light plane with

Michael Roberts, an Australian, waits in his liferaft after ditching his single-engine plane 430 miles northeast of Honolulu. He was quickly located by a Coast Guard C-130 and rescued by the SS *American Trader*, led to the scene by an SAR aircraft.

four men aboard took off from Los Angeles to go east over the mountains to Fresno, California. Three hours later, it ditched beside a freighter 200 miles west of Santa Barbara!

More and more small light civilian planes are flying the oceans, and in many cases it is only a slightly modified form of Russian roulette. With little or no navigation equipment and often only one engine, they take off and head for the other side. Some rely on picking up a radiobeacon or station at the other end, and homing in. One lady, heading for Ireland, landed nearly out of fuel on the northernmost of the Scottish islands. Another bold pilot took off for England with a known 15-degree error in an erratic compass. When he sighted what he thought was Ireland and landed, he climbed out to be greeted by Icelandic Customs officials.

A Navy enlisted man, flying a private plane, departed San Diego to fly 90 miles over the mountains to El Centro. It was his first cross-country flight, and he wandered far off track, finally crash-landing out of fuel in the desert of Baja California—200 miles south of the course line. We searched the mountains for a week with thirty aircraft, extending the search 50 miles to either side of the proposed course. Nothing was found. Several weeks later, the plane was sighted on the desert by another aircraft coming up from Baja California. One of our PBMs landed in the Gulf of California, and four crewmen rowed ashore, towing a metal body box astern of the rubber raft. After a four-mile hike in the burning heat, the landing party arrived at the plane and found the pilot propped against the side. He had taken nine days to die of thirst, and had kept a diary for seven of the days. Staying with the plane is normally a wise move, for it is easier to spot than an individual. Yet, only 10 miles away was a small Mexican village, had he but known where he was!

A year later, a light plane reported that he was lost on top of the overcast in the vicinity of Miami. Lieutenant Ben Weems scrambled in an *Albatross* and soon located him. He decided to lead the amateur pilot into Homestead Air Force Base on GCA if the little boy would fly close on his wing. But this was no fighter pilot accustomed to flying in formation. Two times they started down into the clouds, and each time the civilian pilot popped back up out of the clouds like a drowning swimmer fighting for air. On the third attempt, he stuck close to Benny, who led him down to a landing. It took a lot of guts to concentrate on precision flying with a green and frightened pilot hanging onto you, his prop whirling a few feet from your control surfaces, but Benny was an old pro who didn't shake easily.

Sometimes, help comes from unexpected sources. A Beechcraft Bonanza reported that he was lost *somewhere* in the New York area. Radar finally located him well south of New York, and vectored a Pan American 707 jet to his location. The giant jet slowed down and led the little Beech into a safe landing at Idlewild.

Fortunately for the pride and self-respect of the flying fraternity, they are not the only ones who get lost, though they do so by more spectacular distances. Though traveling at a relative snail's place, the sailors, or their amateur counterparts, also wander off from time to time.

A sailing yawl, crewed by several Princeton boys, tried to make Bermuda in time for the Easter doings. They missed the island by 150 miles and realizing that the Princeton curriculum did not cover this aspect of life, broke out the Gibson Girl emergency radio they had purchased from surplus, and began cranking away. The SOS signal was picked up over a large area of the western Atlantic. A rescue aircraft was promptly scrambled. As soon as we were airborne, we tuned our direction finder to the frequency, and the signal was loud and clear. The needle swung quickly to the east, and we homed in, sighting them an hour later. When a cutter arrived to lead them in, they suavely explained that they were "—not lost, but wanted someone to find where we were." The hair-splitting logic escaped me, but we were glad they did what they did. It saved a lot of searching.

These young men could not compare their tribulations with those of the three-man crew of the 45-foot yawl *Galilee*, which sailed from Tahiti on 17 June 1970 bound for Honolulu. After a short stay at Bora-Bora, 150 miles from Tahiti, the boat sailed into seeming oblivion. Harbor checks were made throughout the Central and South Pacific, a radio alert was broadcast to all ships at sea, and an aerial search conducted on the approaches to Honolulu. None sighted the boat, which had in fact run out of food, fuel, and wind well south of Hawaii, though their position was very dubious; their only sextant had been broken. They continued steering a course to the northwest, hoping to see a ship or island. For forty-eight days after their supplies ran out, they lived on sea plants and on algae scraped from the hull and seasoned with spices! When finally sighted by the USS

The cutter *Cape Corwin* relieves the USS *Niagara Falls* of the tow of the sailing vessel *Galilee*, located 250 miles northwest of Honolulu after being missing for two months.

Niagara Falls (AFS 3) in the North Pacific with a sail hanging upside down, they were close to death from exposure and dehydration. Their weights had dropped from 150 to 112; from 162 to 114; and from 120 to 86.

The all-time record for numbers of lost craft may be held by an ill-fated Long Beach to Catalina motorboat race in the late fifties. Over one hundred boats set out for the run, but fog set in, unexpected and heavy. En route from Yuma, Arizona, to San Diego on a routine flight, we were given orders to divert to the Catalina Channel. There were, said the San Diego controller, some boats lost. More information would follow. As we were approaching the channel, San Diego advised that fifty-five boats were missing. Soon the figure was upped to seventy. There was considerable doubt, for the race committee, which was supposed to be checking in the arrivals at Catalina, got tired of waiting and went on up to the barbecue. Flying low over the channel in the fog and darkness, the sight was weird. Flares were being fired all over the area, and several Coast Guard cutters were towing strings of boats that had run out of fuel. All were eventually recovered, but the last was not picked up for three days. He had overshot Catalina by 40 miles.

Some boatmen, hopelessly lost due to navigation errors, or broken down or disabled equipment, are swept along by the ocean currents for vast distances. On occasion, a skeleton in a boat will bear mute evidence to the tenacity with which the sea clings to its victims. The schooner *Viv-Aux* was lucky, for it could have met the same fate. It departed New York on 4 January 1957, en route to St. Thomas, Virgin Islands. On the 22nd, it stopped at Cumberland Island, Georgia. When it failed to arrive at St. Thomas, extensive air and surface searches were conducted, but no trace was found, and the search was abandoned. Weeks later, the SS *Amstelwal* picked up two survivors from the *Viv-Aux* 1,500 miles east of New York! When sighted, the vessel was sinking. The dead skipper was left behind on the vessel. It was a stark demonstration of the transport of the Gulf Stream, and the helplessness of a disabled vessel in the clutches of such ocean forces.

SAR pilots see so much of the results of navigation error that they eventually become fairly expert in avoiding the usual pitfalls. Yet they also encounter periods when they are "uncertain of position." The young pilots are a bit more prone toward this sort of thing. I learned of the misadventure of two of them only after one had been transferred and the other had left the service.

Late on a winter afternoon, we received a call from the district duty officer in Long Beach. A sailor, diagnosed as a homicidal maniac, had tried to kill a shipmate and was now confined in a straitjacket and heavily sedated. It was essential to get him to the psychiatric ward at the Public Health Service Hospital at Fort Worth, Texas, some 1,200 miles away. Could we do the job? Spying the two young pilots in the ready room, I said, "Want a flight to Fort Worth tonight?"

In a second, both were on their feet and off to pack their gear.

"One thing, though," I called, "this patient is homicidal, and you've got to carry him straight through. The sedation will probably wear off after a few hours, and you can't stop for the night with him on your hands."

Arriving at Long Beach, they got a parachute harness on the patient, straitjacket and all. With a hospital corpsman in attendance, they departed for the first fuel stop at Douglas, Arizona. Leaving Douglas an hour behind schedule, they climbed to 13,000 feet to clear Cochise Head, and bore into the night toward Texas. In the cabin, the patient was indeed recovering from the sedation, and twisting in the straitjacket in an effort to get at the corpsman. To add to the troubles of the two tiring pilots, the weather began to deteriorate. Feeling, with complete justification, that thunderstorms over West Texas are not to be trifled with, especially in a Beechcraft, they elected to descend and fly under the cloud layer. As they approached the Fort Worth area, the rain became heavy, but with only a few miles to go, they requested a controlled visual approach from the Fort Worth tower. They were cleared, and told to report downwind for landing. After ten more minutes of groping toward Fort Worth, they sighted the runway lights, and reported downwind.

"I don't have you in sight" said the tower. "Report on final. Cleared to land."

On final approach the tower still did not have them in sight. As they landed, and were rolling out on the rain-soaked runway, radio contact with the Fort Worth tower was lost, but a new voice came in on the guard channel, "Aircraft that just landed at Carswell Air Force Base, turn off to the right at the first intersection, and cut your engines. Air Police and security forces will meet you."

Glancing out, there was now no doubt where they were. Flashing red lights and sirens all over the field made it evident that this unannounced landing at Carswell, a big SAC base, had shaken things up. The thought of explaining how they got there, and further explaining their cargo to a humorless group of security-conscious Air Police was not a pleasant conclusion to the flight. Looking ahead at the remaining 7,000 feet of the long runway, the out was obvious. Forward went the throttles, while 500 yards behind, two truck loads of SAC gendarmes raced, lights flashing and sirens howling. The race was unequal, and ten minutes later, they landed at Amon Carter Field, Fort Worth. The patient was delivered late but safe to the ambulance, and by 0300, the tired airmen were asleep.

As one of the pilots admitted later, "We weren't really lost, just disoriented a little." I smiled. He was now a member of the club.

Not all intercepts involve lost aircraft, though the lost ones are as a rule more spectacular. Many are occasioned by pilots who know where they are, but have some doubt about the safety of their aircraft, usually brought on by engine failure. Reluctant though some are to let the outside world know when they are lost, when an engine fails or other mechanical trouble occurs not involving pilot error, they promptly broadcast the word. After all, it was a failure by Pratt and Whitney, or General Electric, and there is no lost face for the driver.

A four-engine aircraft suffering the loss of one engine is in no real trouble unless the situation is badly mismanaged. However, should a second engine fail, the situation becomes serious, and if the aircraft has a long distance to go, it can become critical. With even one engine out, its fuel consumption per mile will rise, due to the increased power required on the other engines to maintain flight. If another engine quits, fuel consumption becomes a major worry. Should three out of four engines quit, the pilot has a real full-blown emergency. While modern four-engine jet aircraft when lightly loaded will fly on one engine, it is nip and tuck. Most prop aircraft can't hack it. Fortunately, the chance of losing more than one engine is fairly remote, but it can happen. A B-36 shut down eight out of ten engines over the North Atlantic before ditching. The odds against this happening are fantastic, but it did.

A pilot flying twin-engine equipment had better be prepared to shut down an engine several times in his career. Most twin-engine aircraft will fly well on one engine, but it isn't pleasant, especially far offshore or when the aircraft is heavily loaded. Increased power is immediately required on the remaining engine, and with this increase, the chances of the second engine failing rises, as does the fuel consumption. Even if the remaining engine continues to deliver, the fuel supply can rapidly become critical. Far offshore, if you retain enough fuel, the aircraft may be too heavy to remain airborne. If you jettison fuel to lighten the aircraft, the fuel remaining may be exhausted before landing.

Add to engine failure such things as fire, weather-induced structural damage, electrical troubles, and fuel mismanagement, and a lot of pilots who know their business can become candidates for Search and Rescue. Many military commands and commercial airlines have a policy of calling for an SAR escort whenever doubt exists about the plane's safety. The SAR people approve of this heartily. It is better to escort ten planes to a safe landing than to miss being there when one goes down. In the long run, it saves lives and money. A long search for a missing plane can pay for a lot of intercepts.

Not everyone thinks this way. There was the RAF four-engine bomber that lost one engine in bad weather 100 miles off Bermuda. When communications were lost shortly afterwards, we scrambled to intercept him. Repeated calls on the emergency frequencies brought no answer. He wasn't even guarding them. Finally after over an hour of frustrating searching in the soup with no results, we were informed by Air Traffic Control that he had landed, nearly an hour overdue. Not only had he lost one engine, but he was so unsure of his position that he was forced to grope around for some time to find the field. Learning this after landing, I contacted the pilot to find why we had been unable to raise him on the emergency frequency.

"Oh," he said in a polished British accent, "that is the Mayday frequency, old boy. We only use that when we are in trouble."

"But you had one engine out, and were lost."

"Well, we had a bit of a flap with our navigation, but nothing serious."

"Just the same," I said, "with one engine out and with navigation troubles, we prefer to be with you. We'd rather go out a hundred times than not be there when you need us. Call it a precautionary thing if you wish."

"Oh, I see. Well, that's frightfully decent of you chaps. Over on our side of the pond, the RAF types don't come out until one has been in the water for a half an hour."

SAR aircraft didn't always wait for a request. If an aircraft had lost half its power, or had lost one engine more than 500 miles out, they intercepted. In some cases, the pilot was required by company policy to request an escort, regardless of his own opinion. The BOAC Speedbird was such a case.

He had lost an engine at night 300 miles from Bermuda, with a heavy load of fuel and a full load of passengers. A request was made for intercept and escort. Less than an hour later, he was in sight dead ahead, and we talleyhoed him.

"We certainly appreciate your coming out," he said, "but please don't let the passengers see you. Might alarm them."

We obligingly passed well clear, then latched on astern. Shortly afterwards, he commenced a descent, and we followed him down. Tiny droplets of liquid began forming on our windshield. In a few seconds, it was obvious what it was—gasoline! In order to lighten his plane for landing, he was jettisoning fuel. By turning on his jettison system, hundreds of gallons of fuel were pumped overboard through a jettison discharge pipe, and we were letting down through the thin clouds of fuel. A quick turn took us clear of the area. I don't know how explosive these fuel clouds were, but with my own engines belching flames from their exhausts, I had no desire to find out.

Some pilots inform their passengers when they have requested an escort as a safety precaution. One Pan American pilot asked us to come along the starboard side so the passengers could take pictures. After the starboard customers had done their photography, we slid under and flew along the port side.

There is nothing an escort can do to prevent a plane from going down if its power fails. However, an SAR plane could help with navigation and communications, provide illumination for ditching at night, and most important, be there to mark the ditching point and help in rescuing survivors if ditching does occur.

Night illumination was a dramatic evolution. SAR aircraft carried a dozen high-altitude parachute flares for night illumination. Each flare was in a cartridge-type container three feet high, and seven inches in diameter. It was thrown over and the fuse ignited by a ripcord when it was 300 feet below the dropping aircraft. Once it ignited, it hung on the parachute, burning for three minutes and producing a million candlepower source of light. The sea below was lighted brightly when several were burning.

The illumination procedures used to help a ditching aircraft were developed by the Coast Guard after long tests. The SAR aircraft flew three miles ahead of the distressed plane, and dropped a string of five flares, spaced ten seconds apart. The ditching aircraft then touched down under the flares in conditions almost as bright as daytime.

One of the first uses occurred in the night ditching of a Navy P5M some 300 miles east of Miami, near San Salvador Island. The P5M had lost an engine and was in serious trouble when Lt. Bob Livingstone, climbing out of Miami to intercept, established radio contact and urged the Navy pilot to try and stay airborne until he intercepted. Bob went to maximum continuous power. When the P5M reached San Salvador, it circled only 300 feet over the ocean. A night landing, without illumination, off the reef-studded shore would probably be disastrous. But the SAR aircraft soon arrived, and after a hurried consultation, the two pilots agreed on the spot and heading to ditch. Livingstone first laid five water lights to mark the area, then illuminated the water with parachute flares. The P5M landed on the water without damage. A young Coast Guard lieutenant, in command of the Loran station at San Salvador, commandeered a small local boat, and led the P5M through the reefs to a safe anchorage inside. It was a close thing, but completely successful.

Due to the danger of an accident while handling flares inside an aircraft, they are no longer used by the Coast Guard. More sophisticated sensors are used for night searching, but these are of no use to a ditching aircraft.

A pilot being escorted sometimes has exaggerated notions of what the escort plane can do. On a wild night some 200 miles off Bermuda, I was escorting an Air Force C-119, which was on one engine. The wind was near gale force, and even though we were flying a seaplane, a landing would have been utterly impossible, especially at night. No seaplane could begin to survive in such a sea. The C-119 pilot was worried with good cause. He was struggling along with great effort, barely maintaining altitude. I wouldn't have traded places with him for a small fortune.

"This will be the last time I'll ever make a crossing in a twin engine job," he said, airing his pent-up feelings.

"Oh, we do it all the time," I volunteered, "and we've only got two."

"Yeah, but it's a lot different. You can always land down there."

I thought of the raging seas below and guessed it was better not to disillusion him. He already had his problems.

He called back in a minute or so. He had been thinking also. "You can land down there, can't you? In case anything happens, that is?"

At times, little white lies are more humane. I told a whopping big one, "Sure thing. You go in, we go in. No prob."

I was glad he didn't have to take us up on it.

A Navy transport, loaded with dependents, landed at Hilo, Hawaii, after a torturous 800-mile flight on two engines after two had failed in mid-flight. On landing at Hilo, the closest field, he had less than ten minutes' fuel remaining. A MATS C-97 made an equally miraculous landing after flying for nearly a thousand miles on two engines. At first, the pilot estimated that his fuel supply was inadequate to make shore. But by flying just above the water, and taking advantage of the heavier cushion of air within a few feet of the surface, his fuel consumption improved sufficiently for him to make land. Many pilots questioned his judgment, but it was precision flying requiring the utmost airmanship and guts, and he brought in his plane and passengers. On both flights, SAR aircraft provided escort.

The long Pacific air routes are no longer the exclusive domain of the military and the airlines. More and more private pilots are making the trip, and they sometimes overextend themselves. A De-Havilland Dove, fifteen hours out of Oakland for Honolulu, with two persons on board, declared a distress due to fuel shortage. A Coast Guard C-130 turboprop interceptor was scrambled from Honolulu. As soon as he established radio contact, the SAR pilot began a morale-boosting effort. Despite the announced intention of the Dove pilot to ditch, the SAR pilot assured him he could make it. About 200 miles out of Hilo, the C-130 intercepted and locked on. It was the tangible incentive needed. The Dove pilot elected to go for broke. Five minutes before landing, the DeHavilland's fuel gauge indicated empty, but he landed safely.

Not all of them get in. On 21 June 1986, the two-man crew of a Cessna 310 encountered engine trouble four hours into their flight from Hawaii to American Samoa. Lieutenant Charles Holman scrambled from Air Station Barbers Point, Oahu, in a C-130 to assist. Honolulu Air Traffic Control soon reported that they had lost radio contact with the distressed plane, which had last reported that he was only 50 feet above the waves. Soon, however, Holman and his crew picked up the tone from an electronic locator transmitter (ELT). The signal became louder as the big plane sped south, but the weather was rapidly worsening. While flying at 500 feet around the base of a heavy cloud, Petty Officer Dave Earley spotted a smoke trail and then a tiny yellow liferaft. Passing low over the survivors, Holman dropped a large 20-man raft and survival gear. The Joint RCC at Honolulu quickly located a nearby merchant vessel by use of AMVER, and it estimated arrival at 1100 the following morning. The air station then established an around-the-clock plane cover over the survivors. At 2230 that night, a covering aircraft made radar contact with a Japanese fishing vessel only 40 miles from the survivors. It was steered to the scene and picked up the survivors 600 miles south of Honolulu.

Unfortunately, not all escort missions end on such a successful note. Lieutenant Commander Fred Hancox, escorting an Avianca Connie coming back into New York with engine trouble, eased out to the side when the pilot started to jettison fuel to lighten the ship for landing. Probably an electrical spark, or one from the exhaust, set off the discharging fuel. The big Connie was wrapped instantly in flames, and plunged like a rock into the ocean, leaving a long trail of flame through the black night. The SAR crew looked on in horror, but there was nothing anyone could do for the thirty-seven people aboard.

Over the years, hundreds of distressed airmen have been helped in by the SAR escorts. At the very least, they provide welcome company over the lonely oceans. Often their help was essential for the survival of a sorely beset pilot. Now, with better navigation equipment, fewer planes are lost each year. The jets flying the ocean are not greatly affected by the loss of one or even two engines as were their piston predecessors. As a result, fewer requests for intercept are received, but when they are, SAR crews are always ready.

To an SAR pilot, one of the better moments is the period after scramble, climbing to intercept altitude, when the first call is made to the distressed plane, and the worried pilot answers, "Rescue, am I glad to hear you!"

He's still 400 miles ahead, but you know you are going to get him. More important, you are going to get him in. He may be lost, or he may be crippled, or he may just be unduly worried, but for the next couple of hours, you are the shepherd.

4

Needle in a Haystack

Of the two main elements of SAR, search is the more difficult. The rescue brings out the sweat, but the search is the most time consuming. To be rescued, survivors must first be located. If they are located alive, they will usually be saved. The actual pickup is often an anticlimax to days of anxiety, endless planning, and round-the-clock hard work rewarded by a lookout yelling, "There they are!"

Not all SAR requires search. If a vessel knows its position accurately, a rescue unit can proceed quickly to it and render aid. A small boat may break down within sight of a rescue station; there is never any doubt as it sits with a shirt waving from an oar. A helicopter on patrol may sight a boat firmly aground on a sandbar, where it is likely to remain until help arrives. These are the nice, neat cases; they are handled with dispatch and are soon closed.

The problem is almost as simple when the vessel has a suitable radio. Even if the position is unknown, SAR aircraft and vessels can "home" on its radio signals. Each time the distressed vessel transmits, the SAR pilot throws a switch on his radio automatic direction finder, and a needle on the instrument group points toward the source of the radio signal. He merely follows the needle until the vessel is sighted. In fog, storm, or darkness, the needle will swing in a circle, then quickly settle down, pointing aft as the search plane passes over the signal. As long as the radio is working, the search is usually easy. Often, the shore based radio-direction-finder net is able to take a number of bearings from widely separated stations and plot a rough fix before the rescue unit arrives.

But the real problems are the aircraft or vessels that go down without getting out a distress message. The air traffic control center will begin to worry when an aircraft fails to make a required position report. If two reports are missed, an alert is declared and SAR notified. If the plane fails to show up at its destination on time, the plug will be pulled, and an all-out search begun.

A B-50, en route from Savannah to Bermuda, was such a case. It had made a routine position report 100 miles off the Georgia coast, and the next report was not due for nearly an hour. Suddenly the starboard scanner felt a heavy vibration and looked out to see a runaway prop and fire in number three engine. It was bucking badly.

"Fire in number three!" he shouted.

Up front, the aircraft commander had his hands full holding the madly bucking aircraft. "Bail out!" he shouted. The copilot made an attempt to get out a distress call, but was unsuccessful. He pulled himself to an escape hatch and jumped. The fire spread rapidly, and the plane plummeted into the Atlantic.

Two hours later, New York Control, unable to contact the plane, raised the Uncertainty to an Alert phase. When the B-50 failed to arrive at Bermuda, the air traffic supervisor picked up the hot-line phone and told the Bermuda RCC, "Bermuda Control declares a distress on Air Force 65479."

It was no surprise to RCC, where preparations for the worst had been in progress since the first missed position report had created an Uncertainty. When the second report was missed and an Alert was declared, flight crews were briefed and a Track Crawl search planned. It would extend along the entire intended track of the missing plane, and 10 to 20 miles to either side of the track to allow for lateral position error. The survivors would probably still have some pyrotechnics, and should still be in relatively good physical condition during the first hours. Most SAR pilots prefer a track-line search on the first night, especially in rough seas. Lights and flares can be seen when other detection aids are masked by seas, winds, and whitecaps. The seas that night were rough, with swells 15 to 20 feet high.

An Air Force flight crew wave from their liferaft after being found by a Coast Guard PBM far out in the Pacific. They were soon picked up by a cutter.

The search was launched shortly after the B-50 was overdue and paid off in textbook form. In less than five hours, an SAR plane sighted a flare fired by a survivor and dropped a smoke float to mark the spot. By dawn, merchant vessels and other aircraft had arrived in the area, and the survivors were recovered by the merchantmen. Had the distressed plane been able to transmit a distress message, location would have been faster, but just knowing the proposed track narrowed the search area to a size that could be covered quickly and effectively.

Airmen have been filing flight plans, detailing their proposed route, for many years. The Coast Guard encourages boaters to do the same, but does not have the manpower to accept and monitor such plans. They must be left with friends, who can then notify the Coast Guard if the boat is overdue. The importance of this was vividly demonstrated during a visit I made to Coast Guard Air Station Miami in June 1988.

Early that morning, an alert was received on an overdue boat that had been fishing some 50 miles off Key West. When it did not return as scheduled at 1700 the day before, the man holding the boat's float plan called the Coast Guard three hours later and gave them the voyage data. A communications search was made during the night, and when the boat was not contacted, orders were given the Miami Air Station for a morning search. Following flight planning and briefing, a Falcon jet piloted by Captain Kent Ballantyne, the Air Station CO, with me as an interested observer, was airborne at 0842, and at 400 knots was in the search area at 0902. A search was set up along the intended track of the boat, and at 0928, less than a half hour into the search, we sighted the 25-foot fishing boat *Spanish Fly*, with three people on board, waving an orange flag. They had drifted all night with a frozen engine and an inoperative radio transmitter, but had been comforted by hearing the radio calls about them during the night, indicating that people were aware of their predicament. At 2220, a Coast Guard boat took them in tow 60 miles off Key West. The float plan had been well worthwhile.

That afternoon, another Falcon jet from Miami, again dispatched when a boater failed to arrive at the time shown in his float plan, quickly located the drifting vessel 70 miles north of Ft. Lauderdale, and 30 miles offshore, where it was being swept north in the powerful Gulf Stream.

Just before sunset that same day, we were again airborne in another Falcon in search of a large 65-foot cabin cruiser, supposedly en route from Chub Cay to Miami, but the details were vague. After searching for two hours, we made another series of calls on the distress radio channel seeking any information. A fisherman answered that he had seen the missing boat at noon heading for the States. Apparently the yachtsman had changed plans but had not notified anyone. The overdue boat arrived in the States that night, as did we, but we were lighter by several hundred gallons of taxpayers' fuel due to his carelessness.

Even a sloppy float plan is better than none at all. Four residents

A native fisherman is sighted by a search plane after riding the cabin top of a wrecked boat for two days in rough seas. His companion died several hours after the boat went down off the Bahamas.

went fishing off Miami, where the strong Gulf Stream current runs close to shore. After their boat sank suddenly and they were unable to make a call for help, they drifted for fifty-seven hours in the shark-infested waters, clinging to life jackets and seat cushions. In what can only be called a miraculous deliverance, they were sighted on the third day by alert crew members of the CGC *Tampa*, en route from a Caribbean mission to her home port. They were 50 miles north of their boat's sinking. *Tampa* was not aware that they were missing, nor was anyone else! They had filed no float plan nor even mentioned where they were going.

When neither the track nor time of distress in known, the search planners must lay out an area of ocean large enough to include all probable alternatives. The chances of finding a small object in millions of square miles of ocean wastes in such a search is fairly remote.

The yacht *HSH* was such a case and it was ill-starred from the beginning. Owned by a Philadelphia advertising executive and carrying several passengers, the *HSH* had stopped in Bermuda for a short

visit before sailing on to the Antilles. The day before its planned
departure, I was invited by a prominent Bermudian, himself an experienced sailor, to drop by, meet the party from the *HSH*, and discuss the trip. Knowing the weather was worsening, I asked Aerology
to prepare a weather forecast and a weather map. The outlook was
grim. January had been a month of storms, and now another deep
low had formed over Louisiana and was moving into the Atlantic. It
was no time to go sailing. That night, the party from the *HSH* agreed.
Some of them were becoming a little anxious about getting back to
the States for business reasons, but all agreed that the weather was
not to be ignored. After a pleasant visit, we walked to the door.

"It has been a real pleasure," I said, and added jokingly, "I hope
that we never have to meet professionally."

The following day, we were startled to receive word from the har-
bormaster that the *HSH* had sailed. Winds were already gusting to
near gale force. Twenty-four hours later, winds were up to 92 knots
in gusts—full hurricane force. At about 0930, the Coast Guard radio
operator at Bermuda heard a call from the *HSH*; it was a calm, steady
voice.

"Coast Guard Bermuda, this is the *HSH*. Over."

The operator quickly answered, but there was no reply. When
repeated calls failed to raise the *HSH*, two Coast Guard cutters at sea
to the southeast of Bermuda also called, but without success. In their
area, where the *HSH* should have been, the wind was blowing a full
storm force.

When two days passed with no further calls from the *HSH*, we
were concerned, but with four actual distress cases in our area, our
forces were completely committed. There was nothing to spare to
investigate a mere suspicion; in the prevailing weather, moreover, a
search for so small a vessel would have been nearly hopeless. Nevertheless, the RCC controllers started a drift plot on the *HSH*, based
on the assumption that she could have been dismasted the first day
out. For the next eight days, the probable drift was plotted, using
wind and weather reports from ships at sea.

On the ninth day, we presumed *HSH* should have arrived in the
Antilles, and the Coast Guard at San Juan made a harbor check of
the various ports in that area. There was no sign of the vessel. On
the tenth day after sailing, a search was started.

This was no simple track-line search from Bermuda to St. Thomas.

A sailing vessel seldom sails a straight line, but makes good various tracks to take advantage of favorable winds. With the *HSH*, we were assuming a drifting hulk. The night before the search, the drift calculations were again checked, and the enormity of the problem hit us. If *HSH* was still afloat and dismasted, its most likely position was 870 miles east-southeast of Bermuda, in the trackless wastes of the Sargasso Sea!

To search the area would require six hours of flying each way, leaving only two hours on the scene, even with the long-range PBMs. Fourteen hours of flying would be required for each two-hour search. The outlook was bleak, but at 0400 the following morning, I took off in the first aircraft.

Fifteen hours later, with less than two hours of fuel remaining, we sighted the welcome lights of Bermuda. Search conditions had been terrible, there were no navigation aids in the search area, and the weather was worsening. For the next three weeks, the search went on

The author debriefing after a long search flight during the hunt for the yacht *HSH*.

over continually stormy seas. At last it was called off, but was re-opened the following week by orders from Washington. Only after days of intermittent searching was the case finally closed. Not a trace of *HSH* was ever found.

The unsuccessful searches are the long ones. The finds are usually made within three or four days. After that, the chances of success diminish rapidly. But there are too many exceptions to make the number of search days a criterion of when to terminate. Searches have been called off, only to have the survivors located later by a passing vessel. When this occurs, a detailed case analysis is conducted in order to determine why the search failed. The reasons may be valid enough, but these post mortems are invaluable in improving search operations.

I seldom publicly admit a missing man is dead until I see the body. There is always hope—minute perhaps—but some. On the other hand, there is a practical limit to the length of any search. The decision to terminate search operations with people still missing is always a hard one to make.

I learned my lesson the hard way. In 1954, I was off Bermuda on board the CGC *Bibb*, serving as shiprider for coordinated air–ship exercises. A sudden storm moved into the area, and for two days the wind blew at full gale or hurricane force. The seas were mountainous, and the *Bibb*, a fine sea vessel, had to turn and run before the storm. On the second day, word was received that a small 20-foot vessel was missing with two native fishermen aboard. It has last been seen 40 miles west of the island just before the storm hit. After the storm abated, the *Bibb* and several aircraft searched for five days without success. After being put ashore by the *Bibb*, I flew a PBM on the last day's search. We were forced to quit in the early afternoon by a new storm, and the search was terminated.

Later, I told a newspaper reports, "There isn't a chance that a 20-foot boat of that type could have survived. I was out there in the middle of the storm, and it couldn't have stayed afloat ten minutes."

Ten days later, a MAC plane, en route to Bermuda from the Azores, sighted a small sail 20 miles east of the island. A Coast Guard cutter went out, picked up two men, and towed in the boat. It was the missing craft. For two weeks, with only rainwater to drink and two cans of pumpkin to eat, the fishermen had survived a severe storm and a hurricane in a boat that had less than eight inches freeboard!

Most searches for surface vessels are far from spectacular in the beginning. They typically involve a fisherman overdue. There has been no distress message, but a worried wife calls in and reports that her husband should have returned. The caller will be queried about all possible details, but all too often she has little idea where the boat might have gone, or even how many people were aboard. Some don't even know the color or description. A simple float plan detailing the boater's intentions could prevent this void.

The RCC controller then orders an Extended Communications Check (EXCOM). In the area involved, there may be two or three Coast Guard stations, and they are given the information, with a request for an EXCOM. Each station in turn has a list of marinas, docks, harbors, and police departments to check. If the EXCOM turns up no clues, the search moves into the next stage.

An All Ships Broadcast is made to vessels at sea to keep a lookout and report any information. This will often do the trick. If the broadcast and communication checks are negative, actual search operations begin.

Aircraft, able to travel at ten times the speed of vessels, are the primary search tools. For close-in searches, helicopters and boats may be used. Offshore, large cutters work with aircraft as a ship-plane team to search an area with the high navigational accuracy required. In most cases, the missing vessel will be turned up promptly, and a surface unit will be diverted to the spot to tow it in. But offshore or in bad weather, the search can become far more involved. The search planner must ensure that the search area is likely to contain the missing craft; if it doesn't, the probability of detection is zero. To do this, he must have some idea of the distressed craft's position at the time of distress, and how far it has drifted since that time. At sea, a target is continually drifting, and its estimated position must be updated frequently to provide a datum point, on which the search area is centered.

Drift of an object at sea is a complex thing. Oceanographers are in some respects at about the same state of knowledge as were physicians when they treated disease by scaring out evil spirits. The basic knowledge simply doesn't exist, for the ocean is still largely an unknown quantity.

We have elaborate charts that show the ocean currents, but their accuracy at any time is open to considerable question. Local winds change these currents, and scientists are uncertain how much. Near the coasts, the currents are affected largely by tidal waters, and the flow changes hourly.

Having been given the job of writing the search section of the *National SAR Manual,* and being acutely aware of many of the inadequacies in drift determination, I consulted several of the leading oceanographers in the country. One at a leading western university referred me to a colleague at another school; here I was handed off to still another authority. The answers were all inconclusive, ending up with a consensus of, "Well, we really don't know; what do you people think?"

We didn't know either, and decided to shift from a theoretical to a practical approach. By sending a small vessel to the best estimated position of the distressed vessel, and having it stop and drift, we could form some idea about the drift of the distressed craft. The job of "drifter" proved to be highly unpopular. Not only was the vessel forced to lie to, and not permitted to search, but a small vessel lying to in a high sea develops a very sickening motion. I tried it once, and my sea legs quickly wilted.

But a "drifter" sometimes produces highly accurate results. On the approach to New Bedford harbor is an offshore lighthouse, now automated, but at the time of this incident manned by two men. On a stormy winter night, a call came in to the Boston RCC from a young seaman on the lighthouse, reporting that the watch petty officer had returned to the lighthouse in a boat, and while securing the boat, had been swept away by the seas.

I was search-and-rescue officer for the First Coast Guard District in Boston and hurried in to the RCC. Getting the frightened seaman on the phone, I found that the boat was still tied to the lighthouse landing, though partially flooded.

"Go down and cut it loose," I ordered.

"I don't understand, sir," he stammered.

"Don't question me, just do what you are told. Cut the boat loose." He left the phone, cut it loose, and it drifted off into the night. I intended to use the boat as a "drifter." The winds and currents should take it in the direction of the missing petty officer. Word was passed to the parties searching along the beach to look for the boat. Near midnight, a report came in that the boat had been found, and only a hundred yards away was a body, but not that of the missing man. It was a woman!

I called the seaman in the lighthouse again, and questioned him. Reluctantly he revealed the whole story. The petty officer had gone ashore in violation of standing orders (two men must be on the light at all times). He returned to the light with a woman, whom he had met in town, in the boat. As they tied up and started climbing the ladder, a big wave hit the light, and the woman lost her grip. As she fell, she hit the man on the ladder below, and both fell into the water and were swept away. In the bitter winter weather, there was little chance for either. His body was never found.

We have since developed a Datum Marker Buoy. This is a small bomb-shaped device containing a battery-powered radio transmitter. When dropped at the best estimated location of survivors, it drifts at the same rate as a man in the water. A radio signal is emitted for forty-eight hours, and can be picked up by aircraft at 50 miles, enabling them to home in. If the buoy is dropped near the actual position of survivors, it provides an accurate datum point for the search. Dropped too far away from the actual location, however, it can be carried by counter currents and give extremely misleading information.

The Coast Guard has programmed a powerful computer to help solve the drift and search problem. It helps tremendously in the involved calculations, but like any computer, it is no more accurate than the data supplied. In computing drift, we are likely to be dealing in areas of large uncertainties for many years to come.

Even the most accurate drift determination will prove useless if the distress position is inaccurate. Large merchant ships and most large commercial fishing vessels give reliable positions; so do large aircraft. When a fisherman is in trouble requiring only a tow, and has a good Loran position, it is common practice to send out only an assisting vessel, and dispense with an aircraft verification of the position's accuracy. However, if a storm or darkness is approaching, it is always prudent to check the position by aircraft sighting. A radio can fail, or conditions can worsen.

In 1952, the SS *Miget*, carrying a load of lumber, reported that it had water in its fuel tanks, and was critically low on usable fuel in a position 70 miles south of Hatteras. The weather was worsening, and I suggested that the position should be checked by aircraft, even though a cutter had been dispatched to help. The RCC Controller, relying on *Miget's* position, vetoed the idea. That night at about 2200, the *Midget* broadcast a distress call. She had run aground somewhere

The SS *Miget* breaking up after running aground on deserted Portsmouth Island near Cape Hatteras.

along the coast, but had no idea where. The position given earlier had obviously been in error. Quickly we rechecked the weather and found no improvement. The entire coast was now socked in due to fog. We would be lucky to find anything. Moreover, the nearest suitable landing field still open was Memphis, Tennessee. The flight crew had a long night ahead of them. Fifteen minutes later, the PB1G, a rescue version of the Flying Fortress, roared into the air and was quickly swallowed by the storm.

Lieutenant J. J. Lamping, the aircraft commander, intended to start his search at Ocracoke Island, if he could get beneath the low clouds. As he picked up the island on radar, he started descending. At 1,000 feet, he was still in thick clouds. Cross checking between his pressure and radar altimeters, he continued the descent. At 400 feet, he broke clear of the cloud layer; five seconds later, a flare arced into the air under his nose. It was the *Miget*, hard aground on uninhabited Portsmouth Island, on the desolate North Carolina Outer Banks. Lamping took a fix and transmitted the sighting report. At dawn, the ship's crew were removed by Coast Guardsmen from the Ocracoke Station.

The *Miget's* position should have been checked earlier, and we were all lucky that the failure to do so had cost no lives. The crew of the SS *Pennsylvania* weren't so lucky. They reported the ship had a crack in the hull and was taking water in heavy seas several hundred miles off Seattle. Enough daylight remained to check the position, and an aircraft could have quickly homed in on her radio signals. But a decision was made to wait until morning, when the search aircraft could both fix the position and assist a cutter to rendezvous. It was not an unreasonable plan, but the next morning the *Pennsylvania* was gone with all hands. A long difficult search provided no clues. A visual position confirmation on the first day would not have saved the ship, but it might have narrowed the search area down sufficiently to enable survivors, if there were any, to be located.

The SAR controller is pressured from both sides. He knows statistically that a large portion of the alerts will prove to be false alarms or will not require aid. If he responds instantly on all of them, he could soon run out of aircraft and vessels, and be found short when a real screaming case breaks. On the other hand, he runs the risk of a case he feels is not urgent turning out to be a real disaster. It is a matter of judgment, and in judgments involving human life, you had better be right. Personally, I liked to play them all for keeps until sure that the case was a minor one. By so doing, we expended a few hundred more aircraft and ship hours, but it paid off in lives saved.

The call that came in from a worried wife in Maine was nothing to alarm the operations duty officer at the Salem Air Station. She wasn't even sure that her husband was late, but had a feeling that he should be home. He and two friends fished regularly and usually were home by noon. The duty officer promptly sent an aircraft out. A short time later, he followed it with a helicopter. His intuition was working well that Sunday. An hour later, the helicopter found the boat on the beach, with all gear intact. It looked as though the boys had decided to come in for a beer; the beach patrol was notified and, with police, began checking the local cafes and taverns. The pilots, leaving nothing to chance, extended the search out to sea. In a short while, the *Albatross* sighted a body several hundred yards off the beach. Soon, another was sighted. Boats were promptly moved into the area. The men may have been trolling, and one had probably fallen overboard. The others, attempting to help him, had probably also fallen in, and quickly succumbed in the frigid water. The boat continued running until it hit the beach. From start to finish, there had been not a moment's delay by the rescue team, but nothing could have saved the men. Had we waited until nightfall, however, there would have always been the nagging doubt.

In a routine overdue case, the search is started in the most probable area with one aircraft or vessel. If it is unsuccessful, the area is expanded, and more aircraft are fed in. Ideally, the search builds up and expands until the maximum effort over a wide area is made on the last day. By then, the probability of detection should have been raised to the point that an unlocated target can reasonably be assumed not to be in the area. In theory, the search should then be terminated. In actual practice, a couple more days of token effort are occasionally devoted to what is known as a "morale" search. Supposedly, it is to keep up the morale of the relatives. It is a deadly thing on the morale of the search crews, who go through the motions, aware that there is little or no chance of finding anything.

Closing out an unsuccessful case is often heartbreaking. After a fruitless search for a downed Navy pilot had been called off, his father came to the Air Station and requested that we make one more flight so that he could see for himself. I took him out. For five hours we flew over the trackless ocean. Finally he came to the cockpit and said, "We had better go home. Now I know."

The brother of a pilot missing in a transport ditching came 7,000 miles with his charts and computations to ask that we search one last area of ocean. Himself a pilot, he had worked on drift computations for weeks, and six weeks after the plane went down, he wanted to search the one area he believed his brother might be. We searched it with two aircraft. Nothing was found, but he had done what he thought he had to do, and had perhaps achieved some peace of mind.

There are exceptions to the gradual buildup concept. With a declared distress, where someone is definitely in trouble, you empty the hangars. The same reasoning applies when time is short because of approaching bad weather or night. A fast-drifting target requires an early and large effort. The east coast of Florida has afforded some classic examples. There the Gulf Stream flows at speeds of up to five knots. A broken-down boat must be located rapidly, or it will be carried north at the rate of over one hundred miles a day. However, if it is a few miles out of the stream's axis, it moves relatively slowly. With a possibility of either a slow- or a fast-drifting target, the likely area expands by hundreds of square miles a day. On several occasions, a drifting target was carried north of our search units and was found by passing vessels. The lesson quickly sank in, and in subsequent cases, we hit the area heavy and fast. Now, by use of the Datum Marker Buoy, we are able to determine the drift in such cases fairly well, but early search is still a must.

Search planning is an art, not a science, and the planner must always remain flexible, alert to new clues. Though he deals in norms and probability, he must never completely rule out odd-ball behavior by the survivors. At times, even the most expert planning doesn't cover a situation.

The case off Wilmington, NC, started routinely. A southbound merchantman sighted a yawl 100 miles off Cape Fear, wallowing in the swells with a badly torn jib. The larger vessel sounded its whistle several times, and when no one appeared on deck, continued on its way. Several hours later, the skipper thought it over and notified the Coast Guard. A search plane was sent out but could locate no craft in that position. The following day's search was also fruitless. As there were no vessels reported missing or in trouble, it is likely that the matter would have been dropped had not a small newspaper item appeared in a Baltimore paper. It was read by a Baltimore man, who called the Norfolk RCC.

"That yawl answers the description of my brother's boat," he said. "He was en route to the Bahamas. He and his wife have their two small children aboard, and when the weather is rough, they lock the kids below, while they sail the boat. I'm afraid they may have been washed overboard, and the kids are below decks."

A maximum-effort search was ordered. During the night, planes staged in to Elizabeth City from air stations at Salem, New York, St. Petersburg, and Miami. It was a drama that caught the nation's attention. Before dawn, chartered planes arrived with reporters from the big New York papers and wire services. One of them was assigned to my plane. As the first light showed in the east, the big PBMs began sliding into the water, and the land planes taxied out for take-off. It was the biggest sea search since World War II.

Back aft, as we headed out to sea, the reporter banged away on his portable typewriter, describing the pre-dawn briefing, and the dramatic conversations among the plane's crew members as we winged our way to the search area. It was story background, and it was meant for readability, but the only thing I heard on the intercom system were the regular reports between flight engineer and pilots, and one lookout asking, "Where in the hell is the coffee?" Not that the crew wasn't up for the job; it was just too early in the morning for talk, and they were professionals who knew what they were about.

Our search area was 100 miles long by 50 miles wide, and the search legs were so oriented that we hit the coast on each westbound leg. At the end of the fourth leg, the reporter handed me the first press release, and asked that it be radioed in. It was too good to hold back, especially the flattering description of the pilots, but the radio circuit was jammed with priority traffic from dozens of search units. I had an idea. Only ten miles up the coast from our next landfall was a Coast Guard Station. We could drop it there by message block, and they could phone it in to New York by telephone collect. We hit the coast and started north. The release was packaged carefully, and readied for drop.

Just inside the coastline lies the protected Intracoastal Waterway, used by small vessels traveling between Delaware and Florida. As we approached the station, one of the lookouts sang out, "There is a yawl in the Waterway with a torn jib, and he looks like the one we're looking for. He's about eight o'clock now."

We made a turn, and descended for a low pass. The boat answered the description, but the name was different. Still, that torn jib was mighty suspicious. After the third low pass, we notified Elizabeth City. They diverted an amphibian, which landed near the yawl, and the pilot rowed over in a rubber raft to investigate. He questioned the occupants about whether they had been off Wilmington three days before, and if they had heard or seen the merchant ship. They denied it. However, one of the passengers, a woman, shook her head and winked at the pilot. He persisted in the questioning, and the story came out. They had been the boat off Wilmington, but all were below decks, deathly seasick, when the freighter stopped. After the weather moderated, they had sailed on in. This was our missing boat. Later in the day, the boat belonging to the Baltimore family was located safely moored in the Bahamas. Sometimes, you not only have to be thorough, you also have to be lucky. That wonderful newspaper story never got printed, but it served a purpose.

When a Navy or Air Force plane is down at sea, the Coast Guard is charged with the coordination and control of the operation, but the levy for most of the many aircraft needed is made on the parent service. Large-scale ocean searches may use between 250 and 1,000 hours of multi-engine aircraft time. At a cost of over $1,000 per hour for a large aircraft, the cost quickly mounts. The willingness to devote such effort not only pays off by saving air crews who have been trained at great expense (an aircraft commander represents a $1,000,000 investment), but is a tremendous morale factor for the thousands of people whose business takes them on and over the oceans.

A young Navy ensign in a fighter went down some 50 miles off the California coast. A search by nine aircraft during the late afternoon was unsuccessful, and the search for the next day was being planned. Thirty aircraft were available, but a vessel with ample radar and communication capability was needed to handle this large search as on-scene-commander (OSC). The overall plan is laid on by the SAR mission coordinator ashore. The actual detailed handling of the search units at sea is done by an OSC. Whenever possible, he is in a ship, for aircraft have such limited endurance that the command is continually changing.

The planning job was nearly done, but I couldn't find a suitable ship. At 2100, the phone rang. It was the Chief of Staff, Naval Air Force, Pacific Fleet. He wanted to know how things were coming. I explained my problem.

"How about a carrier?" he asked.

It would be ideal, but where would we get one? We had already been told that none were at sea in the area.

"You can have *Shangri La*. She is in Long Beach, and we will chop her to you at 0200; she should be ready for sea at 0400."

Thirty minutes later, he called again, "Can you use a destroyer division?" Assured that we could, they sailed shortly after midnight.

Later in the night, there was another call offering helicopters. They were promptly accepted.

The following day, with the search underway, I called a friend on the Navy staff, and asked who this particular ensign was to warrant such a commitment of forces.

"He's just another ensign," was the answer, "but the admiral wants him back."

The operation had no happy ending. His charts were found and small bits of debris were recovered, but he apparently didn't eject in time. Everything had been done that could be done, but it wasn't enough. Yet there was a small compensation in knowing that we live in a country where such an effort is made to bring back one man who was "just another ensign."

It is natural that the services will go all out to look after their own. But they will also do it for an ordinary fisherman. This one was a Maine man who had lived in obscurity before, and after that day would return to the same status. He had left Portland for Cape Ann in a small fishing boat. En route he disappeared. A search was promptly started using seven Coast Guard and Navy aircraft. Several hours after the search was underway, the new nuclear carrier *Enterprise*, shaking down in the Gulf of Maine, heard of the case. "Can you use us?" they asked. "You bet we can!" was the answer. *Enterprise*, with her air group, started south for the search area. Soon, over 4,000 men would be engaged in looking for one Maine fisherman. Before *Enterprise* arrived, the fisherman was sighted on a raft by a P2V from Fleet Air Wing Three and was recovered by a Coast Guard cutter. In SAR, the Coast Guard would have a hard time without the Navy; they would have a pretty tough time without us. It is a mutual benefit association.

Many others help on the SAR team. The Air Force and many foreign ships and planes contribute freely of their time when needed. Too much praise cannot be given the merchant marine of all nations. The "Good Samaritan" tradition is almost as old as seagoing itself, and the modern sailor, guided in many cases by the AMVER system, proudly upholds the tradition. A diversion by a merchantman to render aid is not only costly, but often involves considerable risk. There is no reward other than the personal satisfaction involved, yet there is seldom any hesitation to respond when needed.

One of the rare instances when a merchantman failed to stop and render assistance occurred off Cape Kennedy after an Air Force KC-97 ditched in a violent storm. A search aircraft located the survivors, and only two miles away was a tanker, heading straight for them. The search plane circled the tanker and signaled them to follow. Flares were dropped, but still the tanker continued at high speed. Other aircraft joined the effort to divert him. He passed the survivors only a mile off and faded into the night. I have never thought it was an intentional thing. More likely, the skipper thought he had blundered into a missile shoot at Cape Kennedy and was hell bent for election out of the area.

A Standard Oil tanker off Hatteras was too cooperative. While looking for a missing yawl, we spotted one answering the description. Several miles away was the tanker, plowing northward with a heavy cargo. Having no direct radio communications with this one, I circled him at low altitude, rocking my wings and gunning the engines, then headed off in the direction of the yawl. It is the international signal by a plane to a ship meaning, "Follow me. I will lead you to a vessel in trouble."

The tanker turned and came boiling after us. Soon we received amplifying information on the yawl and determined that the one we had spotted was not the missing craft. To call off the tanker and allow him to resume his voyage, I flew across his stern, rocking my wings. This maneuver means, "Cancel everything. You are not needed." He apparently wasn't familiar with that meaning. As we headed eastward to resume our search, a lookout reported, "That tanker has turned

A lone survivor sits in the wrecked half of a skiff. He survived by keeping his core body organs out of the water and was sighted by a sharp-eyed lookout. Fortunately, there were few whitecaps to conceal the target.

and is following us." Back we came, and repeated the cancellation maneuver, and departed again. After us came the tanker like a loyal dog. If we kept going, he might follow indefinitely. Finally, we shook him off by dropping a message block on his deck.

Even after search aircraft and ships arrive in the area, there is no assurance that a small target will be detected. A man in the water without detection aids cannot be seen more than a few hundred yards; a raft perhaps a mile; smoke signals can be sighted at five miles. If the winds and seas are high, all bets are out the window. A small target simply cannot be seen among a thousand white caps. Dye markers will be quickly dispersed, and smoke will be flattened along the waves by the wind. In a 50-knot gale, I have flown directly over a large ship without sighting it.

But sometimes a miracle can occur under circumstances when the odds against locating a target would go into five figures. One occurred the night of 15 November 1962. That day, the distress frequency was saturated with six distress cases in the western Atlantic, caused by a severe storm that had moved in with little warning. The fishing vessel *Monte Carlo* had called for help, and a cutter had been dispatched, but later her radio transmissions ceased. In the raging storm, there seemed little chance of finding her without a radio signal on which to home, but sometimes you have to go out anyway. By the time we had cleared Nantucket, we were fighting through the hurricane at an altitude of 200 feet, and our wings scraped the base of the clouds.

We were relying on the radar altimeter, for the pressure gradient was so steep that the barometric altimeter could not be trusted. The mountainous seas seemed to reach for the aircraft, and the rain hit the windshield like the discharge from a firehose. In the deluge of water, the cylinder head temperatures dropped dangerously low. The aircraft bucked and slammed, and everyone except the pilots was sick. We were too busy. Arriving in the search area, we turned to commence the search, and the sensation was sickening as the aircraft drifted sideways in the 80-knot winds on the crossleg. On the third leg of the search pattern, I considered abandoning the search. It was now dark, and the plane and crew were taking a terrible beating. There was no sense risking an entire crew when it was impossible to see anything. Suddenly, just under the bow, we saw a small light, tossing wildly in the rolling hills of water. It was the *Monte Carlo*. A

An Albatross amphibian searching low over windy seas with numerous whitecaps. Seeing a small target in such seas is very difficult.

quick fix, and a position report was transmitted to the oncoming cutter. The following day, she reached the position and when the seas abated, took *Monte Carlo* in tow. The odds, as occasionally happens, had been wrong.

A small target in rough seas is hard for anyone to see. The fatigue state and motivation of the lookouts are critical. After two hours of looking among whitecaps for a small target, fatigue sets in rapidly, and at the end of five hours, the effectiveness of a lookout may be almost nil. One can only speculate about how much searching is really done by a crew that has been out fifteen hours.

When a search first begins, the crews are "up" for the mission, and all hands eagerly scan the water. As the days pass and nothing is sighted, disappointment sets in and alertness drops. A remark by the aircraft commander such as, "There isn't a chance they could be in this area," can destroy the usefulness of a crew. A good aircraft commander keeps his crew up by constant pep talks, frequent snacks, and rewards for sightings. I have bought a few cases of beer as sighting rewards over the years, and it has been money well spent. But the biggest booster is to keep the lookouts cut in on what is going on, why you are searching where you are, and why the survivors may be in the area. Visual search for small objects is not too reliable, but in the absence of a survivor's radiobeacon, it is the best detection system we have. Realizing the shortcomings of visual detection, most areas of high probability are searched time and again. What one lookout may miss, another on a subsequent flight may see.

But neither close-track spacing nor repeated searches can guarantee success. Two young men and two women took a small boat out for a picnic on Anclote Key, only three miles off the busy boating port of Tarpon Springs, Florida. The two men started back to shore to pick up some supplies and ran out of gas. The waters were well protected and well traveled, yet no one sighted the drifting boat. After a three-day search, the Coast Guard suspended its efforts pending any further clues. During that three days, the men saw Coast Guard helicopters four times and waved at them. They apparently had no pyrotechnics or visual aids in the boat. On 10 April 1988, after thirteen days adrift in the open 14-foot boat, the nineteen-year-old man was badly sunburned and nearly comatose when sighted by a fishing boat. His companion, twenty-five, had died several hours before. They were 50 miles from where they had started out on the 3-mile trip.

Radar is useful, but it seldom picks up rafts or people in the water. Not enough survivors have emergency location transmitters (ELT), though they are the best detection aids available. Too often, survivors lose their pyrotechnic signals while abandoning the ship or aircraft, or expend them foolishly before search aircraft arrive. A number of far-fetched solutions to the dilemma have been suggested. One scientist offered to train falcons to act as lookouts. They have eyes sharp enough to sight a mouse from a thousand feet, and could, he said, be conditioned to react when they sighted an object such as a liferaft. The Coast Guard did start such a research project, using pigeons that had been trained by the Navy Ocean Systems Center to recognize and react to the colors red, yellow, and orange. Project Sea Hunt was started at the Air Station, San Francisco, in 1982. Placed in a pod, the birds were taught to peck on a key when the colors were sighted, this key in turn illuminating an indicator light. In early tests the birds detected the targets in 90 percent of the passes, compared with only 40 percent for humans. Colors, of course, are not always the same as real-life targets.

Most of the recent technical advances have been in the field of night vision and electronic detection. This has included Side-Looking Airborne Radar (SLAR), which has a range several times as great as conventional maritime airborne gear; Forward Looking Infrared (FLIR) sensors able to detect bodies with temperature differences at a range far beyond human night vision; and Active Gated Television (AGTV), which can be used in the passive mode to enhance night images, or with laser for a better picture when the target is pinpointed.

Night Vision Goggles (NVG), which amplify any ambient light, have now been supplied to Coast Guard aircrews largely through the efforts of Stephen M. Hickok, a young Coast Guard helicopter pilot who experienced the torment of searching for his own father, missing in a boat at night, and finding his body near the capsized boat. Convinced that NVGs might have located his father sooner, Hickok began a one-man campaign, which lead to tests that convinced authorities to outfit helicopters with the special goggles.

None of these high-tech devices offer as much promise, however, as the Emergency Location Transmitters (ELT) in aircraft, and the Emergency Position-Indicating Radio Beacons (EPIRB) in ships and boats. The use of electronic locator aids dates back to the bulky "Gibson Girl" hand-cranked transmitters of World War II. Using long antennas carried aloft by a kit or balloon, its transmission on 500 kHz could be heard for hundreds of miles, and the endurance of the signal was limited only by the crew's stamina and ability to keep an antenna aloft. Manually cranked homing devices were soon replaced as aircrew equipment by small hand-sized personnel locator beacons, and on the aircraft by ELTs that are automatically actuated, in the event of a crash, to send out a distress signal on the civil and military VHF/UHF emergency frequencies that are routinely guarded by other pilots in flight. Though the automatic actuation by heavy G-forces is essential in a crash, the large number of aircraft false alarms may be saying something about the landing techniques of some pilots!

It was only a matter of time until a maritime equivalent, EPIRB, emerged. The Class-A EPIRB, automatically deploying like its aerial cousin, operates on the same frequencies and in a like manner. The Class-B EPIRB differs only in that it is manually deployed and must first be actuated by a switch. It is the type usually carried by yachts. An unusual double save in November 1985 was credited to EPIRB. The Coast Guard at San Juan, Puerto Rico, picked up an electronic distress signal sent out by the crew of the 60-foot ketch *Sun Quest*, who had taken to their liferaft in the heavy seas kicked up by Hurricane Kate. Jets were launched from Florida and Puerto Rico, and they sighted an orange flare and a liferaft 300 miles northeast of Puerto Rico. Further search revealed not only the liferaft from the *Sun Quest*, but the previously unreported and dismasted sailing vessel *Taxi Dancer* and her crew. A nearby tug and barge were diverted to the scene and recovered the crews from both boats.

During the mid-seventies NASA, with added funding from the Air Force and Coast Guard, began the development of a system for satellites to monitor distress beacons. The design was to be compatible with the existing ELTs and EPIRBs, as well as a proposed new 406.025 MHz EPIRB. The SARSAT (Search-and-Rescue Satellite) package was built to be attached to the NOAA TIROS weather satellites. To service these and process the information, a ground network and processing system was also developed.

During this same period the Russians developed their own COS-PAC (Space System for Search of Vessels in Distress), which was the first to become operational. Both the U.S. and Russian SAR satellites operate in a similar manner, differing primarily in the processing

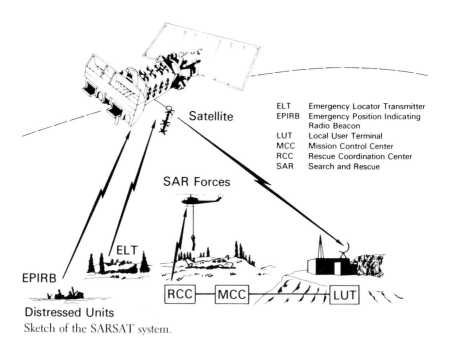

ELT	Emergency Locator Transmitter
EPIRB	Emergency Position Indicating Radio Beacon
LUT	Local User Terminal
MCC	Mission Control Center
RCC	Rescue Coordination Center
SAR	Search and Rescue

Sketch of the SARSAT system.

and distribution of the data generated. They are now combined in one system (COSPAC/SARSAT). France, Canada, Norway, and England are among participating countries. Prior to 1982, most alerts from EPIRBs came from transient aircraft pilots, and the likelihood of being heard by them depended upon the amount of aircraft traffic over the area. Some routes such as the North Atlantic are well covered, while other areas of the world have little air traffic. Most transocean pilots guard the VHF and UHF distress frequencies at all times, just as most good seamen guard Channel 16 on VHF/FM.

At noon on 27 October 1986, the FAA traffic control center in Oakland, California, notified the Joint RCC in Honolulu that several transpacific aircraft had reported picking up an ELT signal about 1,000 miles west of Oahu. An emergency broadcast was made to all ships and planes in that area, and before 1400 an Air Force C-141 confirmed the earlier ELT reports. A Coast Guard turboprop C-130 was dispatched from Oahu, and on arrival at the scene three hours later sighted a large tanker engulfed in flames and a motor lifeboat, with a liferaft in tow, three miles away. Relays of long-range aircraft were kept over the scene until the Japanese fishing vessel *Shoshi Maru* and the Singapore vessel *Dresden* arrived. It was then learned that the burning vessel was the 811-foot tanker O.M.I. *Yukon*, which had suffered a series of engine-room explosions followed by a fire that engulfed the superstructure and control spaces. No SOS could be sent. Four men were killed in the explosion, and thirty-three abandoned ship in mid-ocean. They owed their rescue to the small ELT, a number of alert overseas pilots passing near the scene, and a prompt response by the SAR forces and other mariners.

An ELT might have been just as important to the twenty-eight crew members of the M/V *Tuxpan*, a 474-foot container ship en route from Europe to Mexico with 500 containers stacked seven deep. On 24 February 1987, the vessel reported heavy weather 720 miles WSW of the Azores, and four days later was reported overdue. Coast Guard and Navy aircraft searched over 19,000 square miles without results. Six days later a floating container from the *Tuxpan*, which had been stowed well below the main-deck level, was sighted 150 miles south of the original search area, and another intensive search was conducted. No other trace of the *Tuxpan* or her crew was ever found. The ship was supposed to have an ELT. For reasons unknown, it was not carried on her final voyage, and twenty-eight men may have perished due to the lack of a small device costing only a few hundred dollars.

Racing vessels in some major ocean races are required to carry transponders that relay position and other information when interrogated by the equipment on the satellites. The effectivenss of the system was proven yet again in two nearly identical tragedies at the end of 1986. On 13 November, the ARGOS satellite detected the big trimaran *Royale*, which had been leading the Route du Rhum Race in heavy weather, moving on erratic courses in mid-Atlantic. Another vessel later sighted it capsized, but Luis Caradeo, the sole crew and a world-famous racer, was missing. A month later, *Skoiern IV*, racing in the BOC, was detected by ARGOS wandering off the southwest corner of Australia. When located with sails still up, the sole crewman, Jacques de Roux, was missing. Many racing sailors are also familiar with the 1983 rescue of trimaran designer, builder, and sailor Walter Greene and his crew from the capsized *Gonzo* the day after activating his EPIRB following a capsize on a transatlantic voyage.

More recent cases dramatically demonstrate the potentialities of the satellite detection system. A single-engine Cessna, en route from Monterey, California, to Hawaii, failed to make a scheduled position report. Only moments after the alert was passed by the FAA to Honolulu RCC, an orbiting satellite picked up an ELT signal on the flight path 300 miles northeast of Hawaii. A Coast Guard C-130 was scrambled from Oahu and located the partially submerged Cessna within fifteen minutes after arrival on scene—only five miles from the datum reported by the satellite. Helicopters from Hickam Air Force Base picked up the pilot three miles from the wreck and only two miles from the datum.

On 15 September 1986, the 42-foot motor vessel *Rhea C*, with five persons on board, was reported overdue on a six-day hunting trip from Homer, Alaska, to Port Chatham on the Kenai Peninsula. A composite SARSAT solution was received in the vicinity of Gore Point, and an H-3 helicopter was launched from Kodiak. The helo found all five survivors on the beach only 1.5 miles from the SARSAT indicated position. The boat had sunk five days before after hitting a rock. The occupants abandoned ship in a liferaft, rowed ashore, and were making their way along the beach using the EPIRB.

As of April 1988, over 1,000 lives have been saved by satellite reception of EPIRB and ELT signals. Over 500 involved air crashes, with most others involving marine distress. The processing time will be greatly reduced when the new 406 MHz EPIRBs come into general use. Most of the computations will be done by the satellite computer, and a position accurate within 1–3 miles will be transmitted to the nearest ground station. The new equipment will provide global coverage, which is not possible with the present 121.5/243 MHz. Perhaps equally important is the ability of the new system to send a coded signal giving a boat's or plane's number and nationality, which will allow access to a data bank for information on the craft. This information is important in both SAR planning and in reducing the rash of careless false alarms, which threaten the effectiveness of the entire concept.

In November 1986, thirteen nations cooperated in the first worldwide test of the new 406-MHz SARSAT/COSPAC system. Twenty-four emergency-beacon transmitters on five continents were activated and monitored by three Soviet and two U.S. satellites. Initial results were successful, and final tests are being evaluated.

The effectiveness of this new global system was proven dramatically during the testing phases. Two Belgian racing-car drivers were participating in the thirty-week car race from Cape Town to Cape Horn via Africa, the Middle East, India, China, by boat to Canada, thence to the tip of South America. In a remote part of Africa, one of the cars flipped, severely injuring the driver. The other driver switched on an experimental 406-MHz transmitter. The signal was picked up by SARSAT and "dumped off" at the next ground station. The U.S. notified the French government, whose ambassador arranged for a doctor and medical evacuation to a hospital in Belgium. The driver recovered and later rejoined the race.

With the introduction of the new system, the use of ELTs and EPIRBs will increase greatly. Widespread use promises to have as great an effect on marine and air safety as did the coming of affordable and reliable voice radio following World War II. In a large percentage of SARSAT cases to date, no other distress signal had been transmitted, and authorities were not aware of a distress until receipt of the EPIRB/SARSAT signal. Though this new technology offers tremendous potential for saving lives, its effectiveness and sensitivity in detecting weak signals ironically threatens to nullify some of its promise. In California, the state with the greatest total number of boats and aircraft, the EPIRB/ELT false-alarm rate in 1986 was 98 percent! In September of that year, all nineteen rescue missions stemming from satellite detections were caused by beacons accidently sending out distress signals. Most are caused by human factors, by material failure, or rough handling. The Coast Guard and other federal agencies have started a campaign to correct this problem, and the encoding of the 406-MHz system may be the key.

Not all ideas deal with sophisticated black boxes, however. A suggestion was received, together with supporting literature, to use Extra-Sensory Perception (ESP) to locate survivors. Using this method, the searcher would concentrate on receiving the thoughts of the survivors, thereby determining where they were. One big flaw in this idea, even assuming ESP to be a fact and transmittable over great distances, is that the survivors often have little notion themselves of where they are. On several occasions at San Diego, a woman called and reported that she had dreamed that the crew of a tuna clipper, missing for two years, was marooned on an island near Cape Horn. She was highly incensed when a plane wasn't promptly sent. Another woman called to ask if all of the crew had been rescued from a certain tuna boat. When informed that there had been no word that the boat was even in trouble, she quickly hung up. The following day, the vessel did burn, and the crew were removed by another tuna clipper. The FBI and the underwriters were extremely interested, but only in the possibility that the boat was burned for the insurance.

But "reading a person's mind" can be extremely useful in searching. It is a very pragmatic approach—in his place, what would I have done? By such deductions, the actions of a missing pilot can often be very accurately reconstructed. In many situations, men and women will react in a predictable and uniform manner, especially if they have similar basic training.

On the evening of 5 June 1950, the stillness at the Coast Guard Air Station at Elizabeth City was broken by the clanging of the alarm. As we trotted into Operations, the teletype printer was clacking out a message. A West Air Company C-46, en route from San Juan to Wilmington, NC, with sixty passengers aboard, had lost an engine 450 miles east of Jacksonville, and was turning for Nassau, still losing altitude.

"Bring my fuel load up to 2,600 gallons," I yelled at the line chief, and in minutes the tanker truck rolled alongside the PBM and began pumping in fuel. I tore off the teletype sheet, and ran out to join the rest of the ready crew already in the plane. As soon as the truck moved clear, the engines were started, and the checklist was completed as we taxied out into the seadrome. Minutes later, we were climbing out into the night, heading south. Ahead could be seen the lightning flashes from a storm over the ocean. It was going to be a long night.

Elizabeth City soon advised that the last report from the stricken plane stated he was just above the water, and using max power to maintain altitude. Then there was only silence. He was probably down.

We were told to proceed directly to the last reported position. A search area would be assigned us before we arrived. Other planes were being dispatched from three East Coast air stations. Thirty minutes after takeoff, we were in the storm. The rain came in torrents, and the cockpit lights were turned to full bright to protect us against being blinded by the lightning flashes. All communications with Elizabeth City were lost. Two hours later, we broke out of the cloud area, but still were unable to communicate with anyone. After arriving in the distress area, we established contact with the USS *Saufley*, and she began vectoring us in a radar search pattern. After a half hour, my navigator, Lieutenant Al McCulloch, stuck his head in the cockpit. He had taken several fixes, he said, and was convinced that the *Saufley*'s position was at least 25 miles in error.

"Are you sure?" I said.

"Take a look," he replied, handing me the chart.

His Loran fixes looked good and indicated we were well to the east of the last position of the C-46. Al was a topflight navigator, and I decided to go along with him. We had no search assignment, so would have to lay out our own. What would I have done had I been the West Air pilot? He had made his last report twenty minutes after diverting to Nassau. On single engine, the C-46 was probably making about 100 knots over the ground. We guessed that he may have been able to drag it another 15 miles after the last report. It was a sound theory, and we decided to act on it. Al laid out the track line, and gave me the course to intercept it. Soon we were searching the track. On the third sweep, dawn was just beginning to break in the east. Our fuel supply was getting low, and within an hour we would have to turn for Jacksonville. As we hit the south end of the search, swung over five miles, and then turned north, I said to Al, "This will be the last leg. When we hit the north end give me a course for Jax."

Halfway through the leg, Jim Durfee, my copilot, yelled, "There they are!"

I wrapped the big boat up in a 45-degree bank to the right, and caught a glimpse of two small rafts below. A smoke float was thrown over to mark the spot, but failed to ignite. We came around and dropped another where we estimated the rafts to be. This one lighted off, but no rafts were to be seen. We started a close search pattern, using the smoke float as a reference. After ten minutes and no sighting, I was really worried. Had I really seen the rafts, or was my imagination running wild? But Jim was positive, and we continued searching. Finally we found them again, only a few hundred yards from the smoke float! That Jim had seen them at all in the grey morning light was a miracle. The rafts had no pyrotechnics, and thirty-seven people were packed on the small rafts, so that little of the yellow of the liferafts was in evidence.

"Stand by to drop rafts," I ordered, and Herb Hemingway, the ordnanceman, opened the bomb-bay doors, where six rafts nestled in each bay.

"How many do you want to drop?" he asked.

"Every damn one," I replied. "I'll drop the port load on the first run, and the starboard on the second. First group upwind, and the second downwind. They are bound to get some."

I brought the big boat in at 50 feet over the water, flaps full down, and hanging on its props at 85 knots.

"Stand by. . . . Drop!"

Six rafts went out, inflating as they dropped. The run was repeated and six more dropped. I added power to start my climb, and the starboard prop wound up with a high whining scream. Runaway prop! Jim and I both grabbed for the prop's manual control, and soon had the prop back to 2,600 turns, but we were forced to leave it in manual. The prop governor was shot.

We leveled off at 500 feet and surveyed the situation. The report of the sighting had already been sent out, but the closest aircraft was over 50 miles away. The *Saufley* was about the same distance. Our radioman began transmitting homing signals for the other aircraft. Down below, the survivors were climbing into the rafts we had dropped and were safe for the moment. But they made an awfully small target, and we should stay with them until another plane arrived to take over the guard.

"Sir, you've got three hours' fuel left," warned the flight engineer.

"How long to Jax, Al?"

"If the present winds hold, just about three hours."

Somebody had to make a decision quick, and I knew who had to do it. The seas were about five feet, and we could probably get away with a landing, but I shuddered to think of a takeoff with forty-five people in the plane, and one prop in manual. Besides, the *Saufley* could arrive and have the survivors aboard before I could get them to Jax—if we made Jax. Rule out the open sea landing as too risky for too many people.

How much longer could we stay? If we were lucky, the wind might die down closer to the coast, but I had no idea what the winds were. Strict cruise control might save fifteen minutes of fuel. We could save another ten minutes by diverting to Banana River rather than Jax, but there were no refueling facilities there. I called Lieutenant Commander Bob McClendon, who was in the nearest aircraft and coming fast. Explaining my predicament, I asked when he would arrive.

"Give me ten minutes," was the reply. "I'm at maximum power now." OK, we would stay. Ten more minutes.

A few minutes later, we saw the PB1G boring in. I wrapped up in a tight turn over the survivors.

"They're right below, Mac. Marked by three smoke floats."

"Roger, I've got 'em. You'd better haul tail for the beach."

We didn't need any encouragement. As we settled down for Jax, I reduced RPMs to 1,500, and increased the manifold pressure to 35 inches. It was overboosting, but it saved fuel, and we had a long three-hour sweat ahead. Halfway in, the wind began backing on our quarter, giving us a little more push. It was going to be a close thing. Finally, we sighted the shore, and kept over the St. Johns River, just in case the fuel ran out. Less than thirty minutes remained. After we landed and were taxiing in, I asked the flight engineer, "Reinhart, what's our fuel state now?"

"Oh, we're OK, sir. I held out a hundred gallons that I didn't tell you about. I thought you were never going to leave the scene."

I was too relieved to be angry, but he could have told me on the way in. It would have saved a few more grey hairs.

By the time we arrived at Jax, the USS *Saufley* had arrived on the scene and picked up thirty-seven survivors. The 38th was not so fortunate. When the ship was only 30 yards away, he jumped into the water and attempted to swim to the ship. A large mako shark started for him, but sailors along the rail of the ship opened up with rifle fire, and the shark turned away. But a few seconds later, it turned quickly and hit the unfortunate man, taking off an arm and shoulder. Men from the *Saufley* courageously leaped into the water to help but it was too late. He died shortly after being brought aboard.

It was fortunate that we found the rafts. The sighting by Jim Durfee was an almost impossible feat. Had the rafts been on the down dawn side, they could not possibly have been seen. Without Al McCulloch's superb navigation, we would not have been positioned smack on the track. But the big factor was the agreement of all three pilots in the search plane as to what they would have done had they been in the C-46. It was just what the C-46 pilot had done. Extrasensory perception? No, just the result of common training, an educated guess, and lots of luck.

Captain Paul R. Shook, USAF, made his own luck. Due to engine malfunction, he was forced to eject from his fighter 60 miles off Fort Myers, Florida. The bailout position was well marked by shore radar, and his wingman circled him as he descended. As he hit the water, however, the first break went against him; in getting clear of his parachute harness, he lost his liferaft and with it all his pyrotechnics. But he inflated his lifejacket and waited confidently for rescue. Forty-five minutes later, the first rescue aircraft flew directly over at 100 feet, but failed to sight him.

He spent the first night trying to keep afloat and warm as the seas broke over him. With dawn, his hopes rose, as he saw aircraft searching nearby. During the day, he fought off fish nibbling at his lifejacket. In the midst of this, the sharks came. Captain Shook told of his feelings:

> While engaged in the attempt to scare off the fish I suddenly heard a loud, rushing sound to my left and rear. I immediately froze as I didn't need anyone to tell me what was creating this noise. Two fins came into my peripheral vision and proceeded to within about two feet of me, veered away, made one complete circle around me, and departed. At the time I simply looked off at the horizon and waited for the pain. I thought, "So what, I'll simply bleed to death and it will all be over." Needless to say, they didn't attack. Approximately two

hours later the same series of events occurred, only this time there were three sharks. One of them attacked the fish and was successful. They left as fast as they came and this was my last encounter with them. The remainder of the afternoon I watched in vain for rescue. I saw several aircraft but again they failed to see me.

As the second night in the water began, Shook said:

Again I felt the cold and misery and once more drifted off into fantasy. In what could have been minutes or hours later I sensed something was different. I looked up and saw two lights on the horizon, one above the other. At first I thought they were stars, but after checking the remainder of the sky I noticed a haze layer obscuring the stars near the immediate horizon. Suddenly it dawned on me that this was a ship. I tucked my LPU back behind my arms and started to swim toward the lights. I was swimming against the wind and seas and knew that I had to put all my available effort into the task before me. Periodically I would stop and shout "Ahoy" but they failed to hear me. I was able to get close enough to see the hull reflected in the lights and to discern the running lights. About this time the ship started its engine and departed off to the northwest.

At this point if I had had the means of a sudden end, I believe I would have used it. I had reached my lowest ebb and had completely given up.

Sometime later I noticed two more lights in the opposite direction. I knew it was a ship and started swimming for it immediately. This time I was going downwind with the seas. I remember experimenting with various strokes and decided that the breast stroke and frog kick were the fastest. I had to rest often as the pain in my abdomen was becoming intense. I observed that I was making progress so I pressed on even harder. At last I was able to make out the hull and superstructure. I shouted, "Ahoy, please help me" over and over again. As I closed to within 30 feet or so of the ship, I heard the engines start and it began to pull away. I started shouting again and finally I heard, "Man overboard, all engines stop." The searchlights came on and after a moment they found me.

When he was taken aboard the CGC *Ariadne*, Shook had been thirty-nine hours in shark-infested waters without a liferaft, and lived to tell the story; perhaps he was lucky, but plain guts would be a better explanation.

Some survivors, not trusting luck all the way, have resorted to prayer, with prompt results. I image that there is often more fire-and-brimstone praying in liferafts, cockpits, and on the bridges of ships than at a revival meeting.

Three Arizona men had gone fishing in the lonely Gulf of California. Located between Sonora on the east and Baja California on the west, the gulf is 500 miles of emptiness, without shipping or sign of life. The fishing was good, and the three men failed to notice the approaching storm. It hit with sudden fury, forcing them to run before it, bailing to keep afloat. Several hours later, with fuel exhausted, they drifted helplessly. For the next three days, they drifted over a hundred miles to the south. On the third day, both food and water were exhausted, and the prospect of death by thirst was a grim reality. They made cigarettes out of old coffee grounds and small bits of wood cut from the boat. The taste was horrible, but it was smoke.

The nearest rescue unit was the Coast Guard Air Station at San Diego, several hundred miles away. When the men failed to return to the fishing camp, the Coast Guard was notified. Clearance to enter Mexican territory was obtained, and on the third day after the storm, two planes were launched. All day we searched in a two-plane formation, flying parallel and five miles apart. Late in the afternoon, we were on our last leg and nothing had been sighted. When we reached the eastern end of the leg, we would return to San Diego. The next day, the search area would be shifted farther north. Ten miles before the termination point, the radar operator in the starboard aircraft detected a small target, which quickly disappeared. It could have been a large fish, or a whale. Still, why not be sure.

"Pilot from radar. Small target, zero three zero degrees at four miles. It's faded out now."

Lieutenant Ray Taylor banked and began running down the bearing. A minute later he saw the small boat, with three men waving madly. It was the missing craft. Two minutes later I arrived on the scene in a PBM and dropped a portable radio. It was retrieved promptly and soon we could hear the faint transmission. They wanted to be picked up now, and to heck with the boat. There were no surface craft within a hundred miles, and with dark approaching, the only way to rescue them would be by an open-sea landing. Having the larger aircraft, I decided to land. After setting down, we taxied in close and put over a rubber raft. All three men were soon aboard, and we were airborne just before dark.

After drinking large quantities of water and eating our leftover flight rations, the men came up to the flight deck. They were sunburned and beaten, but happy.

"You know, Commander," said one, "I thought we were goners. I really did. I got down on my knees, and I really prayed for the first time in years. I said, 'Lord, get me out of this mess, and I am through fishing on Sundays, through drinking, through cussin. Give me one more chance, and I'm a changed man.' You know, while I was on my knees praying, I heard those engines, and I looked up. That plane was just turning toward us. When I think about it, it's right frightening."

Ingenuity may be as important as prayer, though I do not discount the latter. Some years later, two men found themselves adrift in a 16-foot boat in that same remote and lonely body of water between Baja California and the Mexican state of Sonora. Food is seldom a problem in the first weeks of survival, but water deprivation can prove quickly incapacitating in such hot climes. As the days passed and thirst built up, the men constructed a still to convert salt water to fresh. The boiler, a used one-gallon gas can partially filled with seawater, was set atop two one-quart oil cans in which a mixture of oil and gasoline was burned. The salt-free distillate was caught in a plastic jug sitting in a seawater-cooled fishing tackle box. Three times the still caught fire in the small boat and was extinguished each time. On the last day of a three-day air search, started after they were discovered missing, the men were located by a Coast Guard aircraft and picked up by a helicopter. They had drifted over 200 miles in ten days, but were little the worse for the experience.

There is an old saying, "The Lord helps him who helps himself," and it has a lot of substance. Some survivors have extricated themselves from tight spots with no thanks to the SAR people. At Shannon, Ireland, a passenger plane crashed shortly after takeoff, coming to rest on the mud flats near the airport. No one was injured. The tower was not aware that anything had happened. Several departing aircraft noticed lights on the flats, and one notified the tower, but no action was taken. Two hours after the crash, an angry, mud-covered copilot walked into the terminal and demanded action. He got it.

Few men walk in from the sea, but they do come down from the hills. Not only is walking faster than swimming, but the survivors are not carried hundreds of miles by ocean currents. Yet land searches can often be more trying than those at sea.

Sighting survivors in mountain country is extremely difficult. Flying in mountain turbulence quickly ages a search pilot; it requires a special technique, and a positive aversion to blind-end canyons. In heavy wooded country, one can fly over a wreck fifty times, and not spot it. On one search, we found an F4U that had been missing for six years. A skeleton was in the cockpit. In the Laguna mountains of California, a hunter found two F4F fighters that had disappeared on a flight from the East Coast nearly fifteen years before. A Coast Guard aircraft was recently found in Alaska forty-two years after it disappeared!

Mountain searches are not for amateurs. A California couple, en route home from the East Coast, crashed in the Laguna mountains in a storm. For five days, a search was conducted using several dozen aircraft. On the fifth day, one of the search aircraft sighted a wreck, and pinpointed the position. When the sighting report came in, we were puzzled, for the color of the wreck didn't fit the description of the missing aircraft. That night, a ground party got into the wreck. It was not the plane for which we were searching, but one flown by a private pilot who had decided to join the search without asking permission or telling anyone. He had flown up a blind canyon, and unable to turn around, had crashed. All four men in the plane were dead. One of the ground search party suffered a heart attack during the night and had to be evacuated by helicopter.

The original missing plane was sighted the next day by a CAP plane at the 4,500-foot level of a large mountain. With dark approaching, a helicopter was needed quickly. We hopped into an HO4S and started for the scene. There was no place to land near the wreck, so we landed down below and ran panting up the mountain, while Coast Guard and small CAP planes buzzed the wreck. Shortly after dusk, we sighted the first wreckage, a piece of wing in the top of a tree. The trail of wreckage led for several hundred yards, and the fuselage was at the end of the trail, wedged upside down between two small trees. There were no signs of either occupant, and we decided to go back down the mountain and get a search party together. It was dark and had started drizzling. Before leaving, I decided to take one last look at the fuselage. Lying on my back, I worked my way under the cockpit, then asked my copilot for a flashlight. He handed it to me, and I flashed it on. A foot in front of my face was the dead girl, still hanging strapped in her seat. I snapped off the light and squirmed out.

"The girl's in there, dead," I said.

"What about her husband?"

Reluctantly, I took the light, and again worked under the wreckage. Shining the light around, I finally sighted his arm.

"He's dead too. Let's get out of here."

The trip down the mountain was a nightmare, as we slipped and fell in the rain and darkness, and it took three times as long as the trip up. An hour later, we walked into a small mountain village. After a phone call to the sheriff, I walked into the small store and said, "We need a drink, bad."

The owner was sorry, but he could only sell beer to take out. It couldn't be opened in the store. We bought six beers, and a can opener. Outside, we sat on a box in the drizzle, and slowly drank it all. It was not a night to remember.

Some land crashes are incredibly hard to locate. An Arizona couple en route from Guaymas, Mexico, to Douglas, Arizona, disappeared in their light single-engine plane in the wild and mountainous Yaqui River country of Sonora. We staged aircraft into Douglas to commence the search. Several local pilots volunteered to help in the search and gave us a briefing on the country.

The turbulence in the mountains was pretty bad, they said, and search in the heat of the afternoon was impossible. Furthermore, the charts couldn't be relied on, for they weren't too accurate. If thunderheads started to form, get out. If you had a forced landing, there weren't many places to set down; even if you found one, the Indians were a pretty hard lot.

They weren't fooling. The wild terrain and turbulence lived up to advance billing. By early afternoon, the turbulence was so severe that the aircraft had to be recalled. During several days of searching, we saw no signs of Indians, nor any other civilization. The aircraft was never found.

The Florida Everglades presents a special problem. There is a great deal of vegetation and growth to conceal a wreck, and close navigation over the area is difficult because all landmarks look alike. It is almost like searching over rough water.

On one search, we spotted a missing light plane upside down, and quickly landed the helicopter near it. I should have waited until another plane arrived to cover us, for I had no idea within 10 miles where we had landed. However, we feared that the occupants might be pinned in the wreckage and decided not to wait. The fears were unfounded. The cockpit was empty, there was no blood, and the magnetic compass had been removed from the plane. They were walking out. I followed the footprints for several hundred yards through the dense growth before losing them in the shallow water. I thought about the snakes, and the place suddenly looked snaky. I beat a hurried retreat to the chopper, and headed for the highway to muster a tracking party. The sheriff could get Seminole Indian trackers, and they were certainly better qualified than I. Soon after we arrived on the highway, however, the two pilots walked out several miles down the road and were picked up by a sheriff's deputy.

Several months later, a Marine F9F dived into the Everglades and disappeared completely in the soft ooze. The spot was sighted by an alert helicopter pilot who noticed the mud oozing back into the hole, and a small puddle of blood. A half hour later, not a trace of the crash site stood out from the surrounding terrain.

Desert searches are yet another thing. Survival time can be short in hot weather, and precise position fixing is difficult. Even a thousand feet over the desert, the heat is sickening. When you are also forced to operate from a makeshift base, conditions can be trying.

A search just before Easter 1957 combined all of these elements. A college teacher and two students had gone 200 miles into Baja California on a hiking trip and had failed to return. The Mexican authorities had no aircraft, but provided ground parties and an Army communications unit. From San Diego, we sent a helicopter, a fuel truck, and several light civilian aircraft of the volunteer Coast Guard Auxiliary Squadron in San Diego. The base camp was a ranch near the desert. On the second day, a plane piloted by Eileen Saunders, an Auxiliary pilot, sighted one of the men wandering on the desert. Eileen was not only a lovely girl, but an experienced pilot who could fly an aircraft anyplace a man could. But the terrain was too rough for a landing, and she returned to the base camp. While Lieutenant Vic Sutton warmed up the helicopter, Eileen climbed in to show him the way. The lost hiker was picked up and guided the helicopter to a second boy, who was injured and had stopped earlier. Before the day ended, all three had been recovered.

Searching can be a tedious, monotonous, frustrating job. It can also be the most satisfying work imaginable—as it is when you sight survivors after days of round-the-clock effort. Then, there is always the sense of something new and unexpected ahead. Take the Sunday afternoon when two of our aircraft from Miami were searching for a missing boat between Miami and Nassau. One of the pilots came on the radio in an excited voice, saying, "Hey, I've got a boat here, and ten to fifteen survivors in the water. Stand by, I'm going in for a low pass!"

Five miles away, the other pilot banked his plane sharply and poured the coal to the engines as he raced for the disaster scene. The contact plane made a low sweep over the ocean, pulled up sharply into a chandelle, and dived back down toward the scene. This time he passed over the boat at not more than 50 feet.

The second plane nearing the scene, called, "Nine four, what have you got?"

The first pilot, wrapped up in another tight turn low over the water, replied, "I'm pulling up after this pass. You'd better verify this one."

As the second plane dropped flaps and slowed down, the pilots could see a couple of people climbing from the water into the boat. Several others were on the boat waving beer bottles. In the water were about ten people, half of them women, swimming around the beautiful luxury yacht. There were no swim suits in evidence. After a gleeful exchange of messages between the two planes, the contact plane sent a message to Air Station Miami, "SIGHTED 60 FOOT CABIN CRUISER TWO MILES WEST OF CAT CAY. TWELVE PERSONS IN WATER. NO EQUIPMENT OF ANY KIND RE-PEAT ANY KIND. SIX MALE SIX FEMALE. NO IMMEDIATE DANGER. EVALUATION TEN PERCENT DRINKING AND NINETY PERCENT SKINNY DIPPING. FUTURE INTEN-TIONS. WILL RESUME SEARCH WHEN LAST FEMALE OUT OF WATER."

5

Rescue the Hard Way

In some ways, the seaplane was an ideal maritime SAR vehicle. It could search for long hours at moderate search speeds, and if survivors were located, it could land on the water to pick them up, *if* the water wasn't too rough.

From a pilot's viewpoint, however, the ocean is usually "rough." Even on the days when no wind is blowing and the surface is unrippled by surface waves, there are underrunning swells, sometimes called "ground swells." Often at a beach, the surf will be high and breaking, even though the wind is calm. The surf is caused by swells from a distant storm, which travel hundreds of miles at speeds as high as 50 knots. They make the ocean surface a long series of hills. Running into one of these hills of water at high speed can occasionally be as shattering an experience as hitting a hill of equal size on land. When hit at 80 knots, a swell has little "give." It took seaplane pilots a long time to find out what was happening. For years they had landed into the wind to keep their touchdown speed as low as possible. More often than not, the wind was running in the same direction as the sea. When the early seaplane pilots pointed into the wind, they also landed into the waves, coming to rest only after bouncing high into the air two or three times as they ran onto the moving hills of water. This produced several hard impacts with the water.

As more seaplane drivers began landing in the open sea, the accident rate went up. Too frequently, pieces of essential metal and fabric from the plane were left behind. Occasionally, a wing float would be torn off, and on the arrival of a surface vessel, the soggy crew would be sitting on the inverted hull, conferring on how to explain it to the skipper when they got back. One redeeming feature of the early seaplane was its relatively slow landing speed. By touching down just beyond one crest, the pilot could sometimes get the plane slowed down or stopped before hitting the next one. It was two-thirds luck and one-third skill.

Luck wasn't good enough. In the 1930s, the blossoming Coast Guard air arm made several successful seaplane landings in rough water to remove sick and injured seamen. The success was heady stuff. Here was search and rescue wrapped up in one package—relatively speedy and long-ranged. It looked like the answer. But the odds caught up. Two aircraft taking off in the open sea were smashed by the waves with loss of lives, and enthusiasm dampened. The dangers

An early-model Coast Guard seaplane takes a patient aboard from a merchant ship's boat. Though the seas here were moderate, the plane was small and underpowered, and required brave men to fly it.

involved were reappraised, and a more conservative policy emerged. Open-sea landing would still be used, but only in cases of grave emergency.

With World War II came bigger and faster seaplanes, rugged and better able to withstand the impact of the sea. They had to be, for with their higher landing speeds, they hit harder. Open-sea landings still had to be considered an emergency maneuver, often the equivalent of a controlled crash.

During World War II, merchant vessels were torpedoed and sunk by the hundreds, and the nation's expanding air forces were spreading out over the oceans. Many craft went down at sea. The seaplane boys went out to get them, and many didn't come back as the relentless sea took its toll. There had to be a better way of doing it, and some veteran seaplane pilots thought they had the answer. Quit beating your head bloody against the oncoming swells, they said, and land parallel to them. In this way, you could avoid going up and over the hills.

It was a plausible theory, but unproven. Perhaps, said the skeptics, it might work with no wind, but who wants to land with the wind abeam or on the quarter? Furthermore, there are often several swell systems running in different directions. What do you do then?

Commander Donald B. MacDiarmid, USCG, then commanding the Coast Guard Air Station at San Diego, California, thought he had the answers, and he wanted to prove it. In 1944, he got the go-ahead and a big rugged PBM, which was fully instrumented to record the deceleration forces involved. He went to work—out in the open sea.

Before he was through, Mac was a legend among seaplane pilots everywhere. Like many pioneers, he was not only a dedicated man, but one of single purpose. To him, rescue at sea was the ultimate attainment, and the seaplane was the means. He became the prophet.

Had he never climbed into a cockpit, D. B. MacDiarmid would have probably been remembered as one of those colorful characters around whom sea stories and service lore are built. Immediately after Pearl Harbor, antisubmarine patrols were being pushed far offshore, but not far enough for MacD, who was then commanding the Coast Guard Air Station at Port Angeles, Washington. When the pilots protested that they needed some fuel reserve in an area noted for its bad weather, MacDiarmid took his operations officer out to show him how he wanted it done. After takeoff, he shifted both engines onto the starboard tank, and flew due west until the tank ran dry. When both engines coughed due to lack of fuel, he shifted over to the full port tank and returned home. Getting out of the plane after landing, he said, "That's what I mean by offshore!" It was no way to operate day after day, but it was a way of proving a point.

MacDiarmid was the epitome of the gung-ho pilot, and there was never any abatement in his enthusiasm. When the alarm bell rang, he led the troops.

The mad dash of flight crews for the ready plane was a MacDiarmid trademark, and five minutes was all he would allow to get a PBM airborne. When he first arrived at Elizabeth City in 1952, he was loud in his criticism of the slow scrambles. I went to work with a stopwatch and clipboard on a time-and-motion study. We ran drill after drill after drill, with a five-second delay eliminated here, a little faster way of doing something there. Finally there was no safe way of cutting things down further. I called the Old Man on the intercom box and told him that we were ready to demonstrate if he would like to observe.

"OK, sound the alarm. I'll go along."

We sounded the alarm, and the crew broke for the plane. Mac came trotting out of the administration building with his cigar clamped between his teeth. Just as he reached the starboard side, the ladder was yanked in and the hatch slammed closed in front of him. He ran around to the port side, but that hatch was closed, too. The plane began to move, while he shouted and pounded on the side. Suddenly, the hatch opened, and two strong pairs of arms grabbed him and yanked him aboard. His feet were dragged through the hatch just as the plane slid into the water. It was quite an entry for a four-ring captain. When they returned, he came into Operations.

"That's fast enough," he said, and walked out. I suspect he didn't want it any faster for fear he might not make the plane on future scrambles.

Over the years, I have formed some reservations about the need for such fast scrambles, especially if shortcuts are made with safety, but I've never downgraded the need for the spirit behind them. You can be eager and still be safe. It's much easier to hold back an eager pilot than to kick a reluctant bird out of the nest.

To Mac, people were grouped in two categories—they were either eager rescue pilots or they weren't. If you were in the former, you could do little wrong. If not, things were rocky. Flying came first and paperwork second. Nothing interfered with SAR. In an era where the way to success is increasingly paved with whisk brooms and copies of innumerable reports, MacDiarmid is remembered with nostalgia whenever old SAR pilots congregate and swap stories. They tell of the time he was ordered to Washington as a member of a personnel board, headed by a rear admiral whom Mac considered to be a "first-rate clerk." When he walked into the board room carrying a brown paper bag, the admiral looked and said, "Captain, why are you bringing your lunch? In the big city, we have restaurants."

"I don't have lunch in the bag," replied MacDiarmid, placing it carefully on the green-covered table.

"Oh?" said the great man, obviously curious.

Six Navy airmen, rescued after their plane crashed in the Pacific, with their rescuer, Commander Donald B. MacDiarmid (third from right, standing). His copilot, Lieutenant John (The Greek) Vukic (far left), was another outstanding open-sea pilot.

"No sir. Before this board is over, I'll probably want to puke. The bag is for that."

His irreverent attitude never endeared him to the powers that be, and but for his concrete operational accomplishments, he would have likely been banished to some remote Siberia. He proudly maintained that his medals and commendations always barely outnumbered his reprimands.

Single-minded, controversial, and with a zealot's drive, Mac-Diarmid was the man who more than any other made the seaplane and rough water compatible. When he had finished his work, he had proven and documented in hundreds of landings that the seaplane could be landed in rough water by paralleling the swell system, accepting the crosswinds that resulted. For the next ten years, he was a fiery evangelist, spreading the doctrine wherever seaplane pilots gathered. But along with it, he also preached sea evaluation, for unless the pilot could determine what, where, and how fast swells were running, the procedures were useless. Many a pilot mistook the relatively harmless wind-driven surface chop for a swell and landed, only to find after touchdown that he had run into a mean fast swell, hidden under the surface chop. Dogmatic and opinionated in many things, when it came to the sea and seaplanes, Mac was first and always the student, looking for a new angle.

In 1946, I brought four ships of Escort Division Forty-two into San Diego from the western Pacific, and we moored off the Coast Guard Air Station. Before the chain had been fully paid out, an invitation came out from the Air Station for lunch. It was my first meeting with MacDiarmid. His first question was about the long swells of the far Pacific, and two hours later he was still talking about waves and the sea. At the time, I wasn't a pilot, but that wasn't the point. He wanted to know about the sea. It is indicative of his pursuit of the subject that I never really knew much about wave generation and motion until after I became an aviator, and then I learned it primarily from him.

Largely as a result of MacDiarmid's work, seaplane rough-water landings after 1945 became safer—not safe, but safer. It is probably correct to surmise that with a few disastrous exceptions, most landings since that time have been made in accordance with the concepts developed by him. Many a downed airman or sick seaman owes his life to those procedures. But they probably don't equal in number the

A PBM Mariner picks up speed for takeoff.

persons on ditched aircraft who have lived because of the ditching techniques developed from the seaplane rough-water procedures. A ditching landplane is different from a seaplane; it won't take off again. But similar deceleration forces apply on touchdown and landing, and a proper heading is essential. In the two decades following World War II, Coast Guard aviators provided leadership in the development of aircraft emergency procedures over water, basing their teachings not only on their experience in aiding distressed aircraft, but on their operation of seaplanes in rough water. Regular training classes were conducted for the other military services and for domestic and foreign airlines as well. The payoff in lives saved was appreciable.

In 1959, Captain MacDiarmid retired. He didn't make flag rank, nor did his strongest admirers think he would. Controversial characters with stars are pretty rare specimens in peacetime, and some conformity is required of an organization man. But wherever ocean pilots gather, his name still comes up, and it is a fair bet that more aviators know his name than the names of the commandants during those years. He is not the type you forget.*

I was thinking about MacD as we picked up speed down the sealane and the floating seaplane lights flashed by. You always do when you think of open-sea landings, and I had been thinking of them all afternoon.

"Flaps up!" I called to my copilot as I reduced the throttles to

---

*In 1986, Captain Donald B. MacDiarmid, USCG (Ret.), was posthumously inducted into the Naval Aviation Hall of Fame.

climb power, and started a gradual left turn to follow the channel past North Island. As Ballast Point slid by under my right wing, we began a climb to 8,000 feet. The panel clock read just after midnight, and it was going to be a long ten hours ahead. The mission—a medical evacuation case at sea. The place—off Baja California, several hundred miles south of San Diego. As we completed the climb checklist, I gave the order to light the smoking lamp, and the flight engineer reported that the coffee was perking and would be ready in a couple of minutes. Would I like any now? You bet your bottom dollar I would, for there wouldn't be any sleep tonight with the roar of the 2800 dash 74 engines outside, and the thoughts of an open-sea landing at daybreak. Thinking about an open-sea landing itself is enough to rob a man of sleep, for in a rough sea, even with a rugged seaplane like the PBM, it is at best a controlled crash, hopefully without damage; at the worst—well, let's not think about the worst. After quite a few, I appreciate them less all the time. When we get back, we will have been nearly thirty hours without sleep, the medical officer will shake his head in disapproval, and the flight safety officer will say that we have exceeded crew limits, but search-and-rescue flying is different from running an airline.

As we level off at 8,000 and go into long-range cruise control, I detect the aroma of coffee on the flight deck, and shift the plane onto autopilot. Reclining in the pilot's seat, I prop one foot on the center instrument pedestal, pick up the mike, and call, "After station from pilot, ask the doctor to come up to the flight deck, please."

"After station, aye."

A minute later, the young flight surgeon, on loan for this flight from the Naval Air Station at North Island, climbs up to the flight deck, and the radarman hands him a cup of coffee.

"Doc, have you had a chance to look over the messages on this case?" I asked.

"Yes, sir, I think I have them all," he said, taking several yellow copies from the pockets of his flight jacket.

The messages had started accumulating nine hours before when a tuna clipper had recovered a badly injured man from the water after he was crushed between two boats. They determined that his condition was serious, and called the Coast Guard by radio. The radio operator at the Coast Guard Radio Station at Long Beach placed the message on a teletype printer to the Rescue Coordination Center at Long Beach, where it was quickly shown to the duty controller. Picking up the phone, the controller called the staff medical officer and read off the message, describing what had happened. The staff medical officer suspected that the case was serious, but he needed additional information and dictated a number of questions to be sent by radio to the tuna boat. When the answers came back, the doctor told the controller, "I suspect a fractured pelvis and probably internal injuries. He should be evacuated to a hospital as soon as possible. In the meantime, I am going to prescribe some medication. I imagine a tuna boat will have a standard medical kit aboard."

Ten minutes later, the hot line from the RCC to the Coast Guard Air Station at San Diego was busy as the controller gave the air station the information on the case. It was then 1700, and too late for takeoff. An open-sea landing is risky enough in daylight. At night, it is suicidal. It would have to be carried out at first light, which would mean a midnight departure from San Diego.

Two of us were on duty as PBM aircraft commanders, and we both wanted the job. Taking out a coin, I suggested we flip.

"Tails," he called. It was heads.

Turning to the assistant operations officer, I said, "I'll take only a copilot, and a minimum crew. We want to be as light as possible, so let's strip the ship of all unnecessary gear. I'll give you my fuel requirements later when we've worked it out. I guess we can blunder through without a navigator."

The crew is kept to a minimum to lessen the number of people exposed to danger, as well as to lighten the ship. A heavy aircraft must land faster, and is more difficult to bring to a stop than a lighter one. The quicker it stops, the less pounding you endure from slamming into six-foot waves.

I got the chief ordnance man on the phone and asked him to ensure that the JATO (jet assisted takeoff) circuits were thoroughly checked out before departure. The four bomb-shaped JATO bottles, each loaded with over a hundred pounds of propulsion chemicals, would provide an extra 1,500 pounds of thrust for our open-sea takeoff, shortening the takeoff run and the agony.

While the duty section was getting the aircraft ready, I picked up the phone to make an important call. I needed to hear from the staff medical officer how serious this case was, for in about twelve hours, I was going to have to make a critical decision, and I would need all the facts.

After the doctor's briefing, I hung up the phone. Now I am holding the bag, but I won't make a final decision until I hear the latest condition of the patient and see the condition of the seas off Baja California at daybreak. As the patient was apparently in shock, we asked for a flight surgeon, and one from Naval Air Station, North Island, arrived an hour before the flight. One of our hospital corpsmen climbed on the plane with him to check the medical supplies.

Now, as we drone along, the flight surgeon is standing just behind the cockpit, sipping coffee as he leans on the radar set. I brief him on what we face and give him the beginner's course in open-sea landing problems. Essentially, a 30-ton aircraft traveling at 70 knots hitting a six-foot swell moving at 20 knots is a nearly irresistible moving mass hitting a series of objects that don't wish to be moved from their course either. If we are lucky and skillful, in that order, no pieces of metal fly off our iron bird; if not, well it's a long way home without your faithful seaplane, as several of my friends have found out. The doc's eyes widen a bit, but he is game.

Hour after hour we fly southward. After Ensenada, the last town, Baja California consists of 500 miles of sand, desert, and mountains. We stay about 20 miles off the coast, holding our distance and navigating by radar. There is no life, no lights, no navigation aids, nothing. The Southwest must have been like this when the cavalry rode in.

The night slips rapidly by, and I have been dozing lightly when the radar operator reports that we are leaving Turtle Bay abeam to port. I bring my seat up erect, open the side window to let the slipstream rush by, and call for another cup of hot coffee. Already I can see a trace of light on the eastern horizon. Down below in the galley, the ordnanceman, drafted as the cook for the flight, is starting breakfast, for we must finish it and have all dishes and loose gear secured before arrival. A small object in a rough-water landing can fly around and become a lethal missile.

After breakfast, we go through abandon-ship drill, just in case this landing becomes the last one for this plane. As the copilot calls off each man's name, he responds with his raft number and the equipment he must provide. The answers are sharper and more positive than usual. I tell the doctor to follow me should we have to abandon ship. He is still game, and even sounds enthusiastic, and I think of the blind faith I used to have in men with wings before I was a man with wings.

I search anxiously for my first glimpse of the surface of the water, for there will be revealed much of the answer about how tough the landing will be. I can't tell too much at this altitude and start descending to 2,000 feet. Soon I can see the surface more clearly. Doesn't look too bad. Very little wind, nor did I expect much. By afternoon, however, it could be up to 20 knots. There is a swell or wave system, but it appears to be moderate.

Arriving over the vessel, I drop a smoke float nearby and time the swells passing it to estimate their speed. No secondary system is apparent, and that is better still. With little wind, and only one swell system, we will land parallel to the swells, rather than buck into them. Anyone who has driven a car across a plowed field on a cold frozen morning will appreciate the difference between paralleling and bucking.

The copilot has radio contact with the clipper and finds that the patient is in a coma. We call the doctor, slip a headset on him, and hand him a mike. There follows a medical consultation by radio, with delays while the clipper captain takes the patient's temperature, examines the abdomen for discoloration and swelling, checks his breathing rate, and answers various other questions that the doctor asks. Taking off the headset, the doctor says, "I can't be sure until I see him, but it sounds as though he has a crushed ureter, and the bladder will not empty. If we don't get him off, he might not last too long."

My decision process is nearing completion. The seas can be landed on. I feel confident of myself and the aircraft, and with luck can get down and off again without damage. The patient's condition warrants the risk. Now for the other eight men anxiously awaiting my decision. "OK, boys, this man needs to be taken off or he probably won't last. The seas don't look too bad. We may get a bad bump or two, but this bird can take it. I don't want anyone to get out of their seat after landing until I give the word. Remember that we could get two or three jolts. When I call for full flaps, brace for impact. OK, landing in two minutes. Strap in!"

As we turn downwind, the copilot puts on his crash helmet, as do the rest of the crew. I never wear one, for I need to hear the copilot call off air speeds while I keep my eye on the water outside. I remove my radio earphones, so that they won't be jarred off my head on impact, and give a final pull on each shoulder strap until they dig into my shoulders.

We turn on final, and drop full flaps. At 100 feet, I begin to rotate the nose up. "Eighty knots," chants the copilot, "eighty knots. Seventy-eight knots, seventy-seven knots——." I hit the trim tab, and rotate the nose higher. Twenty feet above the water, the big seaplane is at a high angle of attack and hanging by her props. "Sixty-five knots!" Now, just ahead, a smooth spot! With one continuous movement, I throw the throttles back into full reverse position while we are still 10 feet in the air. You stop fast this way—both flying and forward motion! The ship pays off in a stall, I pull the yoke back into my chest, and we are on! A jolt, she careens shuddering into the air, and I slam the yoke forward to check her rise, quickly coming back on it as she settles onto the water again. A series of bumps, and then we are stopped with the props still howling in full reverse and throwing a dense cloud of spray around the cockpit. I ease off the power, and the copilot is laughing and slapping me on the shoulder. Relief is written all over him—relief from hours of worrisome wondering. I pick up the mike, and order, "All hands check ship for damage and leaks."

The reports come in. No damage. Everything fine. The ordnanceman tells me that he forgot to take the coffee pot off the stove, and somehow it didn't spill. "Well, I'll use you as a witness if anyone ever claims I've never made a smooth landing," I tell him, laughing.

"Open up aft," I order, for I can see a boat casting off from the tuna clipper with a loaded stretcher in it. As it gets closer, I cut my engines, and everything is strangely quiet except for the auxiliary power unit purring away in the aft end of the plane. The plane pitches gently on the swell, and cocks slowly into the light breeze. I don't want the small boat to come alongside, for an aircraft has very thin skin, and the bow of the boat could easily push a hole in the hull. Instead, we will inflate a rubber raft, pay it out on the end of a line, and when the patient has been placed in it, will pull him to the plane. One of our men will go in the raft to help steady the stretcher and patient.

Within five minutes, the stretcher is aboard and placed in the after station. The patient is so badly crushed that we do not attempt to transfer him into one of the bunks. While the doctor goes to work, the ordnanceman speedily completes the mounting and hookup of the JATO bottles.

Starting both engines, we complete the open-sea takeoff checklist and review takeoff procedures. In common with many open-sea pilots, I feel that takeoff is tougher than landing, and I'll only breathe easy when we are passing 1,000 feet. We taxi on various headings at progressively higher speeds to get the feel of the sea. The same heading we used for landing looks good and feels good. We have a last brief confab to make sure we have our plans straight, and I flip the three switches arming the JATO bottles. As soon as we get onto the step, start planing, and have obtained directional control with the rudder, I will hit the JATO button mounted on my control yoke. Once I have pressed that, we will be committed—for better or worse—for with the added 1,500-pound thrust, we can't stop until the JATOs are expended.

Jockeying slowly onto the takeoff heading, I gradually increase speed to about 30 knots, and the ship begins to pound. Slugs of water hit

A PBM Mariner making a JATO takeoff in protected waters. In the open sea, it was far more difficult.

the windshield and the copilot starts the wipers. There is a smooth spot ahead; I shove the throttles all the way forward and feel my copilot's hand backing me up, holding them full open. Shifting both hands to the yoke, I glance at the air speed at 40, and then a big one hits us. The plane is literally thrown into the air, and I slam the yoke forward with full strength to hold her down, and at once shift it back full as she starts back down. Another hard slam, my thumb finds the JATO button and I press it. The JATO thrusts against my back and pants as we accelerate, and as the plane again settles, I haul the yoke back into my gut. She hits, skips lightly once, twice, and then we are in the air. We are living again! As the JATOs burn out, I roll the tab forward, picking up speed just above the water, and start milking the flaps up. We pick up climb speed and head for altitude. I notice for the first time that sweat is running into my eyes, and that my flight suit is soaked. An artery in my neck is throbbing violently and my breathing is rapid; in fact I am just slowing from a pant. I begin to uncoil slowly, and as soon as we have reduced to climb power, call for a cup of coffee. In a few minutes, the ordnanceman brings up the pot, and as he pours it, I grab his hand to steady it. That makes two of us who have had a scare.

At 6,000 feet, I turn the controls over to the copilot and walk aft to see how the patient is doing. To save time, we are going to climb over the southern mountains of Baja California on a straight course for San Diego. At 10,000 feet, the turbulence is fairly heavy and I hang on a couple of times as I work my way aft. The doctor and corpsman are laying out a sterile field of towels on the patient, with a tray of instruments beside them.

"How's he doing, Doc?" I ask, looking around at the deck of the aircraft, which was rapidly assuming the appearance of an emergency treatment room.

"He's holding up OK, but I have to relieve the pressure on the bladder, so I am going to pass a catheter tube," he said as he finished the sterile field and started slipping on his rubber gloves.

As the realism of the scene surpassed anything on television, I decided to observe for a while, meantime wondering how delicate the procedure is, for the turbulence is now heavy. Suddenly, the ship gives a lurch, and the doctor sprawls on the deck, the tube sliding from his grip. As he climbs to his feet, it is obvious that the sterile field is no longer sterile. Undaunted, he brushes himself off, puts on a new pair of rubber gloves, and two minutes later has to catch himself again as the ship bucks. The last pair of gloves are ruined. Promising to try and find a better altitude, I return to the flight deck, and we climb to 12,000 feet. Here there is a little improvement, so I go back aft again. The Doc is now stripped down to his bare waist, and working with no rubber gloves. Even at 12,000 feet he is sweating, and looks grim and frustrated. The two aircrew members looking on are slightly green. After watching a short while, I also feel slightly tinted, and return to the sanctuary of the cockpit.

Later the Doc comes up front and shrugs. There is apparently a blockage, and he has been unable to complete the procedure. It is urgent that we get the patient into surgery as soon as possible. We prepare a message for the air station, requesting a helicopter be ready to transport the patient to the naval hospital on our arrival. I hand the message pad to the Doc, and he adds a description of the patient's condition.

At San Diego we are lucky, for the early morning fog has burned off, though we can see a fog bank hanging ominously off Point Loma. After landing, and taxiing in at high speed, we are hauled up on the seaplane ramp in jig time. As I finally step wearily out of the plane, I see the helicopter already lifting into the air with the patient, on the way to the hospital where an operating team is standing by. The flight engineer and I walk slowly around the plane, looking for any dents or distortions from the landing. Satisfied that there are none, we start in. "Dave, how about filling out the flight report," I ask my copilot. "I'm not up to the long paperwork ordeal now, for after nearly thirty hours without sleep I am beginning to unglue a bit at the seams." We walk into the officers' mess, and open a beer. I am too tired to stand and too tired to sit. After another beer, I throw myself on a bunk in the BOQ.

The phone rings after what seems like a mere catnap, but I notice it is dark outside. "Commander, this is the duty officer. The Navy Hospital just called and said that the patient should be OK, though he is still in the recovery room. They also said he got there just in the nick of time."

Thanking him, I lie back down, but the aching isn't as bad. It has been a long day's work, and it has been worthwhile.

Not all of them are as successful, nor were some of the others as lucky. The last years of World War II, and the decade after, were the golden years of open-sea operation. The seaplane was the prime recovery craft, but about a six-foot swell was the limit for normal SAR risks, and even then aircraft encountered trouble.

Ira McMullan, one of the finest seaplane pilots, landed 800 miles off San Francisco, had part of his elevator torn off by the sea, and crashed, breaking the fuselage in two. Andy Cupples, landing to pick up a sick sailor from a submarine off Cape Hatteras, dropped heavily into the trough after missing the swell crest, and both engines tore loose from their mounts. Fuel sloshed freely in the hull from broken lines, and the crew abandoned ship. The flight surgeon climbed into the raft, still holding a stretcher, which another crewman threw overboard. Three days later they arrived in Charleston aboard the submarine, wearing submarine dolphin insignias.

Harry Solberg, landing off Bermuda, was on his runout after landing when the bombardier's nose door gave way, and the plane went under without getting its way off. He escaped from the cockpit under water after the flight-deck crew had escaped, using Harry's shoulders as a step to get out!

John Vukic landed in 12-foot seas close under the Red China coast to rescue the crew of a P2V that had been shot down by Communist antiaircraft guns. On the takeoff, just as the plane cleared the water, one engine failed, and they crashed. Four Navy men and five Coast Guardsmen were lost, and the others were rescued only after a miserable cold night in the water. Vukic was hauled into a raft after dark, blinded by blood and a scalp wound. As the freezing night dragged on, one of the Navy pilots said, "Vukic, is it true that freezing to death is painless?" John said that he had heard so. "Well, I'm OK then," was the reply, "because I've never been so damn cold and miserable in my life."

The continuing loss of seaplanes in open-sea landings brought a predictable reaction from the top. In too many cases, after a plane was lost, the intended evacuee recovered very nicely without help. The price being paid was too steep. In the future, before landing, the pilot would have to obtain clearance from the District Commander. This would enable his staff to make a last-minute check on the necessity for landing and check on the availability of other means, such as surface vessels, to do the job. It was not a bad step, for it served as a restraint on possible rash or precipitate action by an overeager pilot, but in practice it sometimes bogged things down. Communications were often slow, and the pilot had to circle endlessly awaiting permission to land. The aviators chafed under the restrictions, but they could do little about it. Finally, the matter was brought to a head when a Navy P2V ditched in the Atlantic. The survivors were promptly located by a Coast Guard amphibian, and the pilot requested permission to land and pick them up. The sea was like glass, and there was little danger involved. In the RCC, the plot showed a cutter only 40 miles away. The survivors were in a raft and in no immediate danger. The staff decided that the ship could do the job. Back went the word to the eagerly waiting pilot, "Permission not— repeat not—granted."

When the Navy people ashore, not knowing the circumstances, heard this, they were badly upset. If the Coast Guard wouldn't do it, they would ask the Air Force. An Air Force SA-16A soon arrived, landed while the Coast Guard plane circled in frustration, and picked up the survivors. The Coast Guard crew returned to the Naval Air Station and got silently out of their plane. Nearby, the Air Force crew was standing with a crowd of Navy people and the survivors. It was a bitter moment for proud men. That night, someone scrawled a biting epitaph on the Coast Guard ready-room door. Word of the forbidden landing quickly spread, and loud protests arose from other SAR units.

The commandant modified the directive to give pilots the right to land without permission when, in their opinion, it was necessary to save life. But such a decision put the burden of being right on the pilot. If the aircraft was damaged, the pilot had best be sure the landing was really necessary. This is harsh, perhaps, but the pilot is in command of the aircraft, and when you are in command, you answer for your decisions. If you are right, you are a hero; if wrong, look out.

But it wasn't that simple. Compensation and liability were not commensurate. An open-sea landing is dangerous, and a man who accomplishes one deserves proper recognition. He will be condemned if he fails. Yet for a number of years, medals or awards were refused for even the most difficult jobs. The word seeped out of the boardroom that none would be given because it "might encourage pilots to make open-sea landings." If it was said, it was a stupid and outrageous statement. Most open-sea landings are made because the pilots are sent out by their superiors for that specific purpose. Very few pilots will needlessly make a landing and risk a crew just for a ribbon and a piece of metal. For a critically ill or drowning man, yes. For ribbons or money, not on a bet. They are just too dangerous. But many dedicated officers and men risked their lives and careers during those years and never received so much as a thank-you message for their troubles. It was a shameful thing that fortunately has been largely corrected.

By 1960, the helicopter was coming of age and was able to pick up people close in to shore who in former years would have required a seaplane's help. As the range of the helicopter increased, seaplane landings became even less attractive. Damage was frequent. Jim Swanson and I landed 300 miles off Hatteras, hit heavily, bounced 20 feet into the air, bounced again badly, and on the third bounce I threw the props into full reverse. When we smacked down again, she stayed on with the prop digging into the water. One float was damaged and the horizontal stabilizer smashed upward eight inches. It was a close thing, but the reversing props were new, and we didn't know much about them.

There is no time for decision once you touch. You make up your mind before touchdown whether or not you are going to stay on. If you can't make up your mind, you shouldn't land. One young pilot, attempting a landing, couldn't decide even after three bounces. He never reversed, left partial power on throughout the pounding, and finally gave up and took off again. His machine was considerably bent when he returned to base. The idea is to shorten the runout as much as possible, and to do that the props should be reversing as you hit. The PBM props required seven seconds to reverse, and the sharp boys soon learned to reverse in the air before touchdown, so that they would be just entering reverse as the plane touched. With the P5Ms and Albatrosses, the reversal was almost instantaneous, and was not used until touchdown. It was much more comfortable.

In February 1952, we were operating out of Naval Air Station Norfolk during fleet exercise Convex III. We had the new reversing props, which the Navy didn't. They were anxious to see how it worked, and we promised to demonstrate the next time we came in. Returning from a twelve-hour convoy escort mission, we called the tower and they passed the word down to the ready room. A crowd of Navy pilots had gathered at the seawall as we started our final approach. With professional pride egged on by service esprit de corps, I was determined to give them a good show and stop the plane within three lengths. I came over the seawall at 70 knots, hanging on my props. Twenty feet in the air, and right over the wall, I slapped both props into reverse. The plane quit flying right there, and we barely cleared the seawall and spectators. It was spectacular, it made a real impression, and it was utterly stupid. I shouldn't have done it for show at any time, and I should never have even thought of it when my reflexes were slowed down by fatigue. Reversal in the air is a thing for emergencies only, and with the later fast-reversing props, it was seldom needed for that. A lot of us have survived at times by luck rather than skill.

The PBMs were replaced with the more expensive and bigger P5M Marlins, which were a nightmare to maintain. By 1959 the number of open-sea landings had diminished to the point where the use of the big Marlins no longer justified their expense. They were all given to the Navy and replaced with the smaller Albatross amphibian.

The Albatross (HU-16) was developed initially for the Air Force. It was much smaller than the PBM and P5M, and about a three-foot sea was its safe limit. At first, the Air Force boys wouldn't admit it, however, and their losses in the open sea were heavy. Several of these losses were unnecessary, but the pilots learned by trial and error as did the rest of us. One HU-16 was sent out to remove a soldier from a troop transport. In attempting to place the man aboard the plane without using the usual rubber raft, the boat struck the plane's propeller, damaging it so badly that it was unable to take off. A Coast Guard PBM had to be sent out from Salem, Mass., to bring the man in. Another Air Force Albatross, despite warnings by experienced pilots on the scene, landed in 15-foot swells off Georgia to pick up survivors of a bomber crash and lost a wing float in the process. It was a needless waste of a new aircraft, because ships were already on scene, larger and more capable seaplanes were overhead, and the seas were too high for any plane to land. The merchant vessels had to interrupt the rescue of the bomber survivors to recover the crew of the rescue aircraft.

Sometimes, however, the circumstances justify unusual risks. In June 1965, two SAC B-52 bombers were lost at sea as the result of a collision while en route to Vietnam for the first controversial raid on empty woods. An ARRS Albatross landed in 14-foot swells to pick up survivors, but was damaged and unable to take off. The plane had to

A Grumman Albatross amphibian on takeoff run. This plane was known to later generations of pilots as a "Goat." The term was an affectionate one.

be abandoned, but the crew and the four SAC airmen they had saved were recovered by a Navy ship.

ARRS pilots have performed dozens of splendid rescues at sea, including several hair-curlers off Vietnam. They were fortunate in having greater freedom of action than the Coast Guard pilots. Their seniors, being aviators, better understood some of the problems peculiar to seaplane operations and left final decisions on operational matters to the squadron commanders. But ARRS, like the Coast Guard, conceded the limitations of the Albatross for their changing mission, and replaced many of them with four-engine land planes and helicopters. The Albatross was a fine plane in moderate seas, and has done excellent work around the world, but it was not up to really rough water.

I have only done three rough-water landings in the smaller Albatross, and every one has been a chore. The last in five-foot seas was the toughest of all, and the takeoff so rough that I had difficulty getting my thumb on the JATO button. Having done my share of rough-water landings and frightened myself and crew on too many occasions, I say, "Good Riddance!" Helicopters spoiled me. Open-sea landings were rescue the hard way.

6
Choppers and Rotorheads

What MacDiarmid did for the seaplane in rough water, Captain Frank Erickson did for the helicopter in rescue work. Like MacDiarmid a dedicated and single-minded individual, Erikson grasped the implications of the helicopter for rescue when it was still in its infancy. Within two years, he had helped develop the helicopter hoist, the rescue basket, shipboard operating procedures, a stabilization system for hands-off flying, and many other improvements still in use today. He started the first school for helicopter pilots at Floyd Bennett Field, and most of the early Coast Guard and Navy helicopter pilots were Erickson-trained men. In December 1944 he made the first helicopter rescue, removing injured men from a Navy destroyer after an ammunition explosion.

Few in number, and frail and underpowered, the early helicopters performed a number of rescues in the following months, but they were generally looked upon by other airmen as freaks. The pilots, called "rotorheads" by their fixed-wing contemporaries, were likewise regarded as an odd lot of zealots; they weren't quite socially acceptable. But on 18 September 1946, Erickson and his boys got their big chance. They were ready.

On that day, a Belgian Sabena Airline DC-4, making an instrument approach to Gander, Newfoundland, crashed into a heavily

Commander Frank A. Erickson, USCG, the father of the operational helicopter.

wooded wilderness 15 miles from the airport. At the time of the crash, neither the Newfoundland nor the Canadian governments had helicopters with which to perform the rescue work. The Coast Guard volunteered the use of its helicopters, and the United States Army provided the large air transports needed to get the helicopters quickly to the scene. Army personnel and trappers quickly reached the site of the plane crash, but so severely injured were many of the passengers that any form of transportation other than by air would have been fatal. The surroundings would not admit landing any of the conventional types of planes.

Gander airport, not many miles from the crash, afforded landing

Picked up at the scene of the crash, this woman was flown by helicopter to this wooden platform by a lake, from which she was taken by an amphibian to Gander.

facilities for large land planes and amphibians. A lake nearer the scene permitted the landing of amphibians, and a small clearing even closer to the wrecked plane, to which the survivors had been carried, afforded a landing for helicopters.

Coast Guard helicopters were partially dismantled at the Coast Guard Air Station, Brooklyn, N. Y., and flown to Gander Airport by Air Transport Command planes. There they were reassembled. In making the rescue, the helicopters flew the survivors from the small clearing near the scene of the crash to a point on the lake where they were transferred to a Coast Guard PBY amphibian. The PBY, able to land on water or fields, in turn transferred the patients to the Gander Airport, where hospital facilities were available. As it was imperative to move the patients at the earliest practicable moment, the

From the wooden platform set up by the lake, victims are rowed out by inflatable rafts to a waiting amphibian.

Starting with its fine 327-foot *Campbell*-class cutters of 1936, the Coast Guard pioneered the use of aircraft on small vessels. Here a floatplane is being hoisted on board one of the new cutters.

helicopters were used only between the small clearing and the lake site, thus saving much time. Eighteen passengers were rescued from the crash.

The rescue received worldwide attention, and the helicopter's status as a rescue vehicle got a big boost. For the next four years, they were used, mainly by the Coast Guard, on an increasing number of rescues. They were short-range machines, but were invaluable in rescues close to shore, in flood evacuations, and in inaccessible wooded areas. The Navy, realizing their potential, soon placed them on carriers for rescue of pilots who crashed while landing and taking off. They also replaced floatplanes on cruisers and battleships, for they could take off without a catapult and land on the deck rather than on the sea. After the 1946 expedition to the Antarctic, they were used in lieu of floatplanes as scouts on the icebreakers.

The Korean War established the helicopter as the primary rescue machine. Starting with only a few "choppers," the Air Force's Third

Soon after delivery of the first early helicopters, they were being tested on board the CGC *Cobb*. Soon afterwards, one was deployed on a merchant ship in a convoy to England. Though unarmed, it served as a scout and marked the first use of a helicopter in ASW.

Air Rescue Group quickly demonstrated the almost incredible versatility of the helicopter in combat. Over 900 United Nations personnel were rescued from behind enemy lines, but the biggest contribution was in ferrying the wounded. Nearly 9,000 wounded men were flown from the front lines to hospitals, and largely as a result of this, the mortality rate was only half of that experienced in World War II.

In Vietnam, with vastly improved helicopters in a country with few roads and usually inaccessible terrain, the use of helos multiplied. Not only did they prove to be excellent troop carriers and as-

An H-65 Dolphin prepares to land on board a *Hamilton*-class cutter. Nearly all cutters built in the last 30 years have the capability of carrying and operating helos.

An HH-52 hoists a man from a housetop following a hurricane on the Gulf coast.

sault machines, but their rescue and medical-evacuation capability afforded support to front-line elements never dreamed of before. However, operating behind and over enemy territory, the helicopter casualties sometimes reached alarming proportions. But its great utility more than compensated for such vulnerability, and today the helicopter not only constitutes the mainstay of SAR, but thousands are used as combat and ASW (antisubmarine warfare) weapons by the services.

In 1945, Commander Erickson confidently predicted the bright future of the chopper. He was scoffed and laughed at by some, but within ten years, the helicopter had exceeded his most optimistic prophecies. Like MacDiarmid, he was quietly retired, but he had the satisfaction of having helped provide the service and the nation with the means that has saved thousands of lives. He was decorated by two foreign governments, but the Coast Guard never accorded him any formal recognition for his work. As in biblical days, "a prophet is not without honor, save in his own country."

The helicopter's forte is its ability to hover motionless in space. By lowering a sling or basket, it can pick up people from ships, land, or water, or land in confined spaces with no takeoff or landing roll. In 1962, the first amphibious helicopters, able to land at sea in waves that would destroy a fixed-wing aircraft, went into service.

The helicopter quickly replaced the seaplane in most aerial rescues of persons from the water and in the evacuation of medical cases from ships at sea. The early models were limited by their range, lifting capability, and inability to fly in bad weather. Over the years, the range has been steadily extended, and modern twin-engine machines can navigate as far as 350 miles offshore and return. Since 1960 all-weather instrument flight has become a reality, and seldom is the weather bad enough to ground the modern choppers. Along with their increased size has come vastly increased lifting and weight-carrying ability.

The helicopter emerged early as an ideal vehicle for flood relief. Storms unprecedented in number and fury hit Northern California around Christmas 1955. Hundred-mile-an-hour gales brought the area more than twice its normal fall of rain. In one locality, 31½ inches fell in thirteen days. Rivers swelled and overflowed, and man-made levees burst. Whole communities were cut off from the outside world, and many villages were totally destroyed. Fifty thousand families fled. Six thousand homes were washed away, and the total dollar loss in property may have reached the quarter-billion mark. Nearly a hundred people perished.

Rescue efforts by federal, state, and local agencies and by uncounted civilian volunteers helped prevent a greater loss of life. The Army, Navy, and Air Force together rescued some thousand persons, mostly by helicopter, while the Coast Guard saved over 500 by helicopter and boat. Of all the tales of rescue that so far have arisen out of California's great freak flood, few compare with the record established by one of six Coast Guard helicopters, the HO4S CG-1305, piloted alternately by Lieutenant Commander George F. Thometz, USCG, and Lieutenant Henry J. Pfeiffer, USCG, with Aviation Mechanics Joseph Accamo and Victor Roulund taking turns as crew.

The flood was nowhere worse than around Yuba City and Marysville, where the Feather and Yuba Rivers join. Late on 23 December, the Feather River levee south of Yuba City burst, and a wall of water swept the town, covered it to 20 feet, and left hundreds trapped, marooned, or dead. Helicopter CG-1305 was the first rescue unit to reach this dark disaster scene. It arrived in the terror-filled early morning and, working without let-up, hoisted 138 persons to safety within the next twelve hours.

Fifty-eight of these were removed by the light of the Aldis lamp (a small hand-held searchlight) from positions of peril among chimneys, television antennas, and trees. The Coast Guard pilots' refusal to quit while any person was known to be in danger, together with their own and their crews' readiness to accept great personal risk as the price of saving others, followed the proud traditions of their service.

Here are a few notable instances from their log:

24 December 1955

0435   Pfeiffer, pilot; Accamo, crew. Over Yuba City, having been advised that the levee had broken and city was flooding. Observed numerous lights, hundreds, blinking from rooftops, second-story windows, trees, telephone poles, etc. Commenced hoisting from nearest rooftop, in darkness, among tall trees and TV antenna, crewman using Aldis lamp.

0444   Landed at local airport with three men hoisted from rooftop.

0447   Hoisted three adults, five children, one dog.

0505   Mr. R. W. Dingeman, hoisted from a trailer rooftop, advised that his wife, a paralytic and unable to move, was marooned inside trailer, floating around on mattress. Directed Roulund [crewman] to ready himself with axe and flashlight and prepare to enter trailer through the vent, locate woman, get her out by chopping hole in side of trailer, then signal by flashlight when ready for helicopter pickup.

0519   Lowered Roulund to trailertop. Proceeded to nearby rooftop and hoisted four persons to safety while awaiting Roulund's signal to pick up Mrs. Dingeman.

0528   On Roulund's signal, hoisted Mrs. Dingeman aboard. Her condition prevented her removal from rescue basket; therefore hoisted Roulund by sling.

0536   Debarked rescued persons.

0545   Thometz, pilot; Accamo, crew. Hoisted two adults, each holding a child, from trees in a flooding current of approximately ten (10) knots. Difficulty experienced in hovering in position where basket could be lowered without getting entangled in the tree. Hoisted another adult from top of electric power pole, where he had tied himself with broken wires. Accamo handled hoist most skillfully, avoiding entanglement in broken wires and pole cross-pieces.

0644   Thometz, pilot; Roulund, crew. Hoisted three adults, four children (one being 1½ years old).

0702   Landed at airport. Re-fueled with engine idling to conserve battery.

0704   Hoisted five adults and four children (oldest seven, youngest three).

0715   Sunrise. Re-fueled.

0844   Pfeiffer, pilot; Accamo, crew. Hoisted six adults, one child, from rooftop.

0858   Found polio victim on rooftop, covered with a tarpaulin. High TV antenna prevented close-in hoist, but pilot, having previously cut guy wires of a 50-foot antenna accidentally with his main rotor blades, perceived possibility of cutting guy wires on this antenna. He therefore eased helicopter close to guy wires until rotor blades severed them, then quickly pulled helicopter up so as to blow the antenna over with rotor downwash. Helicopter was then eased down until front wheels rested on roof. Accamo jumped out with stretcher and assisted aged husband get paralytic woman aboard. Proceeded to nearby roof and hoisted four other adults and two children.

0921   Landed at airport and re-fueled.

1001   Lt. Pfeiffer, pilot; Accamo, crew. Hoisted six adults. Advised that Lt. C. R. Leisy, USCG, has been lowered by a Navy helicopter onto an inflated 4-man liferaft and towed by a Hiller helicopter (Phillip Johnson, pilot) under high-tension lines to an automobile roof-top, where a woman was stranded with her baby. Leisy had managed to wedge the liferaft between tall fence posts, but the Navy helo, equipped only with sling, was unable to hoist the woman and baby.

1050   Hovering over position. Hoisted woman, who was unconscious from exposure. Because of her condition, Accamo was unable to get her out of the rescue basket expeditiously so it could be sent down for Lt. Leisy and the baby. Lt. Pfeiffer therefore lowered helicopter until its wheels were in the water; Lt. Leisy handed the child to Accamo and then crawled aboard himself.

1108   Observed man wading neck deep, on highway. Hoisted man in rescue basket. He was incoherent and nearly frozen.

1135   LCDR Thometz, pilot; Roulund, crew. Hoisted fourteen persons, eleven of them children. These hoists were all made by holding the helicopter with the main rotor a few feet above a 40-feet TV antenna, with helicopter's nose one foot from the antenna prongs. Roulund lowered rescue basket to a cupola on the side of the house, where the mothers and children were loaded.

1600   Relief pilots and crews arrived. Total hoists for past 11½ hours: 138. LCDR Thometz: 66 hoists in 10 sorties. LT Pfeiffer: 72 hoists in 13 sorties.

Both George Thometz and Hank Pfeiffer were awarded the Distinguished Flying Cross. It was well deserved.

Ten years to the day later, another storm hit the area. The first helicopter to arrive in the area was piloted by Lieutenant Commander Donald L. Prince. Flying in conditions that would have grounded many helicopters, they rescued eighteen people. Several were hoisted while he hovered in 60-knot gusts of wind between high-tension power lines. As darkness approached, Don took off with his crew and five persons he had rescued to fly to Arcada Airport, where he could get fuel. Due to the low ceilings and heavy rain, he elected to climb up into the clouds and fly on instruments. When abeam of Arcada, he would make a let-down using the Arcada radiobeacon. When almost there, fate played a cruel trick—the radiobeacon at Arcada failed.

Don was a sharp, cool-headed pilot, and with the primary navigation aid out, he requested a radio-direction-finder steer from the Arcada tower, and when it was received, turned in-bound for the field. But the odds were too great. A Pacific Airline captain, flying over the area, reported the weather and turbulence as the worst he had experienced in thirteen years of flying. The helicopter was set to the east by the terrific winds and smashed into the mountains, killing the crew and all five passengers.

The good ones often do die young, because they are always in the front where the action is occurring. There is a famous motto in the Coast Guard, handed down from the surfboat days, "You have to go out, but you don't have to come back." Don didn't *have* to go out that day, but he went because people were in danger, and a job needed to be done. Eighteen other people are alive because he was there that day, and all of us who knew him will always remember a man who stood tall.

Over water, the helicopter is the rescue method par excellence. Hundreds of airmen and seamen have been plucked from the sea by helicopter hoist. If they can be found, the helicopter can get them. Lieutenant Joe Tanguay, on a bitter New England winter night, hoisted nine men off a burning fishing vessel in the surf off Cape Cod, where boats were unable to go. His hoist operator, John Williams, had to lie on the deck of the helicopter to protect himself from the fierce heat of the burning boat. For thirty-five minutes, they worked in the heat and turbulence. Five minutes after the last man was lifted off, the flame reached the fuel tanks, and the boat blew up with a shattering explosion. They had gotten clear just in time.

When the SS *Dynafuel* and the *Fernview* collided in Buzzards Bay, Mass., we dispatched two helicopters from Salem to the scene. They evacuated most of the wounded, then for the remainder of the day shuttled back and forth bringing foam and fire-fighting gear to battle the blaze, and take off more wounded. In one day, the two choppers made 130 hoists.

The *African Queen*, carrying 156,000 gallons of crude oil, ran aground and split in two off Ocean City, Maryland. Fifteen Navy, Coast Guard, and Marine helicopters removed the forty-seven crew members. A Coast Guard helicopter put a crew member aboard the distressed ship as traffic director for the helicopter fleet, and all ship crew members were taken off in less than two hours. It was rescue on an assembly line scale.

A night overwater hoist is always tough, and can get downright grim. On the night of 22 September 1963, a 38-foot yawl went aground off Scituate, Massachusetts, and broadcast a Mayday. We located them on a reef three hundred yards offshore. In our searchlight beam, the vessel was listing 30 degrees, pounding heavily, and was in danger of

An HH-52 helicopter hovers over various Coast Guard vessels while firefighters tackle the flames on the *Fernview* and *Dynafuel*. *(New Bedford Standard Times)*

rolling over at any moment. I maneuvered over the vessel, but had to stay high because of the masts. Once over the vessel, I was entirely reliant on the coaching of my hoist operator, Aviation Metalsmith Jim Rice, because the pilot cannot see directly below. One man was swept overboard by the waves, and we quickly hoisted him. The basket was lowered again, but this time became fouled in the tangled rigging of the vessel, trapping us like a seagull caught on a fishline. We continued to hover while the men on the boat tried without success to free the basket. The strain of hovering in the darkness, while restricted by the hung cable, was murderous. Soon, Jack La-Flamme, my copilot, spelled me off and I rested. For ten minutes, Rice coached us steadily while we held position, then I took over again. We could cut the cable, but then would be unable to hoist the people if the boat went over. I decided to "jump on the cable" to try and break the basket loose. It was dangerous, but so was the situation. First lowering the helicopter slightly to get some slack, I came up sharply on my power and the helicopter jumped upward. The cable came taut with a sharp jerk, but the basket didn't give. The cable, tending to the side, gave us a down and sideways pull, and sheared off the rear end of our starboard float. Rice, seeing the danger, fired the explosive charge to sever the cable. We moved over to the side and examined the damage. The chopper was still flyable, but the two men were still on the boat.

Moving upwind, we dropped a seven-man liferaft, and it floated down to the yawl. The men grabbed it, but a sea came up and tore it from their grasp. We moved downwind of the raft, and attempted to blow it back to them by the wash of air from our blades, but the northeast wind was too strong. Then came the idea. Rice fastened a small anchor to a line, lowered the anchor into the raft to hook it, and towed it back to the boat. This time, both men jumped overboard and swam to the raft. Once in, they started drifting down among the reefs. There was little room and even less time. We moved alongside, and settled down with our keel just touching the water. Rice reached out and grabbed the raft, but the two survivors had had it for the night. They wouldn't turn loose that raft for any reason, not even to climb into the helicopter. Finally, when almost on the rocks, we were forced to lift into a hover. Lieutenant Larry Kindbom arrived in another chopper, and we played our lights on the raft while he lowered a basket. The men still refused to get in. Finally, they worked their way through the reef, and a Coast Guard rescue boat picked them up. It had been quite a night, but the helicopter again proved that there is practically nothing it can't do in a tight spot.

In 1957, the Coast Guard conducted tests on towing disabled vessels with a helicopter. A 900-ton vessel was towed at 9 knots. Over the next several years, a number of spectacular rescues were made by "tugbirds" when time did not permit waiting for a tow by a boat. On two occasions, helicopters towed disabled boats out of high surf off San Francisco when boats could not reach them. Had they failed, death would have been almost certain for the boats' occupants.

There were many tows of a less serious nature. In 1957, while on a routine helicopter patrol, we found a sloop hard aground on a reef in Biscayne Bay, Florida. We lowered a line, pulled him off, and went on our way. An hour later, passing the reef on our return, we found him aground a second time. This time we hoisted the man

An H-52 helicopter hoists crewmen off a fisherman in the surf.

aboard, pointed out on a chart how to avoid the reef, and lowered him back down. Only then did we lower a line, and tow him off again. This time, he stayed clear of the reefs.

On land, the helicopter is as useful as at sea. In dense woods, swamps, or mountains, where ground parties formerly required days to reach a wreck, the chopper can be there in minutes and either land in a small clearing, or hover and lower ground parties. Many aircraft crashes occur near the airport, where the terrain often prevents crash and fire trucks from reaching the scene. At many bases, the Air Force used crash fire helicopters. These versatile birds could quickly attach fire-fighting equipment, speed to the inaccessible crash scene, and spray the burning wreckage with chemicals.

My first personal experience with the helicopter as a crash vehicle occurred at Elizabeth City in 1952. Several of our planes were putting on a rescue demonstration for a group of Academy cadets engaged in summer aviation training. Halfway through the demonstration, one of the aircraft had an engine failure, and returned to the field.

The crash alarm sounded, and the crash trucks and "meat wagon" took station by the duty runway. The cripple passed over the field, and turned downwind, with everything under control. Then, as everyone looked on in horror, the other engine quit, and down he came at a steep angle and crashed in a thick pine woods a mile away. The cloud of dust rose high in the air over the crash scene. I ran for the ready helicopter and piled in beside Ice Sansbury, the pilot. We knew already what we would find—twisted metal and mangled bodies. Looking at a crash involving strangers is bad enough. When you know the crew and their families, you are sick at your stomach.

We landed in a small clearing near the crash and ran to the wreck. The fuselage was still intact, but the rest of the plane was badly torn up. The copilot was standing nearby, apparently uninjured. The pilot was sitting on the ground holding his head. The flight engineer had run all the way to the highway to get help. There were only two injuries. The pilot, looking back over his shoulder as he fled the smoking wreck, had run into a pine tree. After jumping out of the helicopter, I fell into a well-concealed ditch and sprained an ankle. It was a small price to pay in a situation like that.

Hovering over and landing on flat terrain is usually simple, but mountain flying in high winds and turbulence is another matter. Not only is the helicopter a poorer performer at high altitudes, but turbulence produces blade stall, with a resultant momentary reversal of control forces. It is guaranteed to hasten grey hair. New pilots have to learn the peculiarities of mountain flying, and lectures won't do the trick. They have to feel it for themselves. At San Diego we used a beautiful little pasture at the 5,000-foot level in the Laguna mountains to check out new pilots. Then we would take them to a high plateau overlooking the desert, where they could experience the turbulence caused by the hot winds of the desert rising up the nearly vertical cliffs. It was at this spot on a hot June afternoon that I aged considerably.

What had started out as a routine mountain training flight had suddenly turned into a nightmare, with me hanging by a thin cable a thousand feet over the desert, swinging in wide arcs. I hung by a precarious grip to the "horsecollar" sling, and looked up at the thin cable leading to the helicopter 50 feet above. Then I glanced down at the floor of the desert far below. I didn't have a parachute, and I was petrified. In common with many pilots, I get slightly ill changing a light bulb on a high stepladder without an airplane strapped to me. I gripped the cable hook until my hands froze, and resolved not to look again.

Only three minutes before I had been peacefully lying in the shade on a plateau overlooking the Imperial Valley of California, watching a student pilot making hot-weather high-altitude terrain approaches to the plateau. Earlier, I had demonstrated two approaches, and had climbed out and let the new boy try some. "After the third approach," I told him, "come into a hover, and hoist me in the sling to see what a hoist feels like at this altitude."

Soon I saw him approaching for the hover and the sling, called a "horsecollar" because of the resemblance, was being lowered from the helicopter winch by a slim cable. He was far too high on the hover, and would have to be instructed to come in lower. I slid the sling under my arms, the hoist operator took up the slack, and my feet came off the ground as he hoisted me toward the helicopter. So far, so good. Then, to my dismay, the pilot, instead of hovering motionless while I was being hoisted (which is standard procedure), started forward at a good 30 knots toward the edge of the cliff, where the plateau drops 1,400 feet down to the floor of the desert. I was 10 feet above the ground; then as we slipped over the cliff, I was suddenly 1,400 feet up in an empty sky, supported only by a thin strap. After what seemed like ages, I felt the hoist stop. Oh, God, I thought, my eyes tightly shut, let me give back all the flight pay. Then, the crewman grabbed me by the back of my belt, and I felt the jerk as he yanked me into the cabin. Only then did I open my eyes. I looked down at the desert again from the safety of the cabin. My hands were so tired they shook, but they would have shaken anyway. Then with relish, I climbed up into the other seat in the cockpit. I had a lot to

An HH-52 about to hoist a young boy off the face of a cliff near Cape Disappointment, Washington.

say to the student pilot, and a nice long ride ahead in which to say it.

The mountains are a deadlier place to go down in than the sea, for there are seldom any flat spots in the hills to make a forced landing.

One light plane hit the California mountains after diving in from 3,000 feet. I landed on a small ledge several hundred feet above it and scrambled down the rocks. A hundred feet from the crash, I stopped short and looked at something on a flat rock. It was a human brain. It was the largest fragment of body left. The engine had been smashed into a hard metal mass measuring only two feet from the prop cap to the instrument panel. There was little else.

At another crash, there was a large crater filled with smoking metal. Probing in the wreckage, I sighted the collar of a Navy flight jacket and pulled it out. It contained a headless upper torso. A short time later, a hunting guide reached the wreck, and noticing he had to-bacco, I asked for some. The smell of burned flesh was strong. He extended a plug of Apple tobacco, and I bit off a huge chew. It made the work a little easier. I had a big chaw still in my cheek when we walked into the operations office of a Naval Air Station that night and laid a wallet and several ID tags on the desk. You never get used to it, but you learn to endure it.

A small private aircraft on a cross-country flight ran into a thunderstorm and crashed in thick swampland. It had apparently disintegrated in the air, for one wing section was a half mile from the fuselage. The four bodies were scattered over a half-mile area. We found them several hours later, and lowered a crewman down. He placed a body in the basket, we raised it into the cabin, flew to a nearby country road, and laid it beside the road to await an ambulance. Four trips were necessary to get the bodies out.

After the second body was laid beside the road, we noted an old pickup truck approaching. When the driver sighted the bodies, he swerved, then raced away down the road at full speed. It must have been an unnerving experience for him, and he wasn't about to stop.

After the bodies are removed from a crash, the accident investigators go to work, attempting to find out what caused the accident. The work of these experts is a fascinating combination of plain hard work and scientific detection methods. In large crashes, the pieces are often put together on a wire and woodwork frame to afford a rough reconstruction of the ill-fated aircraft. With new-model aircraft, it is absolutely essential to find the accident cause. By so doing, the defects and bugs that are present in nearly all new planes can be corrected. Until the cause is found, there is always the possibility that it may be a recurring thing that can cost other lives. The present high safety standards of commercial aviation are due in no small part to the ceaseless and painstaking work of the investigating teams of the National Transportation Safety Board (NTSB). In recent years, they have been aided greatly by the flight recorders carried on jet airliners. The rugged recorders preserve records of the course, speeds, and stresses of the aircraft prior to the crash, as well as crew conversations.

Considerable effort and risks are incurred by helicopter crews in crash recovery operations, even after it is known that no survivors exist. Determination of the cause of the crash justifies the acceptance of some risks, for other lives may be saved as a result. But risking helicopter crews in a hazardous operation to recover bodies is not justified. In one large airliner crash, helicopter crews time after time narrowly escaped disaster to bring out the mangled and unidentifiable bodies from an inaccessible canyon. They were then buried in a mass grave. After the operation, one veteran pilot said, "If I go down, and there is a chance I'm alive, I want every damn airplane they can scrape up out looking. But if they know I'm dead, leave me there. I don't want some fellow killed trying to get my corpse out."

Before the amphibian helicopter, rescues at sea were made by hoisting the survivor. Occasionally, a man would be injured or so fatigued that he was unable to get into the sling or basket. A crewman

An HH-52 amphibious helo lands in the open sea.

then had to be lowered into the water to help. It was a risky maneuver, and on a couple of occasions the crewman was lost attempting to aid the survivor.

The first landing at sea by an amphibious helicopter on a rescue mission occurred on 22 March 1963, only a month after the first machine was received. We were on a flight off Point Judith, Rhode Island, searching for two men missing from a fishing vessel. The vessel had been found wrecked on the Point Judith breakwater, but no one was aboard. While searching, we overheard a call from a Navy radar ship that had lost a man overboard on the approaches to Newport Harbor. It was a bitter cold day, and a man could not survive long in the freezing water. After a fast run to the area, we sighted the ship, and began searching astern of it. As time ticked away, the chances of the man being found alive diminished rapidly. Suddenly, Jim Webber, our hoist operator yelled, "There he is, close aboard at three o'clock!" His head disappeared below the water. There was no time to lower a basket so we sat down on the water beside him as his head emerged. Quickly rigging out the rescue platform, Webber grabbed him by the shoulder, but he was a big man, and semiconscious. Webber called for help, and I scrambled out of the cockpit and ran aft. Grabbing him by the shoulder, we hauled him in. He was nearly gone.

"Take off!" I yelled to Bob Russell, the copilot. He lifted off, started for the Naval Air Station, Quonset Point, and called for an ambulance. The sailor was blue, and his body shook violently from the cold. We wrapped him in blankets and our flight jackets, but he mumbled incoherently and lapsed into a coma. The pickup had required less than one minute, and in ten minutes he was in an ambulance. As we climbed out of the cockpit the crew of a Navy helicopter landed and came over to look at our new amphibian.

"We were over you when you picked him up," said the Navy pilot. "It's a good thing you were there. He couldn't have been hoisted."

He looked at the boat-hulled chopper again with admiration, and said, "You wouldn't like to trade, would you?"

Not for a lot full of gold-plated Cadillacs, I thought.

Over the next few years, the water-landing ability of the new birds was proven time and again. At New Orleans, one landed beside a capsized boat and rescued a priest and several children who had been clinging to the boat for hours. They were too weak to be hoisted, or even to swim a few yards to the machine. The helicopter hoist operator jumped in and towed them back. The priest still retained his sense of humor. For an hour before the helicopter arrived, he had felt himself getting weaker, and knew he could not survive much longer. He was, he told the helicopter pilot, "at any minute expecting a recall from Headquarters."

The amphibious helicopter can land in seas that would be impossible for a seaplane. The forward speed at touchdown is zero, and the pilot can control the helicopter on the water by varying the lift of his rotor. If the seas are rough, he keeps most of the weight of the hull on the rotor blades, and the hull rides lightly over the swells.

If a pilot, after bailing out, releases himself from his parachute after hitting the water, he can be picked up easily. However, if he is still attached to the chute or entangled in the shrouds, there is real trouble. On several occasions, helicopters have vainly attempted to pick up a pilot with a chute still attached. The pilot was hoisted clear of the water, but the parachute, acting as a giant sea anchor containing tons of water, held him back. He couldn't be lifted farther until the chute was cut free. Often a submerged chute will drag the pilot beneath the water, or if it is still billowing in the wind, it will drag him at high speed through the water until it collapses or the pilot drowns. I arrived over the scene of a bailout off Nantucket just in time to sight the chute 10 feet below the water dragging the pilot down. He was already below the surface. We could do nothing as he disappeared from sight.

If a chute is only partially submerged, it is a dangerous thing. The wind blast from a hovering helicopter can cause it to billow up and be sucked into the blades of the rescue helicopter. One of our helicopters from Houston, attempting to recover a chute, sucked it up into the tail rotor and crashed.

Chopper pilots have long been plagued by their limited fuel. During searches, some of them used to land at filling stations, refueling with high-test auto gas. Lieutenant Bo Korenek made one of the last filling-station stops. Searching for a woman lost in the Everglades, he was running very low on fuel when ground searchers heard her cries. It was a pitch black night, and the ground party couldn't get to her. Bo decided to top off with fuel at a filling station several miles away and come back to hoist her. He was coming in slowly for a landing, when he felt a thump and at the same time saw all the lights at the station go out. He had hit a power line with his tail rotor. Fortunately, the damage was slight, but after that, a ban was placed on shopping at your nearest friendly Esso dealer. Headquarters decided that a tiger in the cockpit was enough. They didn't want one in the tank.

A few months later, Bo had another pressing refueling problem. A Miami High School football coach, en route by plane from Nassau to Miami, suffered an engine failure at sea. Lieutenant Commander Bob Pope, out on a track search soon after the plane was reported overdue, sighted the downed pilot's flashlight signal some 80 miles off Miami. He dropped a float light, and called for a helicopter. Bo scrambled, and headed through the night for the scene. One hundred and fifty miles to the west, while en route from New Orleans to Miami, we heard the radioed sighting report, and headed toward the scene, knowing that over the long stretch of water, the helicopter would need a cover aircraft. We could catch up with him off the coast. But checking our fuel, we found that there wasn't enough for the job. We called Fort Lauderdale tower, and told them we needed fuel and fast. The boys in the tower took over. When we arrived, they cleared us for a straight-in approach, and two fuel trucks were sitting by the end of the runway. We rolled out, cut our engines, and a truck moved in on either side and began pumping fuel. As soon as they pulled away, we started both engines, and were cleared to take off. We were airborne only twelve minutes after landing.

When we caught up with Bo, he was only 20 miles from the survivor, but new troubles arose. The downed pilot's flashlight had burned out, and he couldn't be relocated, even though markers had been dropped by the covering aircraft. For forty-five minutes, Bo searched without success under the light of parachute flares dropped by the two covering planes. Finally, he had to break off and return to North Bimini, a deserted island with an abandoned landing strip. After Bo landed, we set down on the unlighted strip, using our landing lights. We taxied over and discussed the situation. Bo wanted to go back out there, but he had little fuel left. We decided to refuel the helicopter from our tanks.

Using the empty flare-container cans, each of which held two gallons, we drained the fuel from our tanks through the wheel-well draincock. In the darkness, eight men formed a "bucket brigade," passing two gallons of fuel at a time from the plane to the helicopter, and pouring it into the tank through a paper funnel made from charts. After nearly an hour, the chopper was topped off with fuel and took off. At first light, he found the pilot in a raft, and hoisted him safely aboard. It was a real boondock operation, but Bo brought him back alive.

The helicopter has come a long way from Erickson's early rescue birds, but not without cost. The accident rate has been high, for the versatile choppers often go in harm's way. They are also the most sensitive of all aircraft to fly, reacting quickly to the pilot's slightest touch. A large aircraft can be very mechanical in its response to the controls. A helicopter extends right out from the pilot's fingertips.

Flying over the ocean in all kinds of weather in the early single-engine and piston-powered machines, helicopter pilots knew that in case of engine failure they would have not over fifteen seconds to get out after they ditched. By the time the whirling blades stopped, the machine was under water. But the amphibious helicopter with the more reliable turbine engine, and quick-inflatable flotation bags for greater stability, improved the odds greatly, and the longer-range twin-turbine HH-3F was even better. With these improvements, helicopters spread their protective shadows over vast areas of the oceans. The first of the amphibious choppers designed specifically for SAR, the HH-52, was the most successful life-saving vehicle of all time, with

An HH-60 helicopter. Latest in a long line.

An HH-52 lands alongside an exhausted boatman. Recovery was almost assured.

over 15,000 lives saved in its twenty-five years of service before being replaced by the HH-65 twin-engine light helicopter. The HH-3, though still a capable machine, is aging and will be replaced by the slightly faster and longer-range HH-60 starting in 1990. Neither the new HH-65 or the HH-60 are amphibious, though most SAR pilots would prefer a machine capable of landing on the water. But due to the huge development costs of new aircraft types, SAR helicopters, relatively few in numbers, must be adapted from machines designed primarily for other missions, and those do not require an ability to land on the water. Without amphibious capability, a rescue swimmer must be lowered into the water should the victims need help. Two recent cases in Alaskan waters dramatically illustrate the two techniques.

A rescue swimmer is lowered from a Dolphin helicopter to aid a victim in the water. With the passing of the ability to land on the water, this sometimes dangerous tactic will often be necessary.

On 19 December 1986 the 50-foot trawler *Laura* made a distress call, reporting winds of 50 knots and 30-foot seas. A Coast Guard HH-3F helicopter was scrambled from Kodiak at 0604, followed shortly by a C-130. Lieutenant Commander Tom Walters, the pilot, established contact with the *Laura*, while Lieutenant John Filipowicz, AM3 Tony Juan, AT2 Don Nolan, and HS3 John Holcomb prepared to hoist the trawler's two crew members. The weather conditions were obviously too rough for the chopper to land. The ceiling was down to 500 feet, visibility a half mile, and 80-knot wind gusts had created 40-foot seas. In the far northern latitude, daylight would not come for another two hours. In attempting to place the rescue basket on the wildly careening trawler, all three trail lines carried by the helo were snapped, and when Walters expertly placed the basket on the boat without a trail line, it became entangled in the rigging and the hoist hook was damaged. A splice was rigged in place of the hook, and as the two crewmen abandoned ship in exposure suits, the basket was lowered to them in the water. The two got in and the

An HH-3F in a hover. Even should the hoist fail, this machine can complete a rescue by landing.

basket started up toward the hovering helicopter. Suddenly the cable snapped and the men dropped five feet into the cold, raging waters. With fuel running low, Walters had to make a life-death decision. He and his crew did not hesitate—they would go after the men in the water. On the fourth attempt in the howling darkness, the men drifted under the helo. Walters sat the chopper down on the crest of a huge wave and began to slide down its backside. Juan, Nolan, and Holcomb grabbed the two men and heaved them onto the recovery platform. Walters added power, lifting the machine off, and Filipowicz hurried aft to help the other crewmen drag the cold, water-soaked men inside. The day was not done. It would be impossible to reach Kodiak against the 80-knot winds with the fuel remaining. Walters turned east and fought his way through the storm, finally landing on a nameless island at the mouth of Wide Bay. After waiting out the storm, the crew and their two survivors were picked up at sunset by another helicopter. Their own bird was returned the next day.

Almost a year later and in weather remarkably similar and nasty, the fishing vessel *Blue Bird*, carrying Jim Blades and his six-year-old son, broadcast a Mayday. Air Station Sitka, Alaska, received the call and launched an HH-3F helicopter with a rescue swimmer and night-vision goggles on board. With 30-foot seas and 70-knot winds, Lieutenant Commander J. B. Whiddon elected not to attempt a hoist directly from the vessel due to the rigging of the boat. The man and six-year-old boy on the boat went into the water with exposure suits, and ASM2 Jeff Tunks, the rescue swimmer, went into the water to help them. Tunks helped both into the rescue basket, and then was hoisted himself after suffering some injuries in the cold, rough water. The aircraft was grounded on its return due to over-powering and damage in the severe weather.

Whiddon and his crew, Lieutenant G. B. Breithaup, AD1 C. E. Saylor, AT3 M. A. Milne, and Tunks were selected as the 1987 Naval Helicopter Association Aircrew of the Year. Tom Walters and his crew had won the same recognition the year before. Other professional fliers recognized with admiration and respect the superb airmanship and heroism involved in these two cases, chosen from many heroic efforts by naval helicopter crews.

There was more to come. On 3 January 1989, an Air Force F-4 fighter on a training mission developed mechanical problems off the Oregon coast, and the two pilots bailed out. A wingman lost sight of them as they entered a heavy cloud bank at 15,000 feet. Coast Guard Air Station Astoria scrambled a Falcon jet and an HH-65 helicopter piloted by Lieutenant Commander Bill Peterson. Though the ceiling was only 100 feet and visibility a quarter of a mile, the position radioed by the wingman was right on, and the two rafts were quickly located by the helo. Hovering 15 feet above the cold 16–20 foot seas, a rescue swimmer jumped from the helicopter and began swimming to one of the survivors. Though this was not the first time a rescue swimmer had dared death in such conditions, it involved many other "firsts." The rescue swimmer was ASM3 Kelly Mogk, the only female rescue swimmer in the Coast Guard, and the only woman to graduate from the Navy Rescue Swimmer School at Pensacola, Florida. When she reached Lieutenant Mike Markstaller, he was entangled in his parachute gear and was suffering from hypothermia and

RESCUE

ASM3 Kelly Mogk, in a quieter moment, stands at the door of a rescue helicopter.

several broken bones. Mogk began cutting the tangled gear loose, at the same time talking to the pilot to encourage him. After 27 minutes in the frigid water with her exposure suit leaking, Mogk freed the pilot and put him into a hoisting sling. Copilot Bill Harper and flight crewman Reese hauled him aboard and began resuscitative measures. Kelly Mogk was by now also suffering from hypothermia, loss of feeling in her hands and fingers, and an injury to her lower back. Due to the critical condition of the jet pilot, however, Peterson decided to fly him in immediately, leaving another helicopter to search for the other pilot and retrieve Mogk. With the other two members of his crew working desperately on Markstaller, Peterson fought his way through the worsening weather and delivered the victim to a hospital. The other helo located the other raft, but found Lieutenant Mark Baker 12 feet beneath his raft and entangled in his parachute. Despite all efforts by crewmen and a flight surgeon, he could not be revived. Kelly Mogk was awarded a well-deserved Air Medal, and was later flown to Washington, where she was congratulated by President Bush, himself a well-known pilot survivor of an earlier era.

Other crews received recognition from the very top level. Three Air Station, Cape Cod, HH-3 helicopters safely evacuated thirty-seven Soviet crewmen from the sinking 482-foot *Komsomolets Kirgizii* 220 miles east of the Delaware Capes. Working in 55-knot winds and 20-foot seas, the first helo hoisted fifteen people, the second picked up sixteen more, and the third hoisted the final six, which included the master. Three days later, President Reagan invited the Soviet crew to a White House ceremony honoring their rescuers. Addressing the helicopter crews, their commander-in-chief said: "In your courage, your tenacity, your know-how, you summed up all that is best in the American spirit—in a word, all that is heroic."

Storms are often accompanied by multiple cases of distress, and it was another Air Station Sitka HH-3F helicopter that had a busy day

In high winds and seas, an HH-3F hovers over the stricken Soviet vessel *Komsomolets Kirgizii* while hoisting the first fifteen people.

Soviet crewmen crowded into the cabin during the long ride to shore.

in an April 1985 storm. Originally sent out to assist a vessel taking on water, the helo was released by the Canadian RCC at Prince Rupert after a Canadian Coast Guard vessel responded. Returning home, the crew heard a Mayday and diverted to find the fishing vessel *Bethune* awash with four men in the icy water. After hoisting them, the helo proceeded to Prince Rupert, B. C., for fuel. On arrival, the Canadian RCC requested that the Americans assist the vessel *Gibson*, taking on water off Cape Ball, 60 miles to the southwest. Lieutenant Darrell Folsom,the pilot, switched seats with the copilot, Lieutenant (j.g.) Sig Kirchner, who then took off for what was to be his first actual rescue from the pilot's seat. Ceilings were now less than 400 feet, and winds were over 50 knots with heavy turbulence.

En route to the *Gibson*, another Mayday call was heard from the 60-foot halibut boat *Godstad*, and the helo changed course toward her, as her condition was worse than that of the *Gibson*. A Canadian Buffalo aircraft over the scene reported that the *Godstad* had capsized, and the helo crew soon sighted three men in a raft in raging seas. Kirchner lowered the basket, but two men grabbed it and neither would let go. Both were hoisted together and then the third man. Though the victims were suffering from hypothermia, the helo turned and raced toward the *Gibson*. Three men were hoisted from her, and the battered helicopter crew turned for Prince Rupert with six survivors. En route, still another distress call was received, but fuel was now critically low and the helo landed for fuel. A Canadian helicopter was sent instead, but damaged its hoist and injured a crewman in the rescue attempt. The tired Americans were the only help available in time. Having been flying in severe weather for over six hours, the pilot asked his base for a waiver of crew time limits, and soon headed out again into the storm and darkness. Winds were now over 60 knots with severe turbulence, rain, and darkness. The pilot of the Canadian Forces P-3 over the scene said that a hoist was the only way to remove *Miss Rachel*'s crew. Soon a distressed vessel was sighted, but it turned out to be the *Dee Jay*, with four people on board. They were picked up one at a time as they leaped into the water, and all four were aboard in nineteen minutes. Then another call came in! *Miss Rachel*'s anchor line had snapped, and she was drifting onto the rocks. Lieutenant Folsom had a hard decision, but after nine hours of battling the weather, the risk was too great with a fatigued crew. He reluctantly turned for base, landing at Prince Rupert twelve hours after taking off from Sitka. AM2 John Sherman and AE2 James Revis had hoisted fourteen men from 50-foot seas, while flight surgeon Captain James Rahman and hospital corpsman Bonnie Odom had treated them in the cramped tossing aft compartment of the helicopter. In spite of appalling weather, changing conditions, and dangerous fatigue, the crew had performed faultlessly. Their concern over their inability to assist the *Miss Rachel* was soon dispelled when word was received that her crew had managed to restart the engine and work clear of the lee shore.

The numerically greatest rescue of a ship's people by helicopters was also off Alaska. On 30 September 1980, the 472-foot Dutch cruise

Eighteen passengers and two Canadian paramedics await rescue as a rescue basket is lowered into the boat from a helicopter.

vessel, *Prinsendam*, sailed from Vancouver, B.C., for Singapore, with several stops scheduled en route. She had a crew of 205 and a passenger list of 319, most of whom were middle-aged or elderly Americans. Shortly after midnight on 4 October, a fire broke out in the engine room, and was soon out of control. With the main engines out, and the crew unable to start the auxiliaries, water pressure failed.

The big cruise liner sent an SOS, giving her position as 120 miles west of Sitka. The RCC at Juneau, Alaska, ordered aircraft and ships to the scene. The Air Stations at Sitka and Kodiak scrambled four HH-3F helicopters and two C-130s. The large, fast cutters *Boutwell* and *Mellon*, and the buoy tender *Woodrush*, were dispatched, and all were soon rushing toward the burning ship at best speeds, this being over 25 knots for the big cutters even in the rough seas. Merchant vessels also diverted. The closest and, as it would turn out, the most critical to the rescue, was the huge supertanker *Williamsburgh*. Loaded with oil and drawing 65 feet, she had two helicopter pads and was a steady platform. Her 1,095-foot length and broad beam could easily accommodate all the liner passengers—if they could be transferred.

With the fires spreading and still no water pressure, the master of the *Prinsendam* ordered the passengers and crew into six open lifeboats, a motor launch, and a number of inflatable rafts. The abandonment was uneventful, though many people were only lightly clad in pajamas or night gowns.

Survivors from the *Prinsendam* on the forepeak of the supertanker *Williamsburgh*, after being lifted from the lifeboats by helicopters.

The *Williamsburgh* arrived just before dawn and maneuvered her 225,000 tons to provide a lee for the boats, but taking the passengers on board was a slow process and the weather was worsening. Then the four Coast Guard helicopters, two Canadian Forces machines, and an Air Force chopper from Elmendorf Air Force Base at Anchorage arrived, and the tempo speeded up. Hovering over the boats, each helo would hoist a load of victims and then shuttle to the big tanker, where they landed and off-loaded. As each had to leave for fuel, it took a load of survivors in to Yakutat, where a large medical team had been assembled. On the return trip to the tanker, medical personnel and supplies were brought out. Two other merchantmen, the *Sohio Intrepid* and the *Portland*, were now on scene along with the *Boutwell*. In the afternoon, the last of the liner's crewmen who had continued to fight the fire were removed, and by 1830 the rescue was apparently over. The *Williamsburgh* was ordered back to Valdez, Alaska, to off-load survivors. Fortunately, the *Boutwell* remained on scene, for that night Elmendorf AFB reported two para-rescue men missing. The *Boutwell* resumed the search, with illumination being provided by a C-130. Four hours later a boat was located in the 25-foot seas with twenty-two people on board, including the two Air Force men. They were taken on board the *Boutwell*, which started at high speed for Sitka, leaving CGC *Woodrush* to check out the scene. The *Prinsendam* sank while under tow a week after being abandoned. In this textbook operation, involving a vulnerable group of victims in an extremely dangerous situation, the credit must go largely to the helicopter crews, though they would have had a much rougher time of it had the *Williamsburgh* not been there as a huge landing and delivery point. Without her, some passengers would have probably died of exposure due to the delay of flying everyone to shore after pickup. An Air Force and a Canadian Forces helicopter suffered mechanical failures, but this had little adverse effect on the operation. After the arrival of the *Boutwell*, command on scene was firmly established, and coordination left nothing to be desired. It is doubtful, however, had the *Williamsburgh* not been there, that the small flight deck on the cutter could have handled the landing volume in the prevailing sea and wind conditions.

The *Prinsendam* rescue, though not as technically difficult as some, must be regarded as one of the great sea rescues of all times, and that no lives were lost seems miraculous. But as one survivor, quoted in the official *Commandant's Bulletin,* said: "Some may call the rescue a miracle, but it was only accomplished because of the experience and dedication of the Coast Guard."

Frank Erickson would have been proud!

7

The Lonely Vigil

The DC-6 droned steadily westward at 10,000 feet. It had left the Azores five hours before and should be in Bermuda in another seven. The navigator had been unable to obtain fixes since leaving the Azores and was estimating his position by the courses steered and distance he estimated had been made good. The overcast made it impossible for him to obtain a celestial fix, and his Loran gave up the ghost soon after departure, but the crew was not unduly worried. In another hour they should be over the Coast Guard cutter manning Ocean Station Echo, where they would obtain navigation and weather information. The copilot tuned the radio direction finder attempting to pick up the call letters of Echo's radiobeacon—4YE. He frowned, for only static came in, and he should have been able to pick up the first faint signals by now.

A half hour later, concern was beginning to mount in the cockpit. According to the navigation plot, they should be nearly over Echo, but they had been unable to pick up Echo's beacon or contact it by radio. The captain stepped back to the navigator's table, and looked at the plot, then went over the Howgozit curve—a chart of fuel consumption versus distance covered. It was not too meaningful now, because without a fix, they really were only estimating distance they had covered. If the navigator's estimated position was correct, in two hours they would be past the point of no return—the point at which they would have to continue to Bermuda, because the fuel remaining would not allow their return to the Azores. If their actual position varied greatly from their estimated one, a number of unpleasant possibilities were present. These were beginning to course through the crew's minds. Were they so far north or south that they had passed Echo without picking up her beacon or raising her on radio? If so, the problem of finding Bermuda could become a thorny one unless they got a fix and soon, for Bermuda is a very small island with nothing else within 700 miles.

Twenty minutes later the copilot called back, reporting that he had picked up the radiobeacon on Echo, bearing 10 degrees to starboard, and was altering course to pass over it. A bit later, they were in radio contact with Echo, and five minutes after that Echo gave them a radar fix, course, and speed. Quickly the position was plotted, the calculations applied to the Howgozit, and the navigator turned to the captain. They were over an hour behind schedule approaching Echo, and if the present high (and unforecasted) winds continued, they would have a marginal fuel situation at Bermuda. With navigation equipment partially inoperative, could they hit Bermuda right on the nose, or would they have to use precious fuel correcting in once they had the Bermuda radiobeacon?

A check with Echo revealed that the winds at 4,000 were much more favorable; furthermore, Echo advised that an eastbound pilot had reported that weather west of a front 100 miles ahead was clear, which would enable celestial fixes to be obtained. Quickly requesting a descent from Oceanic Control, the DC-4 slipped down to 4,000 feet, where her ground speed picked up by 20 knots as she flew over Echo.

"It's awfully nice to have you people down there," the captain said. "It could have been a very long night without you."

Four thousand feet below, the radar men in the rolling cutter didn't quite know why the night would be shorter. It was just another contact to them, though they knew that the flight was behind schedule. Back in the cabin of the DC-4, most of the forty passengers slept. They didn't even know Echo was there. It was just another routine crossing, and Echo's job was to help keep it routine.

An ocean station like Echo was a stretch of water in mid-ocean, 210 miles on a side. It was differentiated from the rest of the ocean only by a cutter near the center of the square, stationed there twenty-four hours a day, 365 days a year, fair weather or foul. Six of these stations, four in the Atlantic and two in the Pacific, were manned by Coast Guard cutters. Of the other five in the worldwide system, one was manned by Canada and four by European nations. They reported weather, afforded navigation and communications assistance to aircraft and vessels, and rendered rescue services to any that encountered trouble. The cost of operating them was borne by twenty-seven nations, apportioned in accordance with the volume of civil air traffic they had over the oceans and the meteorological benefits they derived. It was an international undertaking that worked for nearly thirty years with conspicuous success.

An ocean station was many things to many men. To the weather forecaster in the Weather Bureau in Washington, it was another reporting station, though one of the most important, because it was his only source of information in thousands of square miles of ocean. To the airline pilot, it was a checkpoint midway on his flight across the ocean. To the young lieutenant flying a fighter across the vast wastes, it was a source of vitally needed information and comfort. To the merchant captain, plowing westward without a starsight for five days, the ocean station vessel afforded a fix. To the men aboard, it was twenty-one days of work between reliefs, often monotonous and

A pulling boat from the cutter *Bibb* prepares to begin removing passengers from the ditched Bermuda Skyqueen in heavy Atlantic seas.

unrewarding, always lonely, sometimes calm and pleasant, and often a roaring maelstrom where storms breed and hang on, pounding the station vessel mercilessly. Seldom, however, did it drive them from their stations.

To airmen, flying over the vast reaches of ocean, an ocean station vessel could become the very center of their existence should an uncontrollable distress occur.

The first case occurred in 1947, when CGC *Bibb*, on stormy station Charlie, rescued all of the sixty-nine passengers and crew members of the ditched flying boat Bermuda Sky Queen. A short time later, Commander Gene Coffin and his crew on CGC *Sebago* rescued the crew of an Air Force C-47 after it ditched at night on Station Delta. The CGC *Coos Bay*, under quiet, capable Jack Latimer, rescued the entire crew of a Navy P2V after it ditched in rough seas on Echo. It was done so efficiently and rapidly that it went nearly unnoticed. Later, my old shipmate Bill "Juggy" Earle and his crew in the cutter *Ponchartrain* would rescue all the crew and passengers of the Pan American Clipper, Sovereign of the Sky, in mid-Pacific after preparing down to the last detail for any eventuality. In a nice display of reassurance and confidence, Juggy casually told the pilot, Captain Dick Ogg, "OK, you can come on in for breakfast. We are

A motor lifeboat from the cutter *Pontchartrain*, carrying an additional inflatable raft, approaches the airliner minutes after it ditched. Most passengers got quickly into inflatable rafts or onto the wing.

putting the eggs on the stove." The quick recovery of survivors could have been used as an example for a seamanship book.

But the toughest assignment of them all would face Commander Bill Vaughn and his crew in the *Coos Bay*. It would be one that would try the souls of a MATS crew, and the Coast Guard crew helping them.* On this stormy January night, the odds wouldn't have tempted a bet from a drinking gambler at ten to one. But odds often don't take into account the human element, and part of the element was Captain Paul S. Evans, USAF.

On that January night 1,000 miles west of the Azores, Captain Evans was looking death in the face. It was staring at him in the light of flickering starshells hanging in the wild night ahead, and represented by big 15-foot swells and a howling gale that blew the tops off the swells and beat the water into a white froth.

"Help me kick it out!" he yelled to his copilot, Lt. Jack W. Suggs, as he stood on the rudder pedal.

In the second or two that remained to them before smashing into the sea, the C-54 had to be straightened out from the terrific crab it was holding to allow for 42 knots of direct crosswind.

Figuratively, the approach that Captain Evans was making had started two months before in Bermuda, when the *Coos Bay* reported to the Coast Guard Air Detachment there for a week of intensive training in how to assist aircraft in trouble, one of the primary tasks of the ocean station vessels. After reporting to us, *Coos Bay*'s crew was given intensive classroom work, then taken out to sea for actual exercises with aircraft. On the final day, a full-scale checkout at sea was given, complete with night illumination exercises. The aviator shipriders leaned over the shoulders of the ship's air-control team, noting each mistake. Following the last exercise of the night, as the ship headed back to port, they rehashed the mistakes with the ship people. The seven-day cram course was over, and the Air Detachment instructors hoped the ship was as ready as she was twenty-two months before when she saved ten men from a ditched Navy plane.

As *Coos Bay* prepared to get underway from Bermuda at the conclusion of training, I bade farewell to her able skipper, Commander Bill Vaughn.

"Bill your ship looked real good, and I hope your people have

---

*MATS—Military Air Transport Service, later named MAC or Military Airlift Command.

learned a few things. I also hope they'll never have to use what they've learned."

Now, only two months later, Captain Evans in MATS 45569 was relying on *Coos Bay*. With her sharp, recently refreshed crew, he had a great deal going for him. He also had nightmarish odds facing him this stormy January night. They had started piling up three hours before.

At 1604 local time, MATS 45569 had passed over the *Coos Bay*, patrolling a lonely and stormy position known as Ocean Station Echo midway between Bermuda and the Azores—a two-thousand-mile route considered by pilots to be one of the loneliest stretches of water in the world. Over Echo, they were ten minutes behind schedule, and Captain Edward T. Cobb, the navigator, noticed that the winds were from 260 degrees at nearly 50 knots, a little stronger than forecast.

Twenty minutes later, Navy Lieutenant Bowen, the lone passenger, walked from the crew compartment to the cabin. He glanced out at the left wing as he passed. Then he looked hard.

It was still daylight, and he could see a heavy flow of vapor, which appeared to come from behind the No. 2 engine. He called Airman First Class Braun, the flight attendant, who looked and immediately went forward and told the aircraft commander, Captain Evans. Sergeant Brooks, the flight engineer, came back and looked.

"Fuel leak and coming pretty heavy," he told Captain Evans. Lt. Suggs came up and took over the controls while Captain Evans looked for himself. With Sergeant Brooks he checked the fuel gauges. No. 2 was lower than the others.

"O.K., left cross feed—No. 2 main boost on."

A good plan, but No. 2 main tank gauge went down faster than gas could be pumped into No. 1. Only 40 gallons were saved—360 were lost.

Now with No. 1 and No. 2 engines both running off No. 1 main tank (No. 2 was now completely empty and cut off), the pilot and flight engineer checked again. It was still there. Same vapor trail. Same spot. The leak was in the engine!

With reluctance, Evans feathered No. 2 engine. It would be touch and go to make Bermuda with these winds. Fuel consumption would rise with the increased power demand on the other three engines.

Another check revealed the fuel leak had stopped. The navigator passed his position and flight data to Airman Hodge, the radio operator. Evans dropped 10 degrees of flaps and slowed to 125 knots to jettison cargo to lighten the ship.

Hodge began transmitting, "Emergency. Mayday. Mayday . . ."

Captain Evans, with five of the men, went to the cabin and with the crew ladder pried open the forward cargo door enough to jettison the cargo.

In fifteen minutes, they had kicked out nearly two tons of cargo, mail, and personal effects.

All this time, Captain Cobb and Lieutenant Suggs were up front checking fuel versus headwind. The loss of No. 2 engine had cut the indicated airspeed down to about 135 knots.

At 1650 (local time), forty-six minutes past Echo, flight attendant Braun glanced out at the right wing. He saw a heavy oil flow coming over the flap behind No. 3 engine and started forward. At the same time, engineer Brooks checked his instruments and saw No. 3 oil pressure drop to 40 pounds. No. 3 oil quantity showed fifteen gallons.

Brooks checked the wing and immediately began transferring from the forty gallons in the auxiliary tank. Even with continuous transferring, the oil quantity gauge slowly dropped to six gallons. The leak was bad. In fifteen minutes, there was no more reserve oil.

Captain Evans watched closely. When the No. 3 manifold pressure started falling and the tachometer started fluctuating, he feathered No. 3 engine.

As they began descending to maintain airspeed, the navigator shouted, "Can't make it to Bermuda anyway with this speed and our present winds. We don't have a chance. Sorry, skipper, that's the best I can do for you."

The C-54, now a sick and ailing bird, began a 180-degree turn back to Echo, an estimated one hour and twenty minutes away. Darkness was descending on a gale-swept ocean below. Hodge got Echo again and advised them that they were returning to ditch. As they continued the descent into the soup, the vacuum-operated flight instruments began getting sloppy. With both No. 2 and No. 3 engines feathered, there was no vacuum pump operating. No. 2 was unfeathered and allowed to rotate to give vacuum, but the drag caused by the rotating prop of the dead engine caused the plane to settle faster. Lieutenant Suggs began transmitting tones on the emergency frequency for DF bearings.

With No. 2 engine windmilling, No. 3 feathered, No. 1 and 4 cowl flaps wide open, and near maximum power, the pilot could only get 105 knots.

No. 1 and No. 4 cylinder head temperatures were at 220 degrees. When an attempt was made to increase air speed and engine cooling by feathering No. 2 propeller, the vacuum instruments again became sloppy.

Outside, there was only solid blackness and clouds. Evans had to have vacuum for instrument power, so again No. 2 was windmilled to provide it.

At 1830, they passed over Echo. No need to check any longer. They could never make it back to Lajes, in the Azores. Evans recalled the only time he had come down on water had been to land an L-20 floatplane in Greenland—in daylight and smooth water.

Aboard the *Coos Bay*, manning ocean station Echo, all hands were now at action stations. Almost one hour earlier, the boys watching the evening movies had jumped as the loud clang-clang-clang of the general alarm sounded throughout the ship, and the speaker blared out, "NOW HEAR THIS—NOW HEAR THIS—ALL HANDS TO DITCH AND RESCUE STATIONS. MATS 45569 DITCHING."

Commander Vaughn ordered all engines ahead flank, and swung into the heavy seas. As speed picked up, the 2,400-ton ship pounded and shuddered as green seas broke over her bow and even her bridge, but Vaughn refused to slow. At 1817, the Combat Information Center had 45569 in radar contact.

The C-54 requested a ditching heading, and *Coos Bay* recommended 130 degrees, gave the wind as 230 degrees at 42 knots, and swells 15 feet high from the southwest. They recommended ditching crosswind and parallel to the swell. MATS 45569 "Rogered."

Minutes later, the *Coos Bay*, heeling in a tight turn, began laying a line of electric float lights. It took only eight minutes to lay them. The ship then moved into position 1,200 yards upwind of the sealane and waited. Boats were lowered to the rail, cargo nets rigged, swimmers with lines attached made final preparations, and the gun and mortar crews closed up as the illumination star shells came up the ammo hoist into the five-inch gun turret. The deck force and gun crews were ready. Now it was up to the boys in the ship's CIC and in the aircraft.

Back in the C-54 cabin, everything was set—liferafts, Gibson Girl (small radio transmitter), Mae Wests—all checked. Jenkins and Braun stowed the Gibson Girl and liferaft by the rear door. Lieutenant Bowen helped them take a crew bunk mattress and place it against the forward cabin bulkhead. They stung a tiedown strap through the rings in the floor for a hand hold. Then they waited.

Captain Cobb secured his navigator's stool and removed the astrodome. He grabbed all of his navigational gear and ditching equipment and went back to the cabin.

Captain Evans gave the word and Cobb and Braun jettisoned the four emergency exits. The cargo door hit the left horizontal stabilizer with a terrific jolt.

Up front the pilots felt the blow. They were tense, wondering just what would happen next. A big jolt, nothing more. Back aft, the impact was felt clearly, and where the door had been now loomed a black gaping hole by which the wind howled. To the tired men, braced and waiting, it was one more blow.

Brooks had left his seat on downwind. He stowed the crew compartment raft on the front of the lower crew bunk. He checked himself and everyone else for ditching gear and climbed in the lower crew bunk behind the raft.

The gutted transport plane now turned onto the base leg. Hodge stood up front and held the mike to Captain Evans's lips. The pilot didn't have enough hands for everything; both he and the copilot were flying the big plane now.

MATS 45569 then turned onto the last final approach it would ever make.

Echo asked, "Have you power for emergency pull up?"

Captain Evans answered, "No."

Lieutenant James A. Kearney, the young air-control officer on *Coos Bay*, commenced instructions for the final approach. He, along with Captain Evans, seven miles away in the crippled plane, were "facing the bull." For the next several minutes, the rest were spectators.

Glancing at the air plot, then at the small blip on the radar PPI scope, Kearney spoke into his mike, "Your heading should 165; crosswind from your right; commence descent at your discretion. Now turn left to 160 degrees. You are on course. You are six miles out and should be passing through 600 feet. The sealane lights are burning brightly. . . ."

At five miles, the darkness around *Coos Bay* was shattered as the mortars and five-inch turret opened fire, pumping flares and star-shells into the sky.

"You are on course. Three miles out. Your heading should be 335. Your altitude should be 300 feet. . . ."

Now ahead, Captain Evans could see the approach end of the sealane bobbing in the heavy seas and the glow from the flares and starshells hanging in the sky. He also saw the huge swells with crests breaking into spray and flume under the drive of the gale-force winds.

Evans brought the transport down slowly, 100 feet per minute, crabbing hard to the right. He dropped 10 degrees of flaps and waited, then 10 more. Two hundred feet off the water, he dropped 10 more and slowed to 85 knots.

Twenty feet off the water, he dropped his last 10 degrees of flaps and slowed to 80 knots. Echo was still firing mortar flares for illumination, so the landing lights were left off.

The last words from Echo were, "GOD BLESS YOU."

At exactly 1905, both pilots kicked hard left rudder. Power came off and they were down. They didn't hit, they skidded. No first impact and then a second more severe impact, just a very rapid, smooth deceleration. The touchdown was so gentle—despite the water hitting the tail—that Captain Evans was able to hold the control column with one hand.

Outside, waves were running 12 to 15 feet; wind was about 42 knots. The aircraft weathervaned as soon as it stopped, and began bucking like a mad Brahma bull.

In the cabin, the lights were still on. Braun and Cobb threw the raft out of the main cargo door. They all held it in close while Lieutenant Bowen climbed aboard. Jenkins managed to climb in. Between them, they got one more man aboard each time the raft moved in.

As soon as all five of them were on the raft, they pushed away from the airplane.

Up front, Captain Evans and Lieutenant Suggs had shielded their faces with their arms as soon as they had touched water. They really didn't need to for there was no jolt, no real impact.

Try as they might, they couldn't get the six-man raft through the astrodome. So, up they went out into the slippery back of their agitated monster. Flat on their stomachs, they were barely able to hold on.

The *Coos Bay* nosed in at high speed as her 24-inch searchlights played on the scene.

The horizontal stabilizer of the aircraft was rising and falling about 10 feet with each swell. The fliers in the raft had drifted back almost under the tail. Each time the tail came down, they managed to push away. They finally cleared the tail, but couldn't return to the aircraft for the other three men.

Hodge advised Echo with the portable emergency VHF radio that all of them were out—five in the raft and three on top of the airplane.

At 1910, Lieutenant Ray Baetsen of the *Coos Bay* had the motor surfboat fighting through the towering seas toward the downed airmen. The boat couldn't get in close enough, so the Coast Guard lieutenant yelled to Captain Evans, Lieutenant Suggs, and Sergeant Brooks to slide back between the vertical stabilizer and wing and jump off into the water.

The three were only in the water (67 degrees F.) for two minutes. One by one the crew of the surfboat lifted them aboard.

Next, the raft was secured, and one by one five more men were dragged aboard. Fourteen minutes from time of ditching, all eight had been hauled into the surfboat.

Baetsen skillfully fought his way back to the *Coos Bay*. Finally, the hookup was accomplished, and at 1942, all were aboard the *Coos Bay*.

MATS 45569 was last seen still floating forty minutes after it hit the water. Captain Evans noted only slight damage as he exited. In fact, a bent prop on No. 2 engine and the loss of its rear cowling was all the damage he remembered.

A nearly miraculous ditching under night instrument conditions and in a full gale had been accomplished by a fine MATS crew with the aid of a crack well-trained Coast Guard cutter. Had any piece of the pattern failed, disaster would have been the result. No one failed.

Two weeks later, Captain Evans and his crew were landed at Bermuda. As we stood on the dock shaking hands, Evans said, "The people on the ship say I owe a lot to the fellows here who train the ships in the instrument ditching procedure."

As I looked at the survivors standing on the dock, I said, "Well, we've devoted a few months to it, and seeing you here sun-tanned and healthy has more than repaid us."

As we started walking down the dock, I felt good. Hell, it was worth twenty years of effort. SAR is the most overpaid work in the world.

But ditchings are not the only distress cases occurring on station. Despite the hundreds of successful ocean crossings by fighter and tactical aircraft, a few losses occur. Most of these flights require mid-air refueling from tanker aircraft. In addition to the aerial tankers and ocean-station vessels, search-and-rescue aircraft, called "Duckbutts," orbit at predetermined positions along the route during the flight in case of trouble. While the deployment and the coverage required for such flights is expensive, the flexibility and speed with which we can react to requirements for tactical aircraft anywhere in the world represents a significant improvement in our military readiness. It allows us to cover many areas with U.S.-based fighters that would otherwise require overseas forces. In any such undertaking, the pilots must know that no effort will be spared to recover them in case of trouble.

The CGC *Wachusett*, on Ocean Station November between San Francisco and Hawaii, provided that assurance to Blackcrow II, an Air Force fighter unable to make Hickam Air Force base due to lack of fuel. The distressed plane turned toward the *Wachusett*, and the pilot and navigator bailed out. Shortly thereafter, the plane crashed. The *Wachusett* quickly found the pilot and took him aboard. Then in conjunction with Northwest Airlines Flight 574, *Wachusett* located and retrieved the navigator. The Northwest flight was then released with its planeload of passengers, who had seen and taken part in the mid-ocean rescue drama.

Not only on station, but en route to and from stations, the ships were ready. Ocean Area Control (OAC) passed an alert to the Coast Guard on a single-engine Bellanca en route from Boston to Lajes, Azores, with a rough-running engine. Its position was uncertain, but it was attempting to return to the mainland. Cutters *Half Moon*, *Campbell*, and *Yakutat*, at sea off Newfoundland, were all alerted. *Half Moon* soon established radio contact and guided the Bellanca to her by radiobeacon and radar. After passing over *Half Moon*, radar contact with the plane was lost at 100 miles. Contact by radio was then established and held by a TWA flight until the *Campbell* gained radar contact and held it until the aircraft was near Halifax. *Yakutat* acted as a communications relay until the plane had landed safely.

In five ditchings beside Coast Guard ocean station vessels, all 125 persons have been saved without a serious injury—a 100 percent record for those planes that reached the ships.

The *Spencer*, on frigid, gale-swept station Bravo between Labrador and Greenland, was not so lucky. A Piper Apache, en route from Gander to Greenland, reported engine trouble and headed for Bravo to ditch. The aircraft, picked up by radar at 100 miles, was given weather and ditching information, but 27 miles from the ship it disappeared from the radar scope. *Spencer* proceeded at maximum speed toward the last radar location of the aircraft, and at daybreak was joined by Coast Guard, Canadian, Air Force, and Icelandic aircraft. Though survival time in those waters without exposure suits is measured in minutes, the search continued for four days. Nothing was ever sighted.

At this point, one may well imagine that the business of the ocean-station vessel was concerned only with aircraft. Actually, more cases involved assistance to merchant vessels. It had to maintain services to aircraft, but if a vessel near the station was in real need, the station vessel would proceed. Many distress cases, however, were handled by ships going to and from stations. At any time, two or three ships were in transit, and these vessels were always available for mid-ocean rescue. Often the nearest cutter in a U.S. port was four days away, while a vessel en route to station was less than twelve hours. It paid off in hundreds of lives saved.

Thirty-three of these were on board the German ship SS *Helga Bolten* on a stormy October night some 150 miles northwest of CGC *Chincoteague*, maintaining her vigil on Station Delta. At 0407 in the morning, the radio operator in *Chincoteague* spun around in his chair as an SOS signal began to bang out in his earphones, and judging by its strength it was close by. The *Helga Bolten* reported, "No. 1 and No. 2 hatches broken in. Need help as quick as possible!"

Quickly acknowledging the message, the radio room sent a message to the bridge, and requested permission to broadcast an auto-alarm signal. As no other vessel had answered *Helga Bolten*'s distress call and her condition appeared serious, Lieutenant Commander Ray Miller, pulling on his oilskins as he climbed to the bridge, gave the radio room permission to sent out the alarm signal to alert other vessels.

As the radio operator began transmitting the signal, and additional radiomen took their positions in radio central for the distress, they

A pulling boat from the cutter *Rockaway* taking aboard crewmen from the sinking *Smith Voyager*. Two rafts can be seen between the boat and the ship. The freighter's loss was caused by the shifting of its cargo of wheat in heavy seas.

felt the movements of *Chincoteague* change—for the worse—for she was now working up to best speed into 25-foot seas and a gale of 40 knots. Holding on whenever the ship hit a really big one, the operator on the distress channel heard the big liner *Mauretania* answering and reporting that she was proceeding at 21 knots. Then *Helga Bolten* began sending long dashes on 500 kilocycles for *Chincoteague* and the liner to take radio-direction-finder bearings. Soon a Coast Guard PB1G four-engine aircraft from Argentia, Newfoundland, reported in by radio, estimating arrival at the scene in three hours.

Two hours later, the *Mauretania* reported she had the *Bolten* in sight and sent an amended position. The weather was worsening, and the wind was now gusting to nearly hurricane force. In view of the situation, Commander, Eastern Area Coast Guard ordered the CGC *Rockaway* to depart Station Charlie to assist. Just before noon the *Bolten* advised that it was impossible to repair the damage, and that they doubted they could reach port. With the position now well established, the aircraft was released to return to base, for there was little that it could do to help now.

In this sea there appeared to be little that anyone could do. Man's vaunted ingenuity and modern equipment are often powerless before the primitive forces of a full-blown storm. In recovering people from the water or sinking ships under such conditions, we have, with a couple of exceptions, progressed little in two hundred years.

There are three basic ways of taking people off a sinking vessel. The oldest method is to launch a boat. Another way is to drift a rubber raft down to the ship with a line attached, and haul it back in when the survivors board it. The third means is to pass a line, having a survivor tie himself to the end, and after he has jumped in, haul away rapidly and get him aboard before he drowns. In a smooth sea on a very few occasions, skippers have put their ships alongside another so that men could jump from one ship to the other, but it isn't done in any kind of a seaway, or two ships may be in distress.

If survivors are already in the water, the rescue vessel can ease alongside and toss them lines; if they are too weak to help themselves,

A crewman from the capsized trimaran *Gonzo* is pulled by line toward the rescue cutter, while two others wait their turn. Though risky, it was safer than putting the cutter close alongside the thin-hulled trimaran.

rubber-suited swimmers are put over to help them up the boarding nets.

Lowering a boat weighing nearly three tons from a vessel rolling 30 degrees can be a feat challenging the finest seaman. In addition to the rolling of the vessel, the rising and falling of the seas complicate the task. One moment the boat is riding a crest, and the next moment the sea has dropped away, leaving the boat hanging from its davit 15 feet above the water. Under such conditions, precise timing is required to let the boat fall onto the sea at exactly the right moment. Once in the water, the boat cox'n is faced with the problem of getting away from the ship. The ship's bilge keel, flashing by less than two feet away as she rolls, can be a chilling sight. On returning to the ship, hooking on the heavy fall blocks to the hoisting eye of the boat is even more difficult, and the handler's fingers are seldom more than five inches from amputation until the ship starts hoisting the boat and has a constant strain on the falls. When we consider the likely results if a 3-ton boat is hurled against the side of a 2,000-ton ship by the force of a mighty 25-foot ocean swell, the dangers cannot be exaggerated.

On the night of 7 February 1943, while serving in the cutter *Ingham*, we came alongside a boatload of survivors from the British SS *Newton Ash*, which had been torpedoed only minutes before. Though the submarine was still lurking in the immediate vicinity, we stopped and rigged boarding nets to bring aboard the men in the boat. As it came alongside, a huge wave capsized the boat. The next wave smashed it against the side of the ship, crushing twelve men. Nine other men were swept away by the sea, and only three were recovered.

Twenty survivors of the Greek freighter *Captain George* came alongside the SS *Virginia* 360 miles off Bermuda after abandoning their burning ship. The boat capsized and only two of the twenty were saved.

After the SS *Bonitas* sank off Cape Hatteras, twenty-five men in a boat approached the SS *President Adams* and capsized in 30-foot seas. Only five were rescued; the other twenty-two quickly perished.

In a 1987 case, 19 crew members of the 345-foot Philippine cargo vessel *Balso 24* abandoned ship in liferafts 500 miles northeast of Bermuda. The winter seas were 45 feet in height and the winds were 60 knots. Coast Guard, Navy, and Canadian Forces aircraft responded to the distress call. The Navy plane dropped another liferaft, and soon all crew members were in either the liferafts or the ship's boat. The Russian *Adler*, the Panamanian *Frisia*, and an Israeli vessel all diverted to help. Air cover was maintained over the survivors throughout the night by Coast Guard C-130s from Elizabeth City, NC. The USS *Scamp*, an attack submarine, and the *Frisia* arrived at first light. The submarine, though ill-suited by its hull shape for picking up people, recovered one person, then the liferaft capsized in the 40-foot seas. The four other occupants were swept away to their death. *Frisia* came alongside the lifeboat, but found only one person. The other occupants had died or drowned during the night. The sole survivor drowned during the attempt to get him on board the *Frisia*. Despite an international effort by hundreds of trained men, only one of the nineteen-man crew survived.

In a heavy sea, the rescue of survivors by ship's boat is an extremely dangerous undertaking, used only when there is no other way to do a job that must be done.

But with the coming of the air age and the rapid technical strides of World War II came the inflatable rubber raft. Able to bob along on the highest waves, unlikely to be damaged by contact with the ship's side, and so light in weight that one man can pull it through the water, it has proved a bonanza to rescuers at sea. By rigging a line to either end, the rescuer and the sinking vessel can shuttle the rubber raft back and forth, transporting persons from ship to ship without the danger of crushing them against the ship's side. Launching a rubber raft is simplicity itself—just throw it overboard. Furthermore, it makes ideal abandon-ship equipment. For the weight of one ship's boat carrying twenty men, enough liferafts can be carried to accommodate 900. Yet, the raft is by no means a sure-fire method. When the *Lionne* sank off Cape Farewell, Greenland, two men were nearly alongside the SS *Nova Scotia* when the raft capsized in 14-foot seas, and both were lost.

In heavy seas, having a man tie a line to himself and jump overboard is extremely risky. During even a short pull, a man can drown, as happened when the *Coos Bay* hauled in survivors of the *Ambassador* by line. The *Acushnet*, pulling in survivors from the *Cartagena* over a distance of only 30 yards, had to apply artificial resuscitation to revive one.

In heavy seas, there is simply no easy method, nor a sure one. Ray Miller knew this. Looking at the *Chincoteague*'s bow rising, then falling and burying itself completely under the towering wind-beaten swells, he made his decision. If the *Bolten*'s crew must be taken off in this sea, it would have to be by unmanned rubber rafts. The cutter's crew started breaking out the two fifteen-man rafts and getting them ready.

Arriving alongside the *Bolten* and maneuvering with great difficulty in the seas, *Chincoteague* fired five heavy line-carrying projectiles, but all were carried away by the winds. Finally, the sixth and last one carried over to the sinking vessel and, after a heavier line was passed, the two fifteen-man rubber rafts were attached, and hauled in by the crew of the *Bolten*. Within minutes, the *Bolten*'s crew began abandoning ship, sliding down lines into the rafts, which were then hauled in by the cutter. An hour after the shot-line was fired, the rafts were alongside the *Chincoteague*. Cuttermen led by Ensign Roger Shannon climbed down into the rafts and into the raging seas

The thirty-two men and one woman radio operator of the German *Helga Bolten*'s crew abandoning ship 400 miles off Newfoundland. They are climbing into rubber rafts near the after mast, as the cutter *Chincoteague* stands by to recover them.

to help aboard the exhausted German crewmen. One raft was damaged beyond repair, but all hands were safe.

That night, the *Rockaway* arrived from Station Charlie, and the weather began to moderate. In the morning, the sea had abated so much that the master and chief engineer of the *Bolten* were put back aboard the distressed vessel by the cutter's boat. The following day, the tug *Ebro* arrived to attempt salvage, and four tug crewmen plus ten of the *Bolten*'s crewmen were placed back aboard.

Then began the long effort to save the ship itself. On the fifth day, the master tried to get more volunteers from the survivors aboard *Chincoteague* to reboard the *Bolten*, but was unable to obtain any. The following day, due to the worsening condition of the distressed vessel, all her crewmen were removed, but four tug crewmen elected to remain. On the sixth day, they also finally abandoned the *Bolten* in the rubber raft and were picked up by the tug. Later, the tug *Ocean*, which had relieved the *Ebro*, placed eight men on the foundering vessel and advised that no further help was required from the cutter.

On the seventh day of the ordeal, the *Chincoteague*, with her weary crew of thirty-three survivors, departed for Norfolk, leaving the tug to tow in the *Bolten*. Shortly thereafter, however, she was diverted to search for survivors of a Navy P5M that had crashed. Released on the evening of the tenth day, she arrived in Norfolk twelve days after the distress call from the *Bolten* was first heard.

As tough as this rescue was, similar ones have since been made: by the *Coos Bay* of the crew of the SS *Ambassador*; by the *Rockaway* of the SS *Smith Voyager*; by the *Acushnet* from the *Cartagena*; and others too numerous to list. Some vessels, such as the *Coos Bay* and *Chincoteague*, seemed to be at the right place at the right time. After rescuing the crew of the *Helga Bolten*, *Chincoteague* in the same year aided the SS *Canadian Observer*, the F/V *Finmore*, and the SS *Finn Trader*.

The *Finn Trader* suffered an explosion in the engine room, severely burning four men, and sent a distress message to *Chincoteague* on station Charlie. As the two vessels steamed toward each other, the medical officer on the cutter sent advice by radio. When they sighted each other, the weather was steadily worsening, with the rough seas still rising. Lowering away a boat, for all the victims were stretcher cases, the cutter's boat crew made four trips between the ships, bring-

Cutter *Coos Bay* moves in close to the sinking British *Ambassador* to place a line aboard. When this was done, a rubber raft was used to shuttle survivors to the cutter. Rubber-suited swimmers, seen on the cutter's bow, had to enter the water to help when the raft was capsized by heavy seas.

ing back a man each time. One patient was dead on arrival at the cutter, and the second died shortly afterwards. After sixteen uninterrupted hours at an operating table that pitched and rolled with the ship, the doctor announced that the other two patients were improving, and the cutter turned for St. John's, Newfoundland, where the patients and bodies were off-loaded before the cutter returned to station.

The *Owasco* also had a serious problem after removing a critically burned crewman from the Norwegian motor ship *Applan*. As his condition worsened, the *Owasco's* doctor advised that he needed whole blood. The nearest source was the naval air station at Argentia, Newfoundland, some 800 miles away. The available supply was promptly flown out by a Coast Guard aircraft from Argentia and dropped to the *Owasco*. In the meantime, blood plasma from Bellevue Hospital in New York was rushed by police cruiser and Coast Guard helicopter to CGAS Brooklyn, by Coast Guard amphibian to Otis Air Force Base in Massachusetts, then by Air Force jet to Argentia, where a

Cuttermen on Station Bravo, between Greenland and Labrador, fight to keep the ship free of ice in mountainous seas and hurricane-force winds.

Coast Guard R5D then dropped it to the *Owasco*. With the plasma and blood administered, the *Owasco* began the race to Argentia and the hospital there. En route she encountered such severe ice that a propeller was damaged, but with aerial reconnaissance from the Coast Guard Air Detachment in Argentia to spot leads through the ice, she arrived and transferred the patient to the hospital four days after the accident.

At times, the storms on station were so severe that even the rugged cutters were damaged. The *McCulloch* had to abandon Station Bravo with a dangerous crack in the hull. Proceeding to a distressed freighter, CGC *Matagorda*, 900 miles off Japan, cracked her hull and disabled one shaft in heavy seas. She limped 1,200 miles back to Hawaii on one engine, fighting heavy seas most of the way.

The general consensus of cutter sailors, however, was that Bravo was the dirtiest station. The Icelandic low generates severe storms that hang on, pounding the vessels on Bravo relentlessly. The frigid Labrador current, never warming up, keeps the station uncomfortably cold. Often the ship coats heavily with ice, and the crew must turn out on the slippery rolling deck with baseball bats to beat off the ice. Clearing ice is an all-hands evolution, and failure to keep ahead of it can result in the ship becoming top-heavy enough to capsize. This is believed to have happened in this area during World War II to one small Coast Guard cutter, and still another on weather patrol disappeared without trace. Cutters going to Bravo go well prepared, and the baseball bats carried in the bos'n's locker are not for recreation.

David Davies in *Owasco* felt the full fury of Bravo's weather in January 1962. Faced with hurricane-force winds and freezing water temperatures, *Owasco* iced up badly despite the round-the-clock efforts of the crew to free the ice. Ice and seas carried away the lifelines and stanchions on the forward half of the ship, making access by personnel extremely dangerous. The big radar antenna cracked and threatened to topple onto the deck. One boat was swept away and another severely damaged. Finally, *Owasco* was forced to abandon station, heavily damaged and coated with ice. The sea is no respecter of ships or persons, and even Coast Guard cutters sometimes throw in the sponge.

But all was not storm and stress. The airliners passing over a lonely ocean station often had celebrities or actresses among their passengers talk with the cutter crew below by short-range radio. If no notables were aboard, the stewardesses would often substitute, to the delight of 125 sailors.

One cold December night as we were approaching Station Hotel on an overseas flight, I heard an Eastern Airlines flight en route from New York to San Juan working Hotel. After the position report was made, the Eastern pilot said, "I've got one of the girls who wishes to talk with you."

"We are all ears," replied Hotel.

"Hi, boys," came the sexy voice of the stewardess, panting softly into the mike.

"Hi, doll," came the reply from Hotel.

"Fellows, I sure wish I was down there with you. It's such a cold night and . . . DAMMIT STOP THAT!"

Then another voice, Texas bred, came in on the radio, "SUH, this is Navy 5228, take your cotton-picking hands off that lady!"

My copilot picked up the mike and added, "Oh for the life of an airline pilot."

From Hotel, conjuring up pictures of the goings on in that dimly lit Eastern Constellation cockpit, came the demand, "Eastern, quit pinching that girl's fanny. We were talking with her."

Then over the air came the same female voice, perhaps a little sexier and sulkier, "Boys, my fanny wasn't what he was pinching." When the last repartee was made five minutes later and routine resumed on Station Hotel, the watch was perhaps a little cheerier and the routine a bit sharper. The story was probably told and retold a hundred times next day aboard the vessel and every detail examined and enjoyed.

Despite the many services performed over the years by the ocean station vessels, by the mid-sixties the need for them was dubious. Jet aircraft, flying at high altitudes and speeds, were much less affected by weather than their prop-driven predecessors, and advanced navigation systems made outside position-fixing help unnecessary. In many locations, offshore weather information could be obtained at much lower cost and effort from large oceanographic buoys that transmitted meteorological data automatically. When a number of the cutters were transferred from the terrible weather of ocean station duty to combat assignments off Vietnam, many crewmen viewed the change as a welcome one. With the wind-down of the Vietnam War in 1971, a close-down of the ocean stations also began. More were discontinued by 1974 as more cutters were required for drug interdiction operations, and the last station, HOTEL, located between the Virginia Capes and Bermuda, was replaced by a 40-ton automatic buoy in 1977.

Though there were moments of high drama, ocean station duty for the average Coast Guardsman was rough, often boring, and the long periods at sea disruptive of normal life. Clearly a necessity when it was established, the ocean station program was ultimately overtaken by time and technical progress. One lingering disadvantage of its termination is the absence today of Coast Guard cutters in many remote sea areas, either on ocean station or en route to and from station. Many seamen and airmen owe their lives to the cutters being nearby when needed. Though the big cutters will still be available for SAR far offshore to the south and east of the United States while on drug interdictions, and in the North Pacific on fisheries patrols, they will be mostly absent from some other crucial areas, especially the North Atlantic, where they have been a presence for over fifty

years. The void will have to be filled by other ships, mostly merchantmen and tankers, that will be requested when needed, using
AMVER information and communications. The feasibility of this
method was demonstrated on 4 November 1985, when a Cessna aircraft pilot en route from San Francisco to Honolulu radioed from a
position 1,100 miles out that he was low on fuel and needed help. A
nearby Navy P-3 closed and escorted the Cessna until a Coast Guard
C-130 arrived from Hawaii. During this time, AMVER had plotted
all shipping along the route, and the C-130 led the small plane to
the SS *Lurline*, 780 miles northeast of Honolulu. The Cessna then
ditched 500 yards from the liner and was promptly picked up by the
ship's lifeboat.

Variety Unlimited

No matter how expert the rescue pilot or skipper is, or how good his equipment, the safest place for a seaman is in his own ship, *if* it can be kept afloat. Most vessels carry pumps for this purpose, and if a leak or hole in the hull can be plugged or partially stopped, the ship's pumps can keep ahead of the water. If the pumps fail, or haven't sufficient capacity, the ship will go down.

Many ships have been saved by cutters arriving with additional pumps, but in other cases help arrived too late. Soon after World War II, some unrecognized genius in uniform came up with the idea of a small portable pump that could be delivered rapidly by air and parachuted to a sinking vessel. Packed in a watertight container, complete with suction and discharge hoses, and a can of fuel, these gasoline-powered pumps, capable of pumping overboard 60 gallons of water a minute, proved immediately successful. In the thirty-five years they have been in use, hundreds of vessels have been saved. Seldom has such an inexpensive piece of equipment been responsible for the saving of so many and so much.

In most cases, they are parachuted by fixed-wing aircraft, and it is not a difficult feat. But Lieutenant Commander Ray Miller had his problems on the night of 17 March 1963. The fishing vessel *Notre Dame* had sprung a leak off Nantucket and was sinking. As the crew ran for the aircraft, the line crew wheeled out a pump container and quickly hoisted the 150-pound load into the aircraft. Five minutes later, Ray and his crew were off from Quonset Point, RI, and climbing up through the clouds. The weather was not fit for seagulls, but they homed in on the distressed vessel's radio signals and soon had it on radar. They commenced a descent, but passing through 500 feet, Ray was still in the soup, and slowed his descent rate, feeling for visual contact under the clouds. At 150 feet, still in the clouds, he gave it up and started climbing. There was no ceiling at all, and to rely on an altimeter at night below 100 feet is stupidity.

The boat reported it was still taking on water. Ray decided to make the parachute drop run on instruments. Four miles out, the rear hatch was opened, the container placed in drop position, and the parachute static cord attached. The radar operator coached him in, calling out small heading corrections, and frequent range marks.

They came over the target, and dropped. The can went out, the chute billowed behind the aircraft, and swung in a wide arc, illuminated by two battery lights attached to the shrouds. Three minutes later, the vessel sighted the container only fifty yards ahead in the fog. The pump was soon in operation, and before midnight the water level was down enough for the plane to return to base. It was a fairly routine operation, but had it failed, the case could have soon become a major one.

One pump was delivered to a leaking fisherman off Mount Desert Island, Maine, and it promptly cleared the hull of water. It worked so well, and the fishing was so good, that the money-conscious Yankee stayed out despite the leak. When the pump burned out from two days' continual use and the water began to rise, he finally came in. The boarding officer had a heart-to-heart talk with him about abusing the pump, as well as staying out for two more days after making a distress call. To make the lesson sink in, the boarding party inspected the boat and slapped him with several safety-equipment violations.

Not all pump deliveries are as successful. A small cargo vessel was sinking off the Florida coast, and a pump dropped to it failed to keep up with the rising water. Two more were delivered, and when these weren't sufficient, a fourth. Early in the morning, she slid slowly under, carrying our station's entire supply of pumps, but they had provided enough grace for a cutter to arrive and take off the crew.

Helicopter delivery is a surer method if the ship is in range. The container is simply lowered to the vessel as the helicopter hovers over head. Yet even this method is not surefire, and we nearly killed three men before discovering a better way.

A small yawl was en route from Bimini to Fort Lauderdale when it was caught in a storm that had come barreling up from the Caribbean. The occupants, who had chartered the boat for a three-day cruise, were amateurs and they knew it. As the sea built up, they became thoroughly frightened and called for help. Thirty minutes later, Lieutenant Commander Bob Pope and I arrived overhead in a chopper and could see why. The winds were up to 50 knots, and the seas were running 30 feet high. They had taken down all sails, and were running with the sea, using their small auxiliary engine. A cutter was coming, but was still about two hours away. We decided to lower a pump to help them keep down the rising water.

We came to a hover overhead, and the hoist operator started his chant.

"Come ahead ten feet and ease right. Hold it there. Now ahead five feet. The pump is out and going down. Come ahead five more feet. Lower it down a bit. The pump is halfway down. Hold your altitude. Right five feet and come ahead ten. The pump is just above the mast. Whoops! It's in the water. Pick it up! Now the pump is above their mast. Steady!"

For two more minutes, the pump was first in the water and then above the mast as the little boat rose on the huge swells then dropped into the troughs. I was pretty slow on my thinking that day. Only after the pump smacked into the water for the third time did I get a sudden mental picture of a wrecking crane demolishing a building by swinging a heavy metal ball against the brick walls. Here we were about to do a similar wrecking job. If that 100-pound container was above the deck when a swell lifted the boat up, it could smash the vessel or the people on it. We hurriedly pulled up, and hauled in the container. No damage had been done, and the cutter arrived soon afterwards. You learn by mistakes and if you are lucky, as we were, by near mistakes. On future jobs of that sort, a line was attached to the container, and lowered to the boat. After the people on the boat had the line, the container was lowered into the water near the boat, so they could haul it in. It is a much safer and more sure procedure in high seas.

Medical supplies parachuted by a C-130 hit the bull's-eye on the British freighter *Trangie* 700 miles east of Midway Island.

Medical supplies, rubber rafts, mechanical parts, survival gear, and food and water are dropped when needed. Sometimes a battery is lowered to a boat with starting trouble. Occasionally we dropped a container of fuel. It's easier than towing in the vessel.

Once in a while a drop backfires. In July 1955 we located three survivors of a missing plane near a lonely lagoon 400 miles from civilization on the coast of Baja California. Before landing in the uncharted water, I wanted to determine the condition of the men. Coming low over the beach, we dropped a portable radio in a container. The static line broke and the chute failed to open. The fifty-pound container sailed in a curving trajectory and hit ten feet from the men in a cloud of sand. They dived in three directions. Somewhat shaken by the near miss, we landed in the lagoon and picked them up. After that time, I always planned my drops so that the container would land well clear if the chute failed.

Others aren't so lucky. An aircraft from Miami located a boat that had been drifting for three days. Thinking that the men would be hungry and thirsty, the pilot came in low and dropped a packet of emergency rations and water. The drop was free fall without a chute, and the packet should have hit downwind where the boat could drift down on it. The pilot was too accurate! The packet hit the boat, knocked a hole in the bottom, and down it went. When a cutter arrived and plucked them from the water, the survivors were angry. They had lost a new boat, they said, and furthermore, they hadn't been hungry. Later, they sued the government for damages.

A drop off Greenland hit the other extreme. One of the ocean station vessels, on station Bravo, had radar troubles and needed a special part. Unless she got it in forty-eight hours, another ship would have to sail to relieve her, for radar is essential on station for tracking aircraft. The part was loaded aboard a PB1G at Argentia, Newfoundland, and started on its way. Four hours later, the pilot instructed the navigator on the drop procedure.

"When I am on final approach, I will raise my arm. When I drop it toss the package out through the bomb bay."

It was a routine procedure. The navigator would stand in the cockpit and throw the packet back through the cockpit door and out the open bomb bay. But this navigator was new at the game.

When they were 20 miles out, the pilot opened the bomb-bay doors. Then he looked aft, and choked. Standing on the narrow bomb-bay catwalk, 3,000 feet over the Atlantic, was the navigator, swaying slowly and tightly gripping the packet. He hadn't quite understood.

"Get back into the cockpit!" screamed the pilot, waving his arm.

As the arm went down, out went the packet, drifting slowly down as the chute opened. The navigator had understood that part. With shaking hands, the pilot hit the switch closing the bomb-bay doors, and the navigator edged back into the cockpit.

When the packet and chute hit 20 miles from the ship, there was at first disbelief on the ship, then a predictable reaction. Having come 900 miles to deliver the cargo, there was nothing for the aircraft to do except circle for over an hour until the ship arrived to retrieve the goods. The circling was punctuated by commentary between the ship and plane relative to the accuracy of airmen in making drops. One hour wasn't enough. The last sarcastic comment was received 100 miles from the ship on the way back, just before the communications finally and mercifully faded out.

As effective as aerial delivery is, other help is needed in many cases. On 13 February 1960, the Japanese freighter *Toyama Maru* called for help 175 miles north of Palmyra Island in the central Pacific. Two cutters, a merchantman, a British Hastings bomber, and a Coast Guard C-130 raced to her aid. It was found by the British aircraft, and the merchantman, the SS *Lombardi*, soon arrived on scene and sent over a party by boat to help make repairs. The Coast Guard aircraft dropped a pump, which held the water level after the *Lombardi*'s engineers made emergency repairs to the hull. The CGC *Bering Strait* arrived, and after an inspection of the damage and repairs, called for more material to finish the job. Ten heavy containers of cement, sand, and gravel were delivered from Honolulu by another C-130. After the material was parachuted, the damage-control party from the *Bering Strait* finished the repairs and the *Toyama Maru* proceeded safely to Honolulu under escort.

When very large loads of fuel are required, aerial delivery is not only too expensive, but is impractical. The British SS *D'Vora*, carrying a cargo of frozen whale meat, reported that she was in a storm off Nova Scotia and dangerously low on fuel. The CGC *Coos Bay* took her in tow, but the towline soon parted in the heavy seas. The following day, another towline was passed, along with a fueling hose. While the cutter towed the *D'Vora*, 12,500 gallons of fuel were pumped to her. After the fueling was completed, the fuel hose and towlines were cast off, and the refrigerator ship proceeded to port under her own power.

One of the really unusual refueling operations took place off the Bahamas after an Air Force amphibian landed at sea to retrieve a component from a missile fired from Cape Canaveral. After getting on the water, the weather conditions worsened, and the plane was unable to take off in the heavy seas. For two days, it taxied toward land until the gasoline was critically low. When the waves finally subsided, there was not enough fuel to take off and make land.

There were no vessels anywhere in the area that had aviation gasoline or facilities for carrying it. The Air Force asked the Coast Guard

Buoy tender *Hollyhock* refuels Air Force amphibian from a tank truck carried on the foredeck.

for help. If no ships were available, what about a fuel truck, someone suggested. In a short while, an aviation refueling truck drove down to the dock and was lifted by crane aboard the Coast Guard buoy tender *Hollyhock*. Two days later, the tender arrived on scene, took the HU-16 in tow, and passed over the gas hose and JATO bottles. After several hundred gallons of gasoline were pumped into the HU-16, the lines were cast off and the following morning the plane took off. It was probably the first time that a seaplane has been fueled from a tank truck 400 miles at sea. It certainly isn't covered in any of the manuals.

These stitch-in-time refueling and repair services can save a lot of trouble later, so when the Gloucester Coast Guard Station received a call from a fisherman that his boat was sinking at the dock, they dispatched a repair party with a pump to help. Repairs at the dock are not a responsibility of SAR, but it was late at night and the caller said he was unable to get help elsewhere. Arriving at the dock, they pumped out the boat, and looked around for the owner, but he had disappeared. Later that night, he called again, and a party was once more sent out. This time, the petty officer in charge was determined to see that the owner stayed with the boat and looked after matters. After pumping it out, he went looking and finally found him, sitting

A cutter tows a disabled trawler off the Grand Banks.

comfortably in a bar having his tenth beer of the evening, while enjoying the benefits of the Great Society. The benefits were quickly withdrawn.

In thousands of cases, repairs cannot be effected at sea, and it is necessary to tow the vessel in. If it is a large vessel and in no immediate danger, a commercial salvage tug is called in for the job, and the owners of the disabled vessel pay a towing fee, which can be steep.

If the vessel is in immediate danger, or is too small to make it worth a salvage tug's time, a cutter will pass a towline.

In an era when damage suits on any pretext have become a way of making a quick buck, the Good Samaritan action is no sure defense. If a vessel is taken in tow and suffers further damage, the owner may claim negligence and sue the government. A number of such actions have been successful. It was, therefore, with some relief that Coast Guardsmen heard the federal judge in one case rule in favor of the government.

"You were in considerable danger already," his honor told the plaintiff, "and probably would have sunk had the cutter not taken you in tow. Your boat sinking in tow was a normal risk of the sea. The Coast Guard, by helping you, does not guarantee that its action will invariably be successful."

This case was thrown out. But it doesn't always turn out this way, and any SAR man rendering help has an added incentive to ensure that no mistakes of any kind are made. It is to their everlasting credit that the risk of legal suits has produced no noticeable timidity about incurring risks when necessary to save people.

SAR forces will act first to save lives, then property when possible. They do not, however, engage in repair and salvage of a vessel once the vessel is removed from immediate danger. This is the responsibility of the owner, just as the owner of any property must pay for his own repairs. Commercial salvage companies exist for this purpose, and most vessels are covered by marine insurance. In exceptional cases, SAR units may engage in limited salvage to prevent further damage to a distressel vessel while awaiting the arrival of a salvage tug, but this is an emergency measure only.

Apparently, one free enterpriser didn't quite understand this when he purchased a luxurious sailing yacht for a song. The vessel was on a reef off a remote Pacific atoll, and had been for some weeks at the time of purchase. The nearest salvage tug was several thousand miles away, and the cost of bringing it such a distance would have exceeded the value of the yacht. But the buyer had an angle. After concluding the deal, he contacted the Coast Guard and requested a tow off the reef. No dice, was the answer. Get yourself commercial salvage. His prompt reply was that no salvage facilities were available in the area, so the Coast Guard had an obligation to help him. It was a good pitch, had the Coast Guard not known that the vessel had been aground when he purchased it. But like many high-flying speculations, this one didn't pan out.

On 15 January 1960, Texas Tower No. 4, located 65 miles east of Barnegat, N.J., collapsed during a severe winter storm. Three of these radar towers had been erected off the northeast coast as seaward extensions of the air-defense radar warning system. Tower No. 4 was known by the men who served on it as "Old Shaky" because of its motion during heavy weather. SAR aircraft fought their way through the storm to the scene, but their radarscopes showed no targets. The huge structure had disappeared completely with all twenty-seven persons aboard. Numerous Navy and Coast Guard ships, including the carrier *Wasp,* searched for days, but only one body was found. The terrible disaster was to have long aftereffects.

As a result of the tragedy, the Air Force, which operated the towers, decided to evacuate them at any time winds were forecast to reach 80 knots. A general feeling existed among the Air Force people concerned that if there were any more casualties on a Texas tower, heads would roll. The Air Force weather forecasters must have been imbued with the spirit, and possibly tacked on an extra 20 knots on each forecast as a safety cushion, for their forecasts of winds consistently ran higher than those of our own weather prophets. All during the winter of 1961–1962, Coast Guard cutters were called out to take over radar surveillance as the tower crews were evacuated time after time. Rarely did the winds reach dangerous proportions, and neither of the two towers was damaged by weather.

During this period, the tower crews spent almost as much time being shuttled back and forth to the mainland by helicopters as they did on the tower. SAR aircraft were called out time and again to escort the loaded choppers. The crews were in more actual danger flying over the water in the single-engine helicopters than they would have been staying on the towers.

The drain on the time of the overworked cutters would have probably gone on indefinitely had the Air Force not finally decided to decommission the towers. A commercial contractor was given the job of demolishing the structures so that they would not constitute a menace to navigation. While the demolition work was going on, a storm moved up the coast, and the contractor asked the Coast Guard to take his men off. Our forecasts indicated that the winds would not exceed 45 knots, nowhere near the danger point for the structures, and the request was denied. The following morning, with the winds rising, the tower workers clamored to be taken off. Pressure was put on Washington, and the pressure promptly came downhill to the operating units. Early in the morning, the men were removed by helicopters from Quonset Point in a dangerous and needless operation. The winds never exceeded 45 knots. A few months later, the towers were completely removed. In their short lives, the three Texas towers had cost millions of dollars, twenty-seven lives, endangered hundreds of others in the many relief and evacuation flights, and drained off hundreds of hours of SAR aircraft and ship time. SAR personnel throughout the area breathed a long sigh of relief.

Nevertheless, the removal of the Air Force's towers did not end the Coast Guard's concern with the structures. Dozens more were being erected to carry out offshore oil-drilling operations, and the Coast Guard itself erected a number to replace lightships off major harbors. Large, movable drilling rigs were also developed, and in early 1982, disaster struck.

The *Ocean Ranger,* the world's greatest semi-submersible oil rig, was a wonder of modern technology. Larger than two football fields, it was 30 stories high from its pontoons to the top of its drilling derricks. Built in Japan at a cost of $125 million, it first was operated in the Gulf of Alaska, then brought around to the Atlantic off Newfoundland by way of Cape Horn, which speaks well of its seaworthiness. In addition to workshops and machinery spaces, there were three decks of quarters for the crew of up to 100 men, including drilling men, engineers, geologists, and administrative people. None were unduly concerned about the dangers of the sea, for like the *Titanic,* this rig was considered virtually indestructible. However, the Coast Guard inspectors had deemed the lifeboats to be unsatisfactory and ordered the operators to provide davit-operated liferafts. The inspectors were due to arrive on 15 February to examine the safety equipment again. The inspection was never to take place.

On 14 February 1982, the Weather Service issued a severe storm warning, predicting the worst storm so far that winter, and by darkness, winds had risen to hurricane force with 30-foot seas. The *Ocean Ranger* disconnected the drilling rig and prepared to ride out the storm. Shortly thereafter, a huge wave broke over the control module of the rig, breaking out a window of reinforced glass, and flooding the electrical switchboard controlling the ballast control valves. The short circuits and resulting fires caused many of the ballast valves to open, admitting water into pontoons randomly. Though the rig itself was structurally sound, its ballast-tank valve system was out of control and its stability threatened by the uneven ballasting. Shortly after midnight, the *Ocean Ranger* began calling for help, sending distress calls to adjacent drilling rigs, to several support vessels helping supply the rigs, and to the Coast Guard's Atlantic Command in New York. Through the howling storm, ships and aircraft responded, though at reduced speeds due to the extreme conditions being encountered. The tender *Seaforth Highlander* was soon in sight of the rig and saw lights in the water and flares arching in the air. A lifeboat was sighted

A Coast Guard helicopter lands on the drilling platform *Canmar Explorer II* to remove an injured seaman.

and the *Highlander* closed in. But as the boat came alongside, it capsized, throwing all hands into the water, and they drifted off quickly into the night. At 0315, the huge rig, with its flotation unbalanced by the runaway valve system, rolled over and turned upside down. An hour later, two transport helicopters from St. John's, Newfoundland, arrived and sighted lights in the water, but they had no hoist equipment and could do nothing. The intensive air and sea search that followed located twenty-two dead in the icy waters, their death attributed to hypothermia. Sixty-two others from the rig were missing and assumed dead. There were no survivors.

Less than two years later, the drill ship *Glomar Java Sea* sank at its drill site in the South China Sea. None of the crew of eighty-one survived. Then on 29 October 1985, Hurricane Juan smashed ashore near Houma, Louisiana, with winds up to 90 knots. A Penrod Oil rig collapsed and drifted into a sister rig 20 miles south of Grand Isle.

Sixty of the crew members were rescued by Coast Guard helicopters, while twenty-five were taken off by civilian transport helicopters. But the worst drilling platform disaster was yet to come, and this was not due to weather.

On 6 July 1988, a huge explosion tore apart Occidental Petroleum's big Piper Alpha oil platform located in the North Sea 100 miles northeast of Aberdeen, Scotland. Apparently caused by a gas leak, the explosion was followed by a raging fire that drove the remaining survivors into the icy waters. Many leaped 150 feet off the platform into a sea covered with blazing oil. When the grim rescue operation was concluded, 67 rig workers had been recovered, 16 bodies had been located, and 148 people were missing and presumed dead—the worst oil-rig disaster of all time. The loss cost insurers in excess of one billion dollars, the largest single unit claim in history. It dwarfed the $172 million in insurance losses in the 1980 capsizing of the Kielland oil rig, also in the North Sea and also with a heavy loss of life. Work on oil rigs, as on tankers, is a dangerous livelihood.

A helicopter circles a burning oil-drilling platform.

Though the big offshore navigation platforms were by no means as dangerous as the oil rigs, the Coast Guard was concerned for the safety of its men when severe weather moved toward them. This problem has been resolved by converting the lights to automatic remote operation, and other than periodic visits by maintenance crews, the platforms are no longer occupied. No structure, however well built, is an absolute guarantee against destruction by the huge forces of the storms in an open sea.

But severe storms can create havoc even in normally protected waters, endangering lives and property along coastal and harbor areas, and stretching Coast Guard resources to the limit. In November 1983, the West Coast was hammered by a severe winter storm. Winds peaked at 74 knots and seas at 33 feet. A total of thirteen lives were saved in thirty-three SAR cases during the storm, and San Francisco Bay was closed to all traffic at its height. Two years later, when Hurricane

A Coast Guard motor lifeboat makes its way through heavy breaking seas entering an inlet. Such severe conditions are common on the Pacific Northwest coast.

Juan hit the Gulf Coast, SAR units responded to seventy-five distress calls and saved over one hundred lives. The following spring, a severe cold front passed through Galveston, Texas, with 30–50-knot winds and high seas. Over seventy SAR cases developed as a result, involving fifty-one vessels and 122 people, while an additional 56 people were removed from the water. Miraculously, there was no loss of life. In August of the same year, Hurricane Charlie side-swiped Nantucket with 65-knot winds. During the wild night of the hurricane, Coast Guard Station Nantucket received twenty-six Mayday calls from vessels anchored within Nantucket harbor. Though seventy-five boats were washed ashore during the storm, again no one was injured or lost.

Underwater accidents are fortunately rare, as the Coast Guard has only limited capability for underwater SAR, but some cases are handled by local ingenuity. At about noon 9 July 1986, the Ft. Pierce, Florida, Coast Guard Station was notified by a tender that a two-man sub was stuck on the bottom off Ft. Pierce with twenty minutes of air left. A 41-foot rescue boat was dispatched, and one of the crew was Storekeeper First Class Dave Lewis, who had his own scuba gear that he used for recreational diving. Fortunately he had brought it along, and by the time the rescue boat arrived at the scene, he was suited up. Diving overboard, Lewis swam down to the wreck and secured a line to the sub. The boat crew began to haul it to the surface.

Just before the hatch cleared the water, one of the sub occupants opened it, the sub filled with water, the line broke, and the sub sank. Lewis dived over and followed it down. Entering the hatch, Lewis grabbed one man and swam to the surface. Turning the victim over to one of the boat crew, Lewis dived again and brought up the other. With both men on the Coast Guard boat, CPR was started by a team headed by Seamen Barry Gladstein; one of the men had no pulse. Thirty minutes after the alarm was sounded, both victims were delivered alive to a Ft. Pierce hospital. They were both released the next day in good condition, thanks to Dave Lewis's quick thinking and courage.

All underwater work involves some degree of risk, even with highly experienced divers. One unsolved disappearance at sea occurred within a few feet of over one hundred men on the Coast Guard Cutter *Rockaway*, on Ocean Station Hotel, 300 miles off Cape Hatteras.

When one of the cutter's propellers became fouled at night, the commanding officer, Commander James R. Hinnant, ordered diving gear and lights prepared and went over the side to examine the screw. He was a skilled diver and had been commended for diving salvage work under fire during the Philippines campaign. Even though it was night, lights over the stern afforded illumination where he was working only ten feet under the water. Numerous crew members lined the rail just above him.

After he had been down for some time, a signal was made by tugging his line to see if he was OK. There was no answer. The officer-in-charge on deck ordered the line hauled in, but the tending crew was unable to budge it. The line was apparently fouled on the propeller shafts or rudder, and there was no other diving rig aboard ship.

A message was sent to the air station at Elizabeth City, reporting that the commanding officer was trapped beneath the ship and requesting that additional diving gear be air-dropped. The Norfolk Naval Base was requested by phone to have the gear at the airport, and we took off in the ready PB1-G. Before we reached Norfolk, however, the ship canceled the request for diving gear. They had fabricated some from a gas mask and hose, and sent a diver down. Hinnant's air hose and line were fouled on the prop shaft, but he had disappeared.

Boats were being put over to search, and the ship wanted illumination by aircraft parachute flares. We turned toward the ship, 300 miles away, and went to maximum continuous power. Less than two hours later, we began dropping flares to light up the scene. Each burned for three minutes, providing a half million candlepower of light. The ship steamed slowly along, with a boat on either beam searching. Over the next three hours, we dropped sixty-five flares, but no trace of Reed Hinnant was ever found.

What could have happened to an experienced diver only ten feet below the surface? Had his retaining line and air hose fouled? If so, he had only to release his weighted belt, take a deep pull of air, flip off the mask, and surface. It is a simple and basic maneuver for a diver. Many speculated that he had been hit by a shark. There are many large man-eaters in that area, and they are attracted to light. Commander Hinnant had been working beneath a large light, and a shark could have come in while he was busy working on the screw.

However, no sharks were seen at any time, and there was no disturbance in the water, nor any evidence of a struggle. No one saw him surface, though many men were watching the water at all times. What happened to him that night will never be known.

SAR men encounter endless variety when the alarm rings. As though shipwreck, aircraft crashes, and Texas towers are not enough, there were the unmilked and stranded cows. During a major flood operation, nearly 1,500 people and over 300 cows were rescued by the relief forces. But some cattle, on land isolated by the flood, could not be brought out. Yet the weather notwithstanding, cows have to be milked. Midwestern farm boys have always been regarded as the finest sailor material, and they once again proved it. The ex–farm boys turned to and milked cows by the dozens. When it was all over, the milk was wasted, but the cows were more comfortable.

A year later, other Coast Guardsmen had a less humanitarian mission. On lonely Santa Rosa Island off the California coast, the Army had built a radar station during the war, and some of the men had brought a few pet rabbits to the island. In the rapid postwar demobilization, the rabbits were left behind on the island. Having little else to do on the barren spot, the rabbits turned to their natural form of recreation. By 1955, the rabbit population had reached such alarming proportions that they were rapidly devouring all the island's vegetation, and with its disappearance came the danger that the island would be eroded by rains and wash into the sea. The National Park Service, which owned the island, proposed to eliminate the rabbits by dropping poisoned feed. The Coast Guard was asked to do the job by plane and complied with several bombing raids. The rabbits, weary of the sparse menu on the island, quickly ate the poisoned food, and most of them died. But a few survived, and within two years, these hardy and virile survivors had built up a new race of super rabbits. The Park Service people came up with a new plan to bomb the island with a deadlier poison, then land an invasion force of employees armed with shotguns to finish off the survivors. It must have been a final solution, for there were no further requests for bombing strikes against the Santa Rosa rabbits. The airmen were just as happy, for their hearts weren't in it. They had nothing against the rabbits. Like all the world, they too loved a lover.

For Whom the Bell Tolls

In the middle of the floor at Lloyd's of London, enclosed by five ornate columns, is the famous Lutine Bell. It was taken from the frigate *Lutine*, lost in 1799 with gold bullion valued at more than $5,000,000, at the time one of the biggest losses ever suffered by the famous insurance underwriters. The bell is tended by a guard in a long red coat. When a missing ship insured by the syndicate is reported lost, a slip is passed to the attendant, who strikes the Lutine Bell once to summon the various underwriters to hear the bad news. Over the years, the bell has rung thousands of times for sunken vessels. Hundreds of them have disappeared without a trace. In many other cases, ships went down without sending a distress message and would have been in the "missing" category had not one or more survivors later been picked up by passing vessels to tell the story of the ship's demise. Hundreds of aircraft have also gone down at sea, and small craft in uncounted numbers have vanished.

Before radio, and even today if the craft sends no radio message, such disappearances are understandable. The sea takes a heavy toll from many causes, and if the mariner in trouble is unable to call for help, the sea will swallow the evidence. Over the years, large vessels of over 1,000 tons have been in trouble at sea almost daily on an average, but thanks to radio, there is usually time for help to reach them or their survivors. When a vessel equipped with a reliable long-range radio disappears, we usually presume that whatever occurred was the result of such a sudden and overwhelming disaster that the stricken ship was unable to transmit even a brief call for help. The advent of reliable ELTs will greatly reduce the number of such mysteries.

On 5 December 1954, the motor vessel *Southern Districts*, en route from Louisiana to Maine with a cargo of bulk sulphur, was sighted by the SS *Gulf Keys* off the Florida coast, and later in the day a shore radio station communicated with her. No communications were ever established with her after 5 December. An overdue report was not filed by the owners with the Coast Guard until the night of 11 December, nearly a week after the last radio contact, and at least forty-eight hours after she was overdue in port. No trace of the *Southern Districts* or her twenty-three crew members was ever found. But the investigators working on the case were not completely in the dark. Only two years before, the *Southern Isles*, a sister ship, had gone down under similar conditions, and but for an alert ship's lookout, would also have been among the missing rather than among those sunk from known causes. At 0340 on the morning of 5 October 1951, the seas 400 miles east of Jacksonville, Florida, were rough, due to a hurricane off Cape Hatteras. The third mate on the bridge of the SS *Charlotte Lykes* had for some time been watching a light about four miles ahead, when suddenly it went out. About thirty minutes later, as they passed the spot where the light was last seen, the men on the *Charlotte Lykes* saw a small lighted ring buoy in the water and heard shouts for help in the darkness. In the next two hours, they picked up seven survivors. They were from the *Southern Isles*, which had been proceeding from Puerto Rico to Chester, Pennsylvania, with a cargo of iron ore. In the early morning darkness, she had broken in two without warning and gone down so rapidly that no boats could be launched or a distress call made. Many of the sleeping crew found themselves in the water without clothing or life jackets. Of the twenty-three crewmen, only seven were rescued, and one of these died soon afterward. But for the alert mate on the *Lykes* freighter, none would have survived.

At the time the *Charlotte Lykes* broadcast the sighting message, I was at Naval Air Station, Jacksonville, with two PBMs that had been evacuated from Elizabeth City ahead of the hurricane. We were aroused by the Air Station ODD, and at 0630 took off and climbed to 11,000 feet en route to the disaster scene. Lieutenant Jim Swanson followed five minutes behind in the second plane. When we picked up the *Lykes* on radar, we let down, breaking out of the storm clouds at 800 feet. Hour after hour we searched at altitudes of less than 500 feet over the big 20-foot swells, but only bodies and bits of debris were sighted. Shortly after noon, I sighted a naked body, and dropped a smoke float as I wrapped the plane up in a tight turn to pass over it again. I had also sighted something else—a huge 15-foot shark only a few feet from the body. On the second pass, the shark was tugging the corpse around, and on the third pass, two sharks were fighting over it. Two minutes later, nothing remained. Only a hundred yards away was another body, fully clothed and wearing an orange life jacket. It was not molested. Only a year before, we had been at this same part of the ocean when an unclothed survivor of an aircraft ditching was killed by a shark. I firmly resolved to keep my clothes on should I ever be unfortunate enough to be adrift in shark-infested waters.

The Coast Guard Marine Board of Investigation expressed the opinion that the *Southern Isle* was overloaded and was carrying a cargo too dense for a vessel of her type. They also felt that her hull, weakened as a result of the loading during this and previous voyages, had failed while being driven at excessive speeds in the heavy seas. As a result, other vessels of this class were restricted as to type of cargo carried, and strengthening of the hull was required. The steps taken, however, were not sufficient to save the *Southern Districts.* Following the second disaster, the Coast Guard withdrew its certification for this type of vessel to carry cargo on ocean or coastwise routes.

There are other "jinxed" types. Between 1951 and 1966, seventeen T-2 tankers suffered major casualties or sank. Four suffered explosions, four split in half at sea, and the *Marine Sulphur Queen* disappeared. On the morning of 18 February 1952, the New England coast was lashed by a 50-knot gale, sub-freezing temperatures, and snow that reduced visibility to a few hundred yards. At the height of the storm, a distress message was received from the T-2 tanker *Fort Mercer,* off Pollack Rip Light Vessel, that she was having trouble, and shortly before noon she advised that her hull was splitting. At Boston, the Rescue Coordination Center realized that in the prevailing weather the situation was critical. The plug was pulled. Cutters

The bow of the broken tanker *Pendleton* awash off North Beach, Mass. No survivors were found on this section.

Eastwind and *Unimak,* 120 miles south of the *Fort Mercer* and proceeding to help another vessel, were ordered to divert to the later and more serious case. In Boston, CGC *McCulloch* was ordered to proceed, as was CGC *Yakutat,* then anchored in Provincetown harbor. Shortly after noon, orders were given to the Chatham and Brant Point Lifeboat Stations to dispatch lifeboats to sea, despite the full gale, freezing weather, and heavy snow. To go thirty miles out to sea in such weather in a 36-foot lifeboat was asking the maximum effort from the boat and crew, but twenty-five minutes later, Boatswain's Mate Bernard C. Webber and his three-man crew cast off. Before they could even get into the open sea, they had to cross the treacherous Chatham Bar, where mountainous seas was breaking. Without hesitation, they pointed their bow toward the bar. The Coast Guard's history abounds with stories of rugged surfmen putting out in their small craft into the teeth of the gale, but none faced greater odds than Webber and his crew that day and the night that followed. They were all young men, but heirs of an old breed and a great tradition.

As darkness approached, and the small lifeboat fought its way through the breakers on the bar, the radar at the Chatham Station picked up two targets off Pollack's Rip. Soon they were visually identified as halves of a tanker. The first reaction was that there had been a mistake in the *Fort Mercer's* position, for the targets were 20 miles west of the position given in her distress message. Soon, however, Pollack's Rip Light Vessel reported that they had the bow in sight, and the name on it was not *Fort Mercer*, but *Pendleton*. Two ships were involved!

A quick check by the Boston RCC with the ship's agent confirmed the fact that the tanker *Pendleton* had been due in Boston the day before, but had not arrived. Now two bows and two sterns were adrift in the wild night.

CGC *Yakutat* was ordered to proceed to the bow of the *Fort Mercer*, and the *Eastwind* and *Unimak* to the stern section. Webber and his little boat headed for the stern of the *Pendleton*, and CGC *McCulloch* went after her bow. Overhead, aircraft from Salem helped direct the cutters in and dropped flares to illuminate the scene. At 1900, Webber worked in close to the stern of the *Pendleton* and removed thirty-two men, but one fell overboard and was lost in the raging sea. Two hours later, the *McCulloch* and Webber's boat were

Cutter *Yakutat* closes the bow section of the broken *Fort Mercer* to remove survivors. Two men are clinging to the rubber raft being shuttled between the ships.

The Coast Guard icebreaker *Eastwind* closes the stern section of the *Fort Mercer* where 34 survivors were stranded. A rubber raft is being shuttled between the ships.

alongside the bow section. One man jumped from the sinking derelict and was lost; there were no other signs of life.

Twenty miles away, the *Yakutat*, shortly after midnight, started taking the men from the bow section of the *Fort Mercer* by rubber rafts. Four men were pulled aboard, but five who jumped in the water were lost in the blackness. Twelve miles farther out, the *Eastwind*, *Unimak*, and *Acushnet* took twenty-one men off the *Fort Mercer's* stern, but thirteen men chose to remain aboard. The following day, a Moran tug took the stern of the *Fort Mercer* in tow and started for Narragansett Bay. The half ship, in charge of the chief engineer, backed slowly into the sea to help the tug. On the 22nd, the stern was moored at Jamestown, Rhode Island, and 45,000 barrels of oil were pumped into a barge and delivered to the Shell Oil Company at Fall River. The bow of the *Fort Mercer*, which had capsized, was still afloat and drifting into the steamer lanes where it would be a menace to navigation. When it was determined that it was not salvageable, a cutter sank it with gunfire. Finally, on the 24th, a crew from the Chatham Station boarded the bow section of the *Pendleton* and removed one body. The Coast Guard closed the case.

Two T-2 tankers, within a few miles of each other, and on the same course, had broken in two at the same time. Had it not been for the distress call sent out by the *Fort Mercer*, and the chance sighting of the *Pendleton* by the light vessel, the *Pendleton* may well have gone into the records as another mystery of the sea.

As weird as were the circumstances, there was to be a sequel. After the stern of the *Fort Mercer* was towed into port, a new forward half was built and attached. The rebuilt vessel was renamed the *San Jacinto*. On 26 March 1964, the *San Jacinto* exploded off the Virginia coast and split in two. The stern half floated and was towed into port. Weak she might be amidships, but the stern section of the *San Jacinto*, née *Fort Mercer*, appeared to be indestructible.

Tankers, of course, carry dangerous cargoes that are highly susceptible to fire and explosion. In addition, the density of the cargo and uneven load stresses can cause strains and weakening of the hull. When an explosion occurs or the hull splits, the radio antennas may be snapped, and the vessel is unable to get out a distress signal. This may have happened to the *Marine Sulphur Queen*, en route from Beaumont, Texas, to Norfolk, Virginia, with a load of molten sulphur. After a radio message on 4 February, she was never heard from or seen again, and no trace of her or the thirty-nine men aboard has ever been found. The Coast Guard Board of Investigation was unable to determine how she was lost, but commented that she may have gone down from an explosion, a hull failure, or capsizing as a result of synchronous rolling in heavy seas.

Twenty-five years after the *Fort Mercer/Pendleton* case, there was an eerie repeat. In late March 1977, a passing merchant vessel sighted the stern section of the 713-foot tanker *Claude Conway* 145 miles southeast of Cape Fear, N.C. Helicopters from Coast Guard Air Stations at Elizabeth City and Clearwater worked with three merchant vessels to remove twenty-seven people from the stern and from the bow section, which had been located some distance away. No other survivors were found by boarding parties placed on the two sections of the tanker or by aircraft searching the surrounding waters. The CGC *Dallas* sank the bow section with gunfire, and the stern was towed in by commercial salvors. The hull split was caused by an explosion rather than hull failure.

In that same winter, the 33,000-ton Liberian tanker *Irenes Challenge* broke in two due to hull failure. Both halves remained afloat 200 miles southeast of Midway Island. Twenty-eight survivors were rescued by the merchant vessel *Pacific Arrow*, but a thorough search by Coast Guard and Navy aircraft failed to find other crew members. The two halves, containing 4.2 million gallons of crude oil soon sank, and the oil slick soon disappeared.

The known facts in other typical cases can be summarized just as briefly. In November 1960, the SS *Iri* departed England for Montreal, Canada, with twenty-three persons on board. On 26 November it was reported overdue, and a search by Canadian, British, and U.S. Coast Guard aircraft as well as three Coast Guard cutters failed to find a trace. Two years later, a Spanish freighter, the SS *Castillo Montjuich*, left Boston for Spain and vanished. Again no clue was ever found. As with the *Sulphur Queen* and the *Iri*, marine accident investigators could only speculate as to what had happened.

In January 1977, the Panamanian tanker *Grand Zenith* was overdue in the North Atlantic. A large-scale search by aircraft from four services and the CGC *Dallas* located only a single life jacket with the tanker's name on it and later an oil slick that scientists identified as being from the missing tanker. A month later the Liberian bulk carrier *Rose S.* disappeared 700 miles northwest of Wake Island with thirty-one people aboard. In February 1987, the 474-foot container ship *Tuxpan*, en route from Europe to Mexico, was last reported 700 miles southwest of the Azores and was not heard from again. An intensive search found nothing, but later a container, which had been stowed far below deck on the *Tuxpan*, was sighted by a passing ship. These random cases of missing ships indicate how little remains or is known after a large ship goes down. The ocean quickly erases the clues!

Sometimes a sinking is discovered only by rare good fortune. On a March day in 1964 a Royal Canadian Air Force aircraft on exercises 300 miles off Nantucket sighted an odd-looking vessel and went over to investigate. It found the drifting stern half of the SS *Amphialos*, which had broken in half without getting out a call. But for the chance aircraft sighting, the crew and vessel may well have perished without a trace. The crew of thirty-five was taken off by HMCS *Athabascan* before the stern sank, but two died later.

On 12 March 1957, the CGC *Castle Rock* was towing a disabled fishing vessel off Cape Cod when a lookout sighted a red flare. On investigation, the cutter found a lifeboat with nine survivors of the SS *Patrick Sweeney* who had been adrift two days in the winter seas. The collier had been en route from New Jersey to Yarmouth, Nova Scotia, when the cargo of coal shifted suddenly, causing the ship to roll over. No distress message could be transmitted, and when survivors were sighted, the vessel was already twenty-four hours overdue at Yarmouth, but neither the owners or agent knew that the vessel was in trouble. The flare from the lifeboat was the first indication to the outside world of any distress.

Improper stowage of cargo is a major cause of accidents at sea, and the SS *Mormackite* was a classic example. She had departed Brazil for Baltimore with a cargo of iron ore and coffee beans. On the morning of 7 October 1954, the cargo began shifting in heavy seas, and forty-five minutes later she rolled over and sank stern first without any preparations to abandon ship having been made or a distress message sent. The Coast Guard was not notified by the owner's agent until the afternoon of 8 October, when the vessel had been out of radio contact for nearly two days, and was one day overdue at Cape Henry. Twelve hours after the Coast Guard was notified, the Greek SS *Makadonia* heard voices in the night off the North Carolina coast and put over boats to investigate. Eleven survivors of the *Mormackite* were recovered by the Greek vessel after they had been in the water for nearly two days. Another "missing ship" case had been avoided only by luck, but thirty-seven men perished in the disaster.

In December 1964, the SS *Smith Voyager* narrowly escaped a similar fate when its cargo of wheat probably shifted. Its distress signal, however, was heard by the nearby SS *Mathilde Bolten*, and she, with the help of the cutter *Rockaway*, saved all but four of the crew when the distressed vessel went down.

One of the most tragic cases of a ship loss due to the shifting of cargo involved the old Victory ship *Badger State*, taken out of mothballs to haul ammunition to Vietnam. On 14 December 1969, the freighter encountered heavy weather in the North Pacific and changed her route looking for better weather. On the 17th, with confused seas of 20 feet, some of the 500-pound bombs below deck shifted, smashing the dunnage, and one bomb began pounding the hull. For a week the situation worsened, with the crew kept busy repairing the damage. On Christmas Day, the weather got worse, with winds of

Two crewmen of the American freighter *Smith Voyager* fight for their lives in heavy Atlantic seas after the ship's cargo shifted and she took a heavy list to starboard.

hurricane force. The old freighter took a 50-degree roll, and gear tore loose in all the holds and stowage spaces. The master requested an escort, and the SS *Flying Dragon* was directed to close her and accompany her to Midway. Early on the morning of the 26th, however, the ship was hit by a mountainous sea that rolled her more than 50 degrees to either side, wrecking a lifeboat and tearing loose several 2,000-pound bombs in No. 5 hold. Sparks flew as the high-explosive bombs smashed into each other and the ship's structure. In a desperate attempt to stop the runaway bombs, mattresses, lines, chairs, and even frozen meats were thrown into the hold. When this failed, the master ordered a distress message sent. The Greek *Khian Star* was only 40 miles away and soon had the stricken vessel in sight. Reassured by the sight of help nearby, the master altered course for Midway and rang up full speed. But an explosion in No. 5 hold blew off the hatch and scattered burning debris around the deck. The crew was ordered to abandon ship, and a lifeboat with thirty-four men aboard was launched with way still on. The boat was carried aft, and when it was abeam of No. 5 hold, a bomb came out through a hole in the side of the ship and landed in the boat, capsizing it! The master and the remaining five men then went over the side into the rough cold water. Only fourteen of the forty men who abandoned ship made it to the *Khian Star*, which had only a nineteen-man crew and was rolling up to 50 degrees. Even so, she made a number of passes retrieving survivors. Inflatable liferafts were dropped by C-130 aircraft, but most were carried away by the 40-knot winds. Seven ships and several Coast Guard and Air Force aircraft searched 8,000 square miles of ocean, but after the first hours, no one else was recovered.

In most of these cases, ships go down without a trace, but a few crew members survive. In a few rare cases, the crew disappears but the ship is found. In what has remained one of the most famous nineteenth century sea mysteries, the American brig *Marie Celeste* was found wandering, under sail, between the Azores and Portugal. The captain, his wife and baby, together with the entire crew, had vanished and were never seen again.

Fifty years later the sailing vessel *Carol A. Deering* ran onto the dreaded Diamond Shoals off Cape Hatteras on a winter night and was spotted from the beach. When boarded soon afterwards by a Coast Guard lifeboat crew, food was found on the table, charts were laid out, and everything appeared normal, except there was no sign of the crew or any evidence of preparations for abandonment. Despite a long investigation, no clue to the fate of the crew was ever found.

On 10 July 1965, the USS *Mount Baker* found the 30-foot sailboat *Geni* adrift 200 miles off the California coast with no one aboard. The ship's log showed that it had departed Neah Bay, Washington, on 22 May for Sitka, Alaska. The last entry was made the following day at a position 75 miles off Cape Flattery. The sole occupant was never found. The boat was towed in, a mute testimony to the danger of going to sea alone on a long voyage.

In numbers and monetary losses, disappearances run a distinct second to collisions between ships and between ships and shore. Despite over a century of effort by all maritime nations to develop foolproof rules to prevent collisions, they occur with alarming regularity. Like vehicle collisions, they are seen most often in areas of heavy traffic. Neither modern equipment nor training seem to guarantee against

A Coast Guard aircraft passes over two large modern ships that tried to occupy the same part of the ocean at the same instant.

this type of accident. Both the Navy and Coast Guard have had their share in recent years, including the *Coral Sea–Napo, Belknap–John F. Kennedy, Wasp-Hobson, Cuyahoga–Santa Cruz II, Blackthorn-Capricorn*, and the *Eastwind* with a tanker. All of these cases involved vessels with highly trained officers and crews and the latest modern equipment. One of the best-known collisions involved the liners *Andrea Doria* and *Stockholm*, but dozens of other collisions between merchant vessels occur yearly. Many result in massive pollution when one or both vessels are tankers and their fuel tanks are ruptured. Some of these collisions can be attributed to an overreliance on radar while maintaining high speed in fog or reduced visibility, but others are the result of inattention or plain human error.

One of the really bizarre collisions involved the distressed Japanese vessel *Suwaharu Maru* and one of her rescuers. She had radioed an SOS from her position 200 miles northwest of Seattle after a fire broke out on board. An AMVER Surpic showed twelve vessels within 300 miles of the burning ship. The American vessel *Transoneida* was closest and was asked to assist. Another Japanese ship, *Kure Maru*,

A rescue vessel lies alongside lifeboats from the *Andrea Doria*, seen sinking after a collision with the SS *Stockholm* northeast of New York.

also raced to assist, as did numerous Navy and Coast Guard aircraft. The *Suwaharu Maru* soon reported that the fire was under control, but then said that the *Mandoil II*, running at high speed to assist the burning ship, had collided with it in thick fog! The *Mandoil II* was enveloped in flames, and the crew abandoned ship. A Coast Guard plane sighted a liferaft containing twenty-nine survivors, and these plus another four were picked up by the *Kure Maru*. No other survivors from the unfortunate Good Samaritan were found. All of the crew of the distressed *Suwaharu Maru* were saved.

Most collisions, however, occur in crowded harbors and shipping lanes. Consider this small sampling on the approaches to, or in, New York harbor: Ambrose Lightship rammed by SS *Green Bay*; CGC *Eastwind* rammed by tanker, thirteen sailors dead; Israeli liner *Shalom* sank tanker *Stolt Dagali*, nineteen dead; tankers *Alva Cape* and *Texaco Massachusetts* collided off Staten Island, thirty-seven dead; container ship *Sea Witch* rammed anchored tanker *Esso Brussels* near Verrazano Narrows Bridge, sixteen dead; ferryboat *American Legion* and freighter *Hoegh Orchid* collided in dense fog, sixty commuters injured. The impact is terrific when 50,000 tons of vessels hit at combined closing speeds of 30 knots. At the very best, there will be injured persons to remove, like the ones removed by helicopters after the *Shalom–Stolt Dagali* collision. One or both vessels may go down, as did the *Andrea Doria*.

Fire is an ever-present threat at sea, especially following collisions and in ships carrying inflammable cargoes. Most well-remembered

Fires frequently occur after a collision, such as this one between the tanker *Keytrader* (left) and the Norwegian freighter *Baune*.

fires at sea have involved passenger vessels with large numbers of people on board. One of the best known was the *Morro Castle*, which burned within view of thousands of people along the New Jersey shore, with the loss of 126 people. Later, the Canadian passenger vessel *Noronic* burned in Toronto harbor with the loss of 118 passengers, but strangely none of the 171 crew members. On 22 December 1963, the 20,314-ton Greek cruise ship *Lakonia*, en route from Southampton, England, to the Canary Islands, caught fire. There were 658 passengers and 383 crewmen on board. Less than two hours after the fire was discovered, the order was given to abandon ship. Four of the ship's boats could not be used due to the rapidly spreading flames, and 155 people perished in the flames or drowned after jumping overboard.

In all three disasters the passengers accused the crews of failing to aid and protect them, and nearly all fatalities were among the passengers. In each case, the shipping companies denied this and cited panic among the passengers. By marked contrast, the passengers of the *Prinsendam* had high praise for the crew. There was no loss of life and no panic. The superb response of the SAR forces and other ships undoubtedly contributed to the fine performance of both crew and passengers. In a similar case on 9 March 1984, the cruise vessel *Scandinavian Sea* caught fire while five miles off Port Canaveral, Florida, but the ship was able to return to port and disembark all 744 passengers and 202 crew members without any injuries or deaths. The fire raged for two days, and Coast Guard personnel from throughout the southeast were flown in to battle the blaze. They were hampered at times by the ship's list, caused by the large quantities of water pumped aboard to fight the fire, which raised concerns about the ship's stability.

Merchant-ship fires with no passengers involved are more easily managed. In February 1970, the 450-foot Panamanian freighter *Grand Ocean* declared a distress with fires in two holds. The CGC *Bering Strait* and aircraft from Honolulu, Guam, and Japan responded. During the three days that the cutter's crew fought the fire, aircraft dropped over 300 rescue-breathing-apparatus (RBA) canisters and gasoline and oil for the firefighters' pumps and equipment. On the third day the fire was extinguished, and the merchantmen was able to proceed under its own power to Los Angeles. In 1981, the 610-foot car-carrier *Blue Hawk* caught fire in the Pacific. The cutter *Morgenthau* and several merchant ships came to her aid. The fire was extinguished after a two-day fight. Three years later a Coast Guard C-130 on patrol witnessed the explosion of the tanker *Puerto Rican* 10 miles outside the Golden Gate Bridge. The first help arrived within thirty minutes and all twenty-nine people on board were rescued. Navy and Coast Guard fire-fighting units fought the raging fire for several days.

When a large tanker catches fire, chemical foam is the most effective extinguishing agent, and thousands of gallons may be required. Most ships carry enough to fight a small fire, but if a large one breaks out, foam must be provided from other sources. The tanker *Amoco Virginia*, loaded with high-octane aviation fuel, caught fire in the Houston ship channel. The huge fire endangered nearby fuel tank farms, and a vast fire-fighting effort was started. An emergency call for foam went out to all military bases in several states. Over 60,000 gallons of the chemical were delivered to the scene in ninety-eight flights by aircraft and helicopters. The fire was finally extinguished after twenty-four hours.

Vessels often burn for agonizingly long periods of time, and with the SS *Margit*, it proved downright embarrassing. On 15 February 1965, she caught fire in mid-Pacific, and the crew abandoned ship. They were picked up by other vessels, and the wounded were evacuated by air. The following day, long-range aircraft from the Coast Guard Air Station at Barbers Point, Hawaii, searched the area and did not sight the vessel. Believing it had gone down, the search was called off. Several weeks later, the *Margit*, still very much afloat and burning amidships, fetched up on Kechairakkui Island, in the Wotje atoll, after drifting 880 miles in twenty-four days. The *Margit*, unlike the proverbial Old Soldier, had simply refused to fade away.

An even longer odyssey was begun by the 250-foot Taiwanese fishing vessel, *Zhe-Sheng*, which was abandoned in June 1988 about 300 miles north of Midway Island after a fire on board. It was later sighted in August drifting in the North Pacific. Finally, in February 1989 the tanker *Arco Juneau* slighted it 400 miles off Cape Flattery, Washington. The derelict had drifted 2,800 miles in six months, and the only apparent damage was a burned area near the stern. It was yet one more case of premature abandonment. The Coast Guard removed the derelict as a menace to navigation.

There have been a couple of man-made fires at sea, started with official sanction. A Coast Guard 83-foot patrol boat ran on a reef in Buzzards Bay, and after being pounded by the sea, was adjudged to be unsalvageable. Rather than leave it there as a monument to a mistake in Coast Guard navigation, it was soaked with fuel and burned to the waterline.

A year later, a Navy minesweeper, the USS *Grouse*, ran on the rocks on a clear night just north of Cape Ann. There was some speculation among the waterfront crowd that the bridge watch may have been "blinded" by the flashing light of the Cape Ann lighthouse, clearly visible dead ahead. For two days, we flew Navy officers and salvage crews by helicopter to and from the vessel, perched high and dry on the rocks. The minesweeper was there to stay, and the tourists flocked to the shore in droves to see it. Like the Coast Guard a year earlier, the Navy was acutely embarrassed. I mentioned to a senior

The buoy tender *Gentian* prepares to attack a fire on the trawler *Shannon* 35 miles off the New Jersey coast. After the five crewmen were removed, the trawler burned to her waterline and sank.

Navy officer on the scene that the Coast Guard had experienced a similar casualty a year before and had burned its mistake. He listened with great interest. Two days later, the minesweeper was quietly burned by the salvage crew.

Tankers, especially the huge jumbo types carrying hundreds of thousands of tons of petroleum, sometimes cause ecological damage far beyond that caused by the loss of the ship and cargo. Because of their size, they are very difficult to maneuver in close quarters and are more susceptible to collision and grounding than smaller vessels. Such accidents more often than not result in oil spills that under some conditions can reach disastrous proportions.

Perhaps the best known of the tanker groundings resulting in massive oil spills was that of the *Torrey Canyon*, which went hard aground near the Scilly Isles off England's Cornwall coast on 18 March 1967. This huge tanker, carrying 119,000 tons of Kuwaiti crude to Milford Haven, Wales, ran into a restricted and dangerous area at 15 knots. The hazards of the Scilly Isles are well known to seamen, for over 250 ships have been wrecked in those waters over the years. Yet in broad daylight with numerous points of reference on which to obtain bearings, the huge tanker ran onto Seven Stones Reef, to the amazement and disbelief of the watching crew of the Seven Stones Reef Lightship. As the wreck broke up, thousands of tons of black oil gushed into the sea and were carried by wind and currents to the British and French coasts. Before the spill was finally contained and the cleanup completed, total losses amounted to some 25 million dollars. The ecological damage has never been accurately assessed.

One year later, on 3 March 1968, the Greek-manned 18,254-ton tanker *Ocean Eagle*, a third the size of the *Torrey Canyon*, went aground while trying to enter San Juan harbor, Puerto Rico, after a series of misunderstandings and navigational errors. As the ship began breaking up, much of its 5.5-million-gallon oil cargo poured into the clear tropical waters. When the broken halves of the tanker were finally floated and towed out to sea to be scuttled, nearly three million dollars had been spent in removing part of the cargo. Damages to the island's economy were over eight million dollars. Only three days after the *Ocean Eagle* piled up, another Greek crew drove the tanker *General Colocotronis* hard aground on Eleuthera Island in the Bahamas, despite lights blazing on shore only a mile abeam and a U.S. Navy radar tracking station dead ahead.

On 15 December 1976, a grounding with the damage potential of the *Torrey Canyon* episode occurred when the Liberian tanker *Argo Merchant* struck a shoal 28 miles southeast of Nantucket Island. Her presence there resulted from another aggravated navigation blunder that is difficult to comprehend in view of the numerous and sophisticated navigation aids available in modern ships. The CGC *Sherman* and CGC *Vigilant* removed most of the tanker crew and placed damage-control parties aboard. Plans to pump out the oil cargo into barges had to be abandoned when the weather worsened, and the ship soon broke up. Fortunately, northwest winds carried most of the oil out to sea, minimizing the ecological damage along the U.S. East Coast.

During the next ten weeks, fourteen more tanker accidents occurred in or near American waters, and ten of these involved Liber-

An H-3 helicopter hovers over the stranded tanker *Argo Merchant* southeast of Nantucket to place aboard members of the Coast Guard's Atlantic Strike Team. In spite of all efforts, the tanker broke up and sank a week after grounding.

ian vessels. This was followed by a predictable public outcry, which led to the Tanker and Vessel Safety Act of 1977, authorizing the Coast Guard to force ships not meeting its standards to leave U.S. waters. It also established a 200-mile pollution-control zone. As one result, American companies owning ships of Liberian registry began to enforce stricter regulations.

Despite these greater precautions and stricter enforcement, accidents to these vulnerable oil giants continued. In a five year period, 1979–1984, five tanker accidents involving the spillage of 13.3 million gallons of fuel occurred in the Gulf approaches to the Mississippi River Delta, and these were only the worst ones. During the same span, the tanker *Puerto Rico* blew up off San Francisco and burned. Then on 24 March 1989, the huge tanker *Exxon Valdez* ran aground on a reef while leaving Prince William Sound, Alaska, and dumped over 10 million gallons of oil into those previously unspoiled waters. In this greatest American pollution disaster, the ship had left the marked

channel to avoid floating ice, the mate on watch was said by company officials not to have authorization to pilot the vessel on his own
in those waters, and the captain was below decks rather than on the
bridge. Five days later the captain was fired after a federal charge that
he was legally drunk around the time of the grounding. Admiral Paul
Yost, Commandant of the Coast Guard, after a fact-finding trip to
the scene, said:

"Obviously, something went very badly wrong. This was not a
treacherous area, treacherous in the area where they went aground.
It's ten miles wide. Your children could drive a tanker up through
it!"

Most of these tanker accidents occurred in waters in which determination of position should have been no problem; indeed, in most
of the world today, no competent mariner should encounter great
difficulty in fixing his position by conventional and electronic methods. Yet the SS *San Patrick* apparently did, with tragic results. On
10 December 1964, the *San Patrick* left Canada for Yokohama, Japan, with a cargo of wheat. No position reports were given her agents
after that. On the 18th of December, the Japanese vessel *Tetsuho
Maru* heard an SOS message from the *San Patrick*, reporting she
had run on the rocks. Visibility was between zero and four miles in
heavy rain, and the 40-knot gale was accompanied by seas of 25 feet.
Soon after that, the *San Patrick* sent the following message: "VERY
GROUNDED AND VERY BAD CONDITION, LIFEBOAT NOT
POSSIBLE, URGENT ABOUT 5 MINUTES STOP ONLY WITH
HELICOPTER POSSIBLE RESCUE PLEASE CALL NECES-
SARY HELICOPTER." A few minutes later, the radio transmission
stopped.

Aircraft could not be launched for some hours due to the weather,
and it was two days before the *San Patrick*, or what was left of her,
was found. She had run at full speed onto bleak and deserted Ulak
Island in the Aleutian chain, 26 miles east of the position given in
her distress message, and 20 miles north of the great-circle route.
Perhaps her navigation was faulty, or her radar or Loran had failed.
The cause will never be known, for all hands perished with the ship.
The impact against the sheer rocky cliff had been so great that the
bow of the 14,000-ton vessel had folded back over the rest of the
hull. The wreckage resembled that of an aircraft rather than a ship.
Knowing there was no chance of getting off in the towering breakers,

A Coast Guard C-130 of the International Ice Patrol flies low while plotting a group of icebergs on the North Atlantic shipping lanes.

the crew had attempted to fire shot lines up over the 150-foot cliff, but there was no way to anchor them on top. A week after the disaster, a plane circled slowly over the stormy scene while a Catholic chaplain conducted memorial services for the Spanish crew and a wreath was dropped to mark their last bleak resting place.

Vessels are still occasionally sunk by ramming into icebergs. There is a popular misconception that no vessels have been lost from this cause since the *Titanic*, due largely to the effectiveness of the International Ice Patrol, which was established after the disaster. The big bergs on the shipping lanes vary greatly in number from year to year, depending on many meteorological factors. None were sighted in the patrol areas in 1966, but six years later a record 1,587 were reported. In 1984, a colder-than-normal year, a still greater record of 2,202 bergs were sighted or detected on the new SLAR (side-looking air-borne radar) carried by the Ice Patrol C-130s. The threat of this number of large bergs sitting astride the major North Atlantic routes can be better understood if we imagine an equal number of unplotted reefs in the same area, for a berg can do as murderous a job on a ship's hull as any reef.

In peacetime, no vessels have been lost by collision with an iceberg in the patrolled area, as the shipping routes are usually altered to the southward when bergs are sighted. In World War II, the patrol was discontinued and several ships struck bergs, but the losses aroused little notice among the hundreds of ships lost to U-boats. A new Danish vessel, the *Hans Hedtoft*, struck a berg south of Cape Farewell, Greenland, on her maiden voyage in 1959, with the loss of all

The 86-foot trawler *John and Olaf* lies on the beach on the north coast of Kodiak Island. Her crew of four abandoned the boat as it became unstable under weight of the ice. The liferaft was found 75 miles away, but the men were never found.

hands. During the several hours between striking the berg and sinking, the Danish vessel transmitted a number of messages, while the
two closest ships, the German *Johannes Kruess* and the CGC *Campbell* battled through mountainous seas and dangerous ice fields to try
and reach her. The *Campbell*, under command of Captain Frederick
J. Scheiber, a resolute skipper with long experience in Greenland
waters, drove through dangerous fields of ice and huge seas in visibility of less than a mile, only to find nothing on her arrival at the
scene. What happened on the Danish ship in the final hours will
never be known. She was outside the Ice Patrol coverage area, and
her government owners had been repeatedly warned of the extreme
hazards of operating in Greenland waters in midwinter. The warnings were not heeded. The terror of those last nightmarish hours can
only be imagined. Unlike the *Titanic*, the launching of boats in the
stormy and icy seas was impossible, nor were there other ships close
by. Men, women, and children must have awaited the end knowing
that there was no hope.

There have been other sinkings by ice outside the patrol area, but
fortunately with happier endings. The motor vessel *Petit Bras D'or*
struck a berg 150 miles off Halifax, Nova Scotia, but all hands were
rescued. On 11 January 1986, the Antarctic Operation Deep Freeze
expedition support vessel *Southern Quest* was crushed by the ice and
sank in the Ross Sea 60 miles north of the U.S. McMurdo Station.
The icebreaker *Polar Star*, operating in Operation Deep Freeze,
launched both of her HH-52 helicopters and recovered all twenty-
one crew members from ice floes.

More people on ships than on aircraft are reported lost at sea, and
considering the total time of exposure, this is not surprising. Air accidents, however, often occur with little warning, and the impact,
even in a controlled ditching, is usually severe. In a ten-year period
ending in 1964, twenty-two United States commercial passenger planes
alone were lost at sea, and nine of these went down with all hands.
On 8 November 1957, a distress was declared on a Pan American
Airways Stratocruiser, Romance of the Skies, en route from San
Francisco to Honolulu with forty-four persons aboard. Eight cutters,
several long-range Coast Guard aircraft, and numerous Navy, Air
Force, RCAF, and Pan American aircraft flew a half-million miles
in the search effort, and eight Coast Guard cutters covered 30,000
miles more. Debris was finally located 60 miles north of the track

line, but no survivors were ever found, and the actual cause of the crash has never been determined. A Northwest Airlines DC-7 disappeared over the Gulf of Alaska on 3 June 1963, on a flight from Tacoma, Washington, to Anchorage, Alaska, with ninety-five passengers and six crewmen. Some debris and a few human remains were finally found, which led investigators to conclude that the aircraft hit the water with terrific impact.

The military incidents have been higher than those of commercial airlines, partly because military aviation is more dangerous than civil transport, and partly because more military aircraft are flying. In scheduled transport operations, however, the safety record of the Military Airlift Command (MAC) is as good as any commercial airline, and better than most.

Of many of the military losses, little can be said. The aircraft simply disappeared without trace. Pogo 22, a SAC B-52, disappeared at sea on 14 October 1961, and a search by seventy-nine aircraft, five cutters, and two merchant ships over an area of 286,000 square miles turned up no trace. A MATS C-118 with twenty-eight persons aboard disappeared between the Azores and Newfoundland on 26 January 1961 and was never found. Later, a C-124 disappeared in mid-Pacific, and 3,000 hours of searching failed to sight even a fragment. On 27 May 1962, a giant C-133 transport, the largest aircraft in use at the time, disappeared between Dover, Delaware, and the Azores. The last report was received as it left the coastline at Cape May, New Jersey. A gigantic search was mounted, extending from Cape May to the Azores, nearly 2,500 miles. On the second day, a nose wheel was sighted and recovered. It proved to be from the missing aircraft. A little more than a year later, another C-133 out of Dover was reported missing on the same route, but nothing was ever found. The cause of both crashes remains undetermined. On 8 January 1962, a B-50 en route from Langley Air Force Base, Virginia, to the Azores, disappeared, and over 1,200 hours of searching by search-and-rescue aircraft failed to sight anything.

An unusual dual disappearance occurred on 28 August 1963, when two huge KC-135 jet tankers were reported missing between Bermuda and Florida. A single plane may go down, but seldom are two large multi-engine craft reported missing at the same time. A search finally located debris near the mid-point of the flight. Enough pieces were recovered to determine that both planes had gone down near the same spot. Investigators guessed that a mid-air collision had occurred while the two planes were flying in formation.

In 1945, a famous multiple air disappearance occurred off the Florida coast, and this involved six aircraft! A flight of five Navy TBM bombers took off for a routine offshore navigation flight and disappeared. When they failed to return, a PBM seaplane was dispatched to search for them. It also failed to return. No trace of any sort was found, and the fate of the six planes has remained a mystery to this day.

The fate of one aircraft was determined only by a quirk of timing. On 6 January 1960, a National Airlines plane was reported missing between Wilmington, North Carolina, and Miami. At 0700 that morning, I had entered the Miami airport terminal to board another National Airlines plane for Washington on a business trip, when a call was made for me over the public address system to phone the Coast Guard Air Station at Miami. When I called, the duty officer advised that a National DC-6 was overdue and search aircraft were being launched. I went to the National ticket counter and observed a number of people standing around awaiting the arrival of the aircraft. They had not yet been told. Calling one of the National agents to the side, I quietly showed my identification and was shown to Operations, where they gave me all the information they had. There was little to go on. The aircraft had reported over Wilmington as it headed out for the over-water flight to Florida, and had not been heard from since. It was nearly an hour overdue. After boarding my flight at Miami, the captain asked me to come up to the cockpit when we were airborne. En route to the coast, he said that he intended to search at low altitude along the track line to Wilmington, and I was asked to join the flight-deck crew as an advisor. The visibility was poor, but we searched along the track, communicating with other search aircraft to maintain traffic separation. Back aft, many of the passengers were sick, due partly to the turbulence, but some perhaps due to the low level at which we were flying. Few airline passengers had ever flown a trip at such low altitude, but most of them were glued to the windows keeping a lookout. Several sighting reports were relayed up via the stewardesses, but invariably turned out to be patches of Gulf seaweed. When we were two hours out of Miami, we were advised that the crash site of the aircraft had been located on land near Bolivia, North Carolina, close to the coast.

CAB investigators later determined that the crash had been caused by a bomb set off in the lavatory by a passenger who, before takeoff, had heavily insured his life. After the explosion, the captain of the doomed aircraft was able to turn toward the coast and keep the aircraft aloft for nearly 20 miles before finally crashing. All aboard were killed. Had the bomb detonated a short time later, the plane would have gone down at sea, and it is unlikely that the cause of the crash would have ever been determined.

With most transocean air traffic now being conducted by jets, a ditching due to loss of power is highly unlikely. Most jets fly well on one or two engines. The great majority of crashes occur during landing and takeoff and within a short distance of the airport. Some large jets have disappeared over mid-ocean, but such an occurrence should always arouse suspicion of terrorism or sabotage. Occasionally, however, cockpit mismanagement can undo even the safest and most sophisticated machinery. A large jet nearly ditched in the Pacific after the crew, attempting to shut down one engine, mistakenly shut down all power. The engines were finally restarted just before the plane would have hit. In another case of cockpit error, a large jet dived thousands of feet before being brought under control. Still another jumbo jet landed in Japan losing power and with its fuel tanks nearly empty after encountering unexpected headwinds on a nonstop flight from the U.S. West Coast. But considering the billions of miles flown yearly, over-water flights are one of the safest means of getting from point to point. The universal use of ELTs combined with the SAR-SAT/COSPAC system and modern communications make it extremely unlikely that we will in the future have aircraft missing without a trace except for those blown up by criminal intent.

Small boats, yachts, and fishing vessels in uncounted numbers disappear, sometimes in groups. For example, in 1961, the ketch *Calista III* disappeared between the Bahamas and Southport, North Carolina. Three years later the ketch *Dancing Feathers* disappeared on the same route under similar circumstances. Long searches in both cases produced no sighting and no clues, only speculation.

The schooner *Windfall* also disappeared, but in this case there was at least a clue. On the stormy night of 15 November 1962, the Belgian merchant vessel *Stad Gent* heard voices in the night and sighted five men in the water 250 miles off Cape Hatteras. In the heavy seas, the Belgian was unable to come about and lost sight of the men. On the following day, the survivors of the schooner *Curlew*, herself a victim of the seas off Bermuda, reported that the *Windfall* had sailed from Mystic, Connecticut, on the same day as *Curlew*, but had not been sighted or heard from since. As the *Windfall* had five men on board, it has been suspected since that the strange night-sighting far off Cape Hatteras was of the men from the *Windfall*.

The fishing vessel *Lynn* was anchored on the night of 29 January 1964 with a half-dozen other vessels in the lee of Monomoy Point on Cape Cod. Winds were high and seas rough. The following morning, the *Lynn* was missing. No one saw it go or knew of any trouble. On the third day of the ensuing search, a bait box was found several miles away, and it was identified as coming from the *Lynn*. No other clues were ever found to explain the disappearance from the midst of the anchored fleet.

As with aircraft, the availability of good communications gear and EPIRBs at affordable prices should result in a marked reduction in missing boats and yachts. However, the pleasure boater is not as regulated as commercial ships and aircraft, and many boaters will continue to sail with only the minimum required equipment, and with predictable results. Captain or seaman, large vessel or small, the sea plays no favorites. Despite the many advances in maritime safety, and the advent of larger, more complex, and safer vessels, the Lutine Bell rings often. In one recent year, 117 large vessels were lost, and over 8,000 suffered disabling damage.

There is also another signal used at Lloyd's—two strokes on the bell when a ship that has been reported missing makes port safely. But the sea is a tenacious adversary. The bell seldom rings twice.

10
The Chamber of Horrors

In 1964, Coast Guard SAR units responded 41,666 times to requests for assistance. Five years before, only 21,337 sorties were made. One observant young officer plotted a curve of the rising cases and compared it with the curve of the gross national product. The shape and rise of the two curves were nearly identical, and the reason was not hard to imagine. With prosperity had come a vast increase in the number of small pleasure boats and a corresponding increase in boating accidents and mishaps. That year there were nearly 8 million small boats in the United States, and over 40 million Americans went out on the water yearly. The exodus to recreational waters was given additional impetus by the overcrowding of recreational facilities on land. The population explosion also helped beget the boating explosion. Only twenty years later, in 1986, the number of boats had doubled to 16.5 million; by 2000, the predicted number will be 20 million.

It has not been an altogether orderly growth. In 1964 the deaths among recreational boaters exceeded our deaths in Vietnam and our military aviation deaths in all theaters combined. At first, this high death rate was attributed to too many amateurs on the water. But that answer seemed a little too pat, so the Coast Guard pulled its accident investigation reports and began to analyze them. The facts were disquieting. From the hundreds of grim case histories in the "morgue," the operation analysts were able to create a composite "corpse." It has not changed greatly since the first such profile in 1965.

The popular concept of a marine distress may be a sailboat fighting for its life in a raging sea, but the actual event is far more mundane and commonplace. Based on the Coast Guard's 1987 Boating Statistics, a composite or typical accident occurred as follows.

The thirty-seven-year-old operator, accompanied by his wife and a child, were cruising in his 20-foot outboard-powered boat, periodically stopping to drift and swim or fish. He was fairly experienced, with some 250 hours of operating time in the boat, but had never attended a formal boating education class. As he cruised along the river, there was no indication of danger. The 60-horsepower motor was running smoothly, pushing the five-year-old fiberglass boat along at 15 knots. Winds were light, the water smooth with a temperature of 70°, and there were no obstructions to visibility. At 1630 on a June weekend, there seemed to be nothing to worry about. Personal Flotation Devices (PFDs) were in the boat, but none were being worn.

Coming around a bend in the river, they were suddenly confronted by another boat coming head on at high speed. They turned hard right at the same time that the speeding boat turned left. No meeting or danger signals were sounded. In the ensuing crash, three people were injured and over $3,500 in damages were incurred. Fortunately, both boats floated after the impact, due to their built-in flotation, and none of the occupants attempted to swim ashore. All were picked up by passing boats and transported to a hospital by the sheriff's department, which also conducted the accident investigation. The operator of the speeding boat was found to have a blood alcohol content of over .10 percent and was by legal standards intoxicated.

In real life, the victims will include men, women, and children of all ages and accomplishments. Fatalities do not conform to the narrow pattern of the composite corpse. They will occur in larger boats, in storms, and in blazing explosions. Some will die before they even realize they are in danger.

Statistics are pretty impersonal. They don't leave the sickening impact that pulling in the drowned bodies of a woman and child does. In the case-file room, known as The Chamber of Horrors, only water accidents are kept. The National Transportation Safety Board has its own chamber for fliers. In addition to the obvious difference in the elements in which they operate, airmen and pleasure boaters have another big habit difference. Airmen discuss and dissect accidents at great length in any bull session, their clinical detachment seemingly balanced between morbidity and pleasure. It isn't morbidity, however, but an absorbing interest in learning by the mistakes of others. When death may be lying in wait at the far end of the next runway, the possibility of a mistake is never far removed from the mind.

Pleasure boatmen avoid the subject of accidents with an equal determination, hoping perhaps that it will go away. Recreational boating is, after all, for pleasure, and why spoil it with unpleasant subjects. But case histories are like vaccinations—a mild exposure may prevent more serious consequences later. The leading cause of death in small boats is capsizing, followed by falling overboard. Thousands of these accidents occur yearly, but let's examine just a few. The lessons should be clear.

Ralph Statts, Jr., was no amateur boatman. He held a mate's license for river, steam, and motor vessels, any gross tonnage. He was a professional. Late on a pleasant afternoon, he took his wife and two sons for an outing on the Ohio River in his 16-foot aluminum boat, powered by a 30-horsepower outboard. Statts knew the boat well, but there were two grave deficiencies. The boat had no lifesaving equipment, and his wife and sons could not swim. There had been blocks of built-in flotation material under each seat, but they had been removed while the boat was being painted and had not yet been replaced. The little boat had crossed the river and had turned for home when a riverboat passed, creating a wake. A following sea came aboard, alarming Mrs. Statts, who stood up and tried to grab her two children. Statts released the tiller to try and get his wife and sons back into the center of the boat, and it rolled over in 30 feet of dark murky water. After repeated dives trying to locate his family, he swam to the river bank, screaming for help. Police arrived on the scene to find him in shock and crying, "God help me." The bodies of his wife and two children were later recovered downriver.

As tragic as it was, this case was soon eclipsed in magnitude. At Lake Talquin, Florida, a church group was having a picnic. Some of the members had rented a 15-foot, flat-bottomed, wooden boat with a small outboard motor. It had only six horsepower, not enough to be dangerous. The weather was ideal, and the water was calm. Many other boats were around. There was no premonition of danger.

Joseph Bouie was a deacon of the church, steady, and widely respected. After taking four teenagers for a ride, he asked the small children around the picnic table if they would like to go. Eighteen of them swarmed aboard. Some sat on the bottom of the boat, while others had their arms and legs dangling over the side. As they left the shore, the boat had only two to six inches of freeboard. There was no lifesaving equipment aboard, and not one of the children could swim!

Exactly what happened is not known, but just as the boat began to take on water, the children started to move around. With so little freeboard, there was no safety margin. The boat went down, and all were thrown into the water. Another boat, only 150 yards away, raced over to the scene and managed to retrieve one boy. The rest, ranging in age from five to fourteen, drowned. Seven children were from one family. The water was only eight feet deep, but it was deep enough. Bouie was a good swimmer. When his body was found, one child was in his arms, another on his back with arms clutched around his neck, a third was holding tightly around his waist, and a fourth clinging to one leg.

Sometimes a well-found boat with adequate lifesaving equipment can be a death trap. In May 1964, the seas off the Merrimack River Bar, north of Cape Ann, Massachusetts, were rough. The boat, fishing off the bar, was equipped with lifesaving gear and was seaworthy, but suddenly was caught beam-on by two closely following seas and capsized. Four people were thrown clear, five others were trapped beneath the boat. In the tower at the Coast Guard's Merrimack River Station, an alert lookout saw it happen and sounded the alarm. The boat crew raced for the boat. A phone call was immediately placed to the Salem Air Station, 20 miles south and the Klaxon rang out there less than two minutes after the boat capsized. At Salem, we knew what the bar was like in rough weather. Lieutenant Roger Frawley and his crewman, Parachute Rigger Russell Yeaton, raced for the ready Sikorsky amphibious helicopter. Two minutes after the alarm rang, they lifted off and Frawley went to 103 percent power on his jet-turbine as he banked toward the Merrimack River. He arrived at the capsized craft at the same time as the rescue boat, which picked up four survivors from the water, but despite efforts by two rescue-boat crewmen who jumped into the chilly waters, they were unable to get to the people trapped beneath the boat. Their pounding and screaming could be clearly heard.

The eight-foot seas and high winds rapidly set the capsized boat onto the huge rocks of the jetty. As it smashed onto the first rocks, Frawley saw an arm sticking out from beneath the boat. Drastic action was indicated. He held the helicopter in a hover just over the rocks, and Yeaton leaped out of the machine. Working his way down among the rocks and breakers, Yeaton pulled two people from the wreckage as the boat broke up. A third man was beyond help. His skull had been crushed as the waves smashed the boat onto the rocks. Despite the rapid response of the rescue forces, and Yeaton's courageous action, three people were lost.

Professional seamen are not immune. In Hampton Roads, a heavily loaded Navy liberty boat swamped in high seas with a heavy loss of life. A Coast Guard boat, servicing buoys in Alaska, capsized, and both men drowned. Dozens of other cases prove that experience alone is no guarantee against capsize.

Next as a cause of death is falling overboard. It does not need to happen in a ten-foot sea. A cabin cruiser was tied up securely to a pier in good weather when, after cocktails and dinner, a guest noted that the flag was still flying from the staff at the stern. The boat's owner explained that the staff was stuck, so the guest jumped up on the stern, grasped the staff, and heaved up on it. The staff came free and the guest went into the drink. He did not come up. When the body was recovered, an autopsy revealed that the guest had struck his head as he fell, probably knocking himself unconscious.

Most deaths from falling overboard occur because life jackets are not worn. The presently approved life jackets are rather heavy and bulky, and they are sometimes uncomfortable in hot weather; regardless of this, life jackets should be worn by or placed near non-swimmers, and small children should never be in a boat without one on.

Fire at sea is a terrifying thing, even on a large vessel. In a small boat, there is literally no place to go but overboard. In most cases, fire is caused by the leaking of fuel into the bilges, where the fuel vapors mix with air to form a highly explosive mixture. Boats are supposed to be equipped with flame arrestors on the exhaust, and with bilge ventilating systems to clear out these fumes. With reason-

Fire is a terrifying thing in a small boat and can become quickly uncontrollable, as in this fire on a 37-foot Canadian boat.

able care to ensure clean bilges and the use of the ventilator fan, an explosion need not occur. If it does, the results can be disastrous. A fuel explosion like the one off Miami Beach is not easy to forget.

The telephone call came in from a guest at the Eden Roc Hotel, reporting an explosion on a boat offshore. We were airborne in less than three minutes, and sighted the column of smoke as we passed over the coastline. Arriving on scene, small pieces of debris could be seen scattered for several hundred yards. The explosion had been shattering. A fishing boat had arrived, and I brought the big Sikorsky chopper to a hover over it. A body was floating by the stern, held up by lines tended by two men on the boat.

Too late, I thought, with a sick feeling. Only eight minutes gone, and too late. But a radio call from the assisting boat raised our hopes. The man in the water was alive but so badly burned that the rescuers were unable to lift him into the boat. The rescue basket was lowered from the helicopter into the water, and they gently eased him in. After a fast flight the basket was lifted out of the helicopter and carried into the emergency room at Mercy Hospital. As we revved up the engine and prepared to take off, the sound of his screams still lingered in my ear, and the stench of burned flesh permeated the helicopter.

How did it happen? He had started the engine without checking and ventilating the bilges. Gasoline vapor had accumulated in the bilges, and a spark from the starter or a backfire from the exhaust had ignited the explosive mixture. TNT could not have done more damage.

Sometimes it is just carelessness. In 1964, two men were trolling off Bodega Bay, California; one took a full tank of gasoline to fill up the outboard motor's tank, and returned the half-empty tank to the cabin. As he took the can back, he carelessly spilled gasoline, leaving a trail of fuel to the cabin. Shortly afterwards, he lit a cigar and threw the hot match on the deck. The spilled gasoline flared up, and the flame followed the trail into the cabin. Within seconds, the flame reached the can in the cabin, and it went off with a violent roar. All the lifesaving equipment was in the cabin. Both men jumped over fully clothed and attempted to hang on to the boat, but were soon driven off by the heat of the flames. While swimming ashore, one man became exhausted and sank from sight.

Accidents can occur in an insidious manner, with little warning. A Coast Guard rescue boat, escorting a cabin cruiser that had been having engine trouble, noticed it steering erratically. Boarding the boat, the escort found the three occupants unconscious, overcome by carbon monoxide fumes from a leaky exhaust. The victims were all revived.

The luxury yacht *Lady D.* was not so lucky. Four occupants were below deck relaxing while a hired professional skipper ran the boat. As the boat approached the dock, he yelled down below for some help in handling the lines. No one answered. He went below and found all four dead, asphyxiated by carbon monoxide. They had no warning. Two were sitting in the lounge, one was in his bunk, and the fourth was in the lavatory.

Though capsizing, falling overboard, and fire are the leading causes of death, the greatest number of boating accidents are caused by collisions. Half of all accidents are boat-to-boat crashes, while 13 percent are boats hitting objects.

As the waters become more crowded, collisions become more frequent. The seriousness is compounded by the high speeds at which many boats travel. Several tragic maimings have occurred when boats

Operating a boat under the influence of alcohol can result in collisions on the water as on the highway. Impact forces at high speed can be awesome.

towing water skiers at high speed ran among swimmers. A boat propeller, turning at high speed, is a lethal butcher tool.

In late November 1987, a high-speed boat ran through a large crowd of boaters who were at anchor and listening to a concert in Miami, Florida. A small inflatable dinghy was struck and the occupant fatally injured. The operator of the fast boat was charged under Florida's new boating homicide law, though he was sober. After conviction, he was sentenced to five years' imprisonment.

Several months later, a boat operated by a Miami man and carrying three British Navy men crashed into the entrance jetty to Miami harbor at 0500. A Coast Guard boat on patrol was flagged down by a Miami Beach policeman, who passed on a witness's report of a crash and cries for help from the south jetty. Less than an hour later, the Coast Guard boat located the wreckage, one survivor, and three bodies. The three Navy men and the local boater had been drinking in a bar on the Miami River. The local man offered to take them back to their ship in his 25-foot open fisherman, which was powered by two 200-hp outboard motors. Though the sea was calm, the wind light, and visibility good, and the boater had been warned by the sailors to slow down, the boat hit the jetty at high speed. Autopsies revealed high blood alcohol in all the bodies.

Two Florida newlyweds in a jet-drive boat crashed into a concrete pier at a speed of over 40 knots, killing the wife. Blood tests showed the husband to be legally intoxicated, and in a plea agreement, the husband pleaded guilty to manslaughter and was sentenced to six months in jail and five years of probation.

Seven people died and nineteen others were injured in three separate boating crashes in a one-month period near Beaumont, Texas, in 1987, and all the accidents involved alcohol.

The Coast Guard receives numerous demands to do something about such accidents and arrest the speeders. Many arrests are made, but the Coast Guard's forces are stretched thin. During a twenty-year period when SAR incidents have nearly doubled, Coast Guard personnel have actually decreased. On the inland lakes and rivers, where many of the speeding accidents occur, Coast Guard forces are meager and are likely to remain so. The Coast Guard has encouraged the various states to take over some of the responsibility for boating law enforcement, and many, usually the ones with heavy boating activity, have responded, especially in dealing with drunken boaters, which is a factor in well over half of the accidents. Enforcement is aimed at those operating in a reckless manner underway while drinking, and not at those who indulge at anchor.

Due to the rapid increase in boating and the prevailing high death rate at the time, the Congress in 1971 passed the Federal Boat Safety Act (FBSA/71). This established minimum safety equipment standards for boats, provided for Coast Guard standards and inspections for such manufactured gear, and established safety education programs for boaters. Partially as a result, the death rate per 100,000 boats dropped by an astonishing two-thirds over the next fifteen years.

All the education, enforcement, and coaxing in the world can do little to prevent the incidents caused by extremes of human behavior. Melvin West of Jacksonville, North Carolina, was an example. Despite warnings by the Coast Guard of the inadequacy of his boat and equipment and his lack of navigation gear, he set out for Bermuda in a 17-foot, 30-horsepower outboard boat. The distance was nearly 700 miles, and that area of the ocean is often rough in the autumn.

When he was overdue, a search was launched. Two days later, a merchant ship located him and gave him supplies after he refused to be picked up. He had no idea of his position. Three days later his family requested further search, and on the third day he was located by Coast Guard aircraft, out of fuel. He still wanted to continue but was refused further fuel, and he and the boat were taken aboard the CGC *Rockaway*. Several months later, he tried again. This time, despite extensive search efforts, he was never found.

After a number of such obviously foolhardy cases resulted in a needless use of vast SAR resources at taxpayers' expenses, the Coast Guard was granted authority to stop unsafe voyages. This power was used to turn back a man attempting to sail from San Francisco to Hawaii in a bath tub, and a man trying to sail from Maryland to Europe in a small catamaran with obviously inadequate supplies and preparation. Dozens of other likely disasters have also been halted early, but it is difficult to stop a person leaving without fanfare or advance notice. Kenneth Maffel, an odd-job laborer from Santa Cruz, California, did just that. He attempted to sail from South Florida to the Bahamas in a small inflatable raft. His formal preparations consisted of a couple of informal classes on sailing and the study of maps and wind and current patterns at a local library before leaving. "I thought I could zig-zag back and forth to get there," he said. When he was picked up by the big supertanker, *Rich Duchess*, after a chance sighting off Cape Hatteras, he had drifted over 650 miles in the clutches of the Gulf Stream, and was emaciated, severely sunburned, and unable to stand.

From his hospital bed, Maffel decided that he would "be staying on land for a while." He also believed that, "Going through life, you take risks. You've got to take chances." True enough, but the odds should give you at least a reasonable chance of success, which wasn't the case in Maffel's odyssey!

While the Coast Guard's authority to prevent obviously ill-considered voyages is reasonably clear, there are many cases where risks are involved that are apparent to the voyager, but do not warrant Coast Guard intervention or the restriction of a sailor's freedom.

A 30-foot sailboat was sighted drifting in the Pacific by the Japanese freighter *Kiyo Maru*. The lone occupant, John Kennaugh of Oakland, California, told a harrowing tale. He had attempted to sail from Seattle to Oakland but was becalmed and drifted helplessly for twenty days. Then a series of storms hit, ripping off the sails and disabling the boat. When he was sighted by the freighter, Kennaugh said that he was "completely shot physically. I just couldn't have survived another storm." He added, "That's the last trip to sea for me, period!"

In a distinct category are the ocean racers, especially the single-handed ones on long-distance races or circumnavigations. The dangers here are clearly recognized, and the participants, almost always experienced and highly skilled, are in a much better position to judge them than any regulatory agency. Years of work and hundreds of thousands of dollars are spent preparing for these events, yet casualties still occur. Those participating take risks, but they do so knowing the odds. That is a different kettle of fish from the amateur setting forth largely uninformed and unprepared, who is likely to end up requiring assistance.

Small boats do not succumb to storms and other natural phenomena as much as generally believed, but it does happen, often abetted

A 52-foot motor lifeboat tackles a breaking sea off the Columbia River near Cape Disappointment.

by human mistakes. Some of the most dangerous stretches of water are not in mid-oceans, but at the entrances to harbors and inlets where swells rolling in from the sea encounter a rapidly shoaling bottom or a fast-ebbing tidal or river current and build to massive heights before breaking violently.

Some of the most dangerous such areas in our North American waters lie along the Pacific Northwest coast, particularly off the Columbia River Bar. Over the years, this treacherous stretch of water has claimed hundreds of ships and lives. On the afternoon of 12 January 1961, with gale warnings flying, the Cape Disappointment Coast Guard Station received a report of the 38-foot *Mermaid*, disabled and drifting toward the breakers. A 36-foot heavy-duty motor lifeboat (MLB) was dispatched, but with the worsening weather and light, probably did not have the speed to reach the distressed boat in time. A faster but less seaworthy 40-foot utility boat was dispatched to try and keep the boat out of the breakers until the slower, heavier boat could arrive. A larger 52-foot motor lifeboat was also dispatched and arrived at the scene after dark. Deeming the bar too dangerous to recross, the big 52-foot lifeboat stood offshore after taking in tow the distressed boat in winds of over 60 knots and 30-foot seas. The 40-foot utility boat, unable to stay at sea, attempted to cross the bar and was capsized. The crew was picked up by the 36-foot motor lifeboat, which then made its way to the Columbia River Lightship before having to abandon ship due to damage incurred in the rescue. The disaster was quickly compounded by news that the rugged 52-foot motor lifeboat had capsized and sunk, with only one man picked up. Another 36-foot lifeboat from Point Adams took over the tow of the *Mermaid*, but the fisherman was soon hit by a series of breakers and disappeared. In that terrible night, the sea claimed two fishermen and five Coast Guardsmen, as well as three Coast Guard boats and the *Mermaid*. It was a chilling demonstration of the power of stormy seas on shoal water.

Today, the National Motor Lifeboat School at Cape Disappointment uses these same waters daily to train Coast Guard coxswains and others from many foreign nations on how to deal with such killer seas. Though equipment and techniques change, the sea remains the same constant threat.

On 16 March 1984, Coast Guard Station Cape Disappointment received a distress call from the 20-foot pleasure craft *Gambler*, reporting he was disabled with engine failure "somewhere north of the Columbia River entrance." Gale warnings were flying.

A 44-foot motor lifeboat with BM3 Gary Fisher, coxswain, was soon underway to assist. A helicopter from CGAS Astoria was launched to locate the *Gambler*. On the Columbia River Bar the MLB encountered long ocean swells. As it turned in the direction of the *Gambler*, the conditions worsened, with the swells increasing to 10–12 feet. The helo located the *Gambler* 12 miles north, and as the MLB headed towards it, the Air Station advised that an approaching cold front contained winds much stronger than forecast.

Fisher passed a towline and bridle, but the inexperienced *Gambler* crewman was unable to attach it. The towline was again passed with a "kicker hook" attached, which was attached to a ring on the king post, and the tow commenced towards the Columbia River Bar.

The weather had now deteriorated, with 60-knot winds and 14-foot seas. The MLB was making 2–3 knots good over the ground, heading into heavy seas and occasional plunging breakers. Driving rain reduced visibility to 50 yards at times. Seasickness was taking its toll on the crew.

One and a half hours after darkness the *Gambler* could no longer withstand the 18-foot plunging seas, and the towline broke. Due to the heavy weather conditions, Fisher turned down sea to bring the line aboard; *Gambler*'s king post was still attached. With nothing left on the *Gambler*'s bow on which to attach a towline, and unable to remove the *Gambler*'s crew in 18-foot seas, BM3 Fisher called for a helicopter to evacuate the two people. The helo arrived on scene at 1935 and attempted a basket hoist. The *Gambler* crewman was unable to retrieve the basket. At 2018, while attempting a subsequent basket hoist, the helo saw a large wave swamp the *Gambler* and directed the MLB to move in to recover the crew from the water. Fisher, who had maintained station 400 yards off the *Gambler*, responded immediately.

The operator of the *Gambler* was separated from his boat, apparently making no effort to swim or save himself. The crewman was clinging to the bow of the *Gambler*, now three or four feet out of the water. Under the helo's "Night Sun" searchlight, Fisher maneuvered his boat through the 18-foot seas to a position near the victim, and the rescue swimmer, SN Geoff Morris, went into the water and worked his way to the operator. They were pulled into the MLB by the other crew members. There the survivor complained of severe back pain; he was stabilized against the bulkhead while the coxswain again moved in to rescue the crewman, who was still clinging to the hulk. He let go of the hull, but appeared to make no attempt to swim. Morris again plunged into the waves to rescue the crewman. They were both pulled aboard by the crew of the MLB.

The MLB arrived off the Columbia River entrance shortly before midnight and was directed by Cape Disappointment to remain out until daylight because of breaking bar conditions. Exhausted and suffering from seasickness, the crew circled off the Columbia River Bar taking turns at the wheel and continuously monitoring the survivors in two separate compartments throughout the night. After daybreak the boat was escorted across the bar and delivered the survivors to ambulances at Cape Disappointment at 0726. They had been underway for sixteen and a half hours.

Foundering takes a regular annual toll. Though it is most often caused by rough water, it can occur in smooth seas if the boat is overloaded. The 63-foot launch *Sno Boy* was reported overdue on a fishing trip out of Kingston, Jamaica. On this small boat were fifty-five people, fifty bundles of bamboo poles, ninety-nine drums of gasoline, sixty-eight drums of water, and nineteen tons of ice! A large search finally turned up only a few pieces of debris. The boat was believed to have foundered with all hands. No bodies were ever recovered.

But even experienced yachtsmen in properly maintained and loaded boats may occasionally have to ride out severe storms or full gales offshore. The experience may be due to an inaccurate forecast, carelessness in keeping an eye on the weather, attempting to adhere to a schedule regardless of weather, or even to a conservative decision not to try a treacherous inlet in adverse conditions.

The three-man crew of the 32-foot ketch *Dibya* did not lack experience as they sailed from Morehead City, N.C., on a December morning en route to the Bahamas. One of the crew, Edward M. "Emo" Osbourne of Easthampton, N.Y., an old friend and shipmate of mine and veteran of many Bermuda races and small-boat Atlantic crossings, is a thorough and conservative sailor, and a World War II frigate captain. That they sailed with forecasts of 25–35 knot winds was partly due to the fact that they would be running before it, but also because their departure had been delayed by mis-routed airline baggage. By the following morning, however, they were 20 miles southeast of Frying Pan Shoals Light with northeast winds of 55 knots and 15–18 foot seas, which carried away their dinghy. Attempts to obtain the latest weather by VHF radio were futile as they were 60 miles offshore and well outside range of the Coast Guard VHF net. Shortly afterward, the little ketch was hit by a rogue sea and rolled 360-degrees, wiping the deck clean of gear and leaving Emo Osbourne paddling 30 yards astern. Acting quickly, Colin Fraser, the skipper, heaved him a line and hauled him to the boat. The boat was without power or lights, dragging a maze of rigging and masts, and one of the crew was injured. No distress call had been or could be sent, nor was an EPIRB on board. For the next day and a half, the exhausted men worked to clear the wreckage and tried to get up a jury rig in order to close the coast, but with little success. On Sunday night, however, they sighted the lights of a ship, alerted it with an SOS signal sent by flashlight, and were soon picked up by the 80,000-ton tanker *Exxon San Francisco*. The boat was lost. Even with the numerous SAR stations along the coast, a sailor in distress must still be within radio range in order to alert them, and *Dibya* was clearly outside that range. When sighted by rescuers, she was 100 miles east of Charleston, S.C. The *Dibya* encountered sea conditions as formidable as might have accompanied such winds in mid-ocean, and one of them proved too much for the little ketch. Though they were undoubtedly concerned about sea room, their distance off-shore precluded VHF contact with shore stations, and they were most fortunate to be sighted by a passing vessel.

This near disaster was to have an eerie repeat. Seven years later, at nearly the same date, the 33-foot *Demon of Hamble* departed Beaufort for Ft. Lauderdale on the same route taken previously by the ill-fated *Dibya*. The weather conditions were similar. The skipper, Angus Primrose, an English yacht designer, was a highly experienced sailor who had recently sailed the boat, one of his own designs, from Plymouth, England, to Newport, Rhode Island, in the single-handed transatlantic race. His crew on this leg was Dereka Dodson, a young British dentist.

The voyage was routine until the afternoon of 23 October 1980, when, at the same position that the *Dibya* had capsized, the wind rose suddenly and the seas quickly built to "monstrous size." As seas began breaking over the small vessel, Primrose told his companion that he thought the boat would capsize, and shortly afterward it did, but soon righted itself. The two launched a liferaft and abandoned the boat. Dodson was soon washed overboard, but was hauled back to the raft by Primrose. Then he was washed over by a wave and disappeared. Five days later, Dereka Dodson, who had survived on a diet of seaweed and rain water, was sighted and picked up by the submarine tender USS *Canopus*. She was in "amazingly good condition."

Not only had the *Demon of Hamble* capsized at the same spot, under conditions nearly identical to those of the *Dibya*, but Primrose was a close friend of Ed Osbourne of the *Dibya* and had designed a 40-foot sailboat for him, which had been built in France. It was named *Primevere*, the French word for primrose, in honor of its designer.

Though experienced sailors such as these occasionally encounter trouble, the fellows who venture out in foul weather in inadequate craft are too numerous to list. So are the inept navigators who, in so many cases, should never be allowed out of the harbor, but who eventually end up at the end of a Coast Guard towline or on a reef.

Occasionally, there are incidents where it is difficult to decide whether to laugh or cry. In September 1965, a yachtsman was cruising 30 miles offshore when he detected gasoline in his bilges. Wisely deciding to drain the bilges of the potentially explosive mixture, he very unwisely pulled the sea plug. Instead of the gasoline draining out, the sea roared in, and in the confusion, the startled yachtsman lost the plug, and the boat went down. He abandoned ship. Over three days later, a search craft located him, suffering badly from exhaustion and exposure. Such a blunder, reminiscent of a Laurel and Hardy comedy, was one of many such unbelievable accidents that occur each year. To call the people involved stupid is, in most cases, incorrect. A man doesn't make enough money to own a large cabin cruiser by being stupid. Perhaps a better classification is that he is ignorant in a specialized area and will not admit that his general experience doesn't extend far enough to cover it.

One alcove in the chamber of horrors needs to be set aside for a special category—the occasional oceangoing yachtsman who fouls up. Not only is there less excuse for one of these lads to get into trouble with his expensive equipment, but the cost of locating and assisting him on a wide ocean can quickly mount into five or six figures. A seagoing yacht usually represents a substantial outlay of cash, and the owner should be willing to put out a reasonable amount of time to acquire some nautical know-how to match it. The ocean is no place for "boots." Fortunately, the majority of ocean yachts are manned by splendid sailors, whose performance can be distinguished from the professionals only because they sail for pleasure rather than pay. Some owners—not sailors themselves—hire professional skippers and crew. These competent types are seldom found in our alcove off the chamber, except for exceptional circumstances of weather and equipment failure.

But there are others who sail in their well-equipped boats into a comedy of errors. It isn't funny to the SAR people or to the taxpayers. There was, for example, the big Canadian auxiliary schooner reported overdue between Nova Scotia and Bermuda. His routing was to be Bermuda, San Juan, Panama, and San Diego. For three days, twenty-five different commands were involved in the case, shipping was alerted throughout the western Atlantic, and dozens of hours of multi-engine aircraft search time were expended. On the third day, he was found peacefully at anchor in the Virgin Islands. The SAR coordinator addressed a message to him, calling his attention to the extensive and useless effort made on his behalf, and suggested he keep interested parties better notified during future changes in voyage plans.

Another yacht sailed from the West Coast to Hawaii, and when it was twenty-eight days overdue, a search was started. It had not cleared with anyone or filed a float plan before sailing, and only by chance did the Coast Guard become aware that it was overdue. It had a poor compass, no chronometer, no radio transmitter, and was using only a large-scale chart of the Pacific with which to navigate. Neither the owner nor the navigator was an experienced seaman. The latter had taken a short course in navigation before sailing but was able to work sun lines only. The third person aboard, the wife of the owner, had never been to sea. There was a very limited supply of line and canvas, and in rough weather, they were often unable to take in sails. They were eventually located, provisioned, and sent on their way to Hawaii, but it required the efforts of two ships and several large aircraft to accomplish it.

While most such cases show a lack of knowledge and preparation, other seemingly inept performances by normally competent sailors are caused by extreme fatigue and seasickness. Many offshore cruisers are manned by male-female teams, often middle-aged or retired people, and heavy weather can quickly exhaust such a two-person crew. The combination of fatigue and seasickness will impair judgment, and even the physical ability and will to take essential steps. But even larger crews in bigger boats can be beaten down by prolonged blows and breakdowns.

The 49-foot trawler-type yacht *Skivy Waver* had departed Montauk, N.Y., for Bermuda in late November 1986, but soon ran into bad weather. The crew decided to turn back, but lost one engine due to fuel contamination and were unable to make headway against the worsening storm. Soon the yacht began taking on water, and a distress call was sent out. A Falcon jet out of Elizabeth City attempted a pump drop, but the four men on the boat were unable to recover it. The men attempted to dewater the boat using hand pumps, adding to their fatigue. More pumps were dropped by an H-3 helo from Cape Cod, and the CGC *Chilula* soon arrived to take the boat in tow. Two men were taken aboard the cutter, but the other two exhausted crewmen were unable to climb the ladder to safety on the cutter. A four-man damage control team from the cutter was then put on board the boat to stay with the two men and try to save the boat. By the morning of 21 November, however, seas had increased to 40 feet and the water-logged boat was rolling 60 degrees. Deeming a boat-to-ship transfer too hazardous, the CO of the cutter called for helicopters, and CGAS Brooklyn launched two Dolphins to the position 130 miles off the New Jersey coast. Two civilians and one cutterman were lifted by the first helo, and the second hoisted the remaining three Coast Guardsmen. Though a difficult rescue in the high seas and 40-knot winds, it was much safer than a surface transfer.

Some distress incidents can be attributed simply to poor planning and carelessness. In the Caribbean, a boat carrying thirteen people was reported overdue at Santo Domingo on a trip from Curaçao. It carried only ninety-six hours of fuel for a trip estimated to take eighty-eight hours. After an unsuccessful five-day search, the vessel was presumed lost. Three days after the search was secured, a merchant vessel chanced upon a boat from the missing craft with five survivors and one body. The boat was 300 miles from the proposed track line! The search was reopened, and the other boat was located 40 miles off Jamaica. The CGC *Sebago* recovered five survivors and learned that two persons had died in the boat.

Perhaps one answer would be to revive a version of the twelfth century Code of Oléron. Under that harsh maritime code, a pilot who ran aground due to his own negligence was expected to pay all costs resulting from the error. This was reasonable enough, but if the hapless mariner lacked the financial means to make good the cost, the captain or the crew were authorized to decapitate him. There is little chance that the law will be revived; few boatmen could afford to pay the cost of a modern air/sea search, and capital punishment seems to be on its way out.

There are also the fiercely independent types who want to do it themselves and refuse all outside help. They are on the whole a most admirable breed, if the attitude is not carried to extremes. The small British sailing vessel and its sole crewman may have stepped a bit over the line of good judgment. On 18 November 1987, the Spanish SS *Pilar* came upon a dismasted sailboat. The sailor had jury-rigged some sails and refused help. When the *Moly* did not arrive at Bermuda, the case was reopened, and two days after that the sailboat was again sighted, this time by the Liberian merchant vessel *Bardu* 290 miles northeast of Bermuda. Again the lone sailor declined help. Two more weeks went by without further word, and on 6 December, Bermuda SAR authorities listed it as overdue and missing. Another two weeks went by, and on 19 December, over a month after the sailboat was first sighted, it was again located, this time by the Cypriot vessel *New Flame*, 120 miles northeast of Bermuda. Like the mythical *Flying Dutchman*, the *Moly* seemed destined to remain forever at sea. This thought may have occurred to the solo sailor, for he at last abandoned ship and went on board the *New Flame*, which deposited him back home in England.

At the other end of the spectrum are the "regulars," the repeat customers—the hypochondriacs of the sea. In every RCC, there is a card file indexed by the names of boats and vessels. Most vessels will have only one case on their card, but a small group will have from five to ten cases each listed. Some are so familiar to the cutter men that when a call comes in, no description is necessary. Many are old and weary commercial fishing boats engaged in a hard and dangerous trade off inhospitable shores. Like any old machinery, they have a high breakdown rate and frequently require help. In most cases, it is machinery, not human failure, that puts them at the end of a Coast Guard towline. But occasionally a real lulu gets loose at sea and creates a one-ship wave of distress cases. Among these menaces to navigation, the *Liki Tiki* may have achieved some kind of water-logged immortality. The Coast Guard won't forget her for a long time, but Coast Guardsmen find it hard to talk about the case without choking up a bit. The *New York Times* summed up their feelings quite well, however:

CHINCOTEAGUE, VA. Dec. 1—The LIKI TIKI, a battered schooner plagued by bad luck, ran afoul again early today.

The vessel's six passengers were plucked from a bobbing liferaft in churning seas about 60 miles northeast of this community. It was the eighth time the Coast Guard has rescued the LIKI TIKI since July 23. Tonight the craft was being towed in by a cutter.

The schooner, owned by the Woodbury, N.J., Skin Diving Club, sailed out of Atlantic City at 3:00 p.m. yesterday and passed the Coast Guard Station there, which was flying a gale warning. Pennants were standing out stiff in the wind.

Although the LIKI TIKI had already run aground five times, and had to be towed in from sea twice in a little over four months, apparently no one aboard was overly worried about the warning.

The skipper was Karl Baker, 35-years old, of Woodbury. He is in the construction business, but says he has been around boats a long time and knows all about them. Mr. Baker's first mate was Elmer Seaman, the 39-year-old Mayor of Barnegat, New Jersey.

Mayor knows things, too.

Mr. Seaman is also in the construction business, sewers mostly, and says he knows a lot about boats, too. He is usually in charge of the maps and charts when the LIKI TIKI puts to sea.

Each time the boat runs aground, the Mayor blames it on sand bars unmarked by the Coast Guard. But, according to a spokesman for the Coast Guard, 'there was definitely some navigation problem there somewhere.'

The four men aboard yesterday were Budd Wilson, 30, of Batso, New Jersey; Oakley Gunther, 52, of Beach Haven; Don Lex, 26, of Morrisville, Pennsylvania, and Steven Bottcher, 32, of Philadelphia.

They were bound for some skin diving off Florida, but as darkness fell yesterday, they were engulfed in a blinding snow storm. In seas 20 to 40 feet high, mainsail, jib, and gaff went overboard; the sea began to pour down the hatch, and everybody soon was violently seasick.

As always, when in trouble, the LIKI TIKI radioed the Coast Guard.

The charts fail again.

The Coast Guard asked where they were, but Mayor Seaman's charts had failed again. He didn't know. Before midnight, two cutters from Cape May, New Jersey, were nearby—thanks to radar—but they could do nothing until dawn. The six LIKI TIKI men passed a desperate night.

At dawn, the Coast Guardsmen tried to get a line aboard.

Finally, the six men leaped off the schooner onto a liferaft thrown over by the Coast Guard, and then a basket was lowered in a 40-knot gale from a Coast Guard helicopter from Floyd Bennett Field, Brooklyn, piloted by Lieutenant George Garbe. The sea was pitching the raft up and down, and Lieutenant Garbe held the copter in place while the basket went down six times and brought up the men.

The helicopter brought them ashore near this town and they dried out at the Russell Hotel here.

The Coast Guard is a little tired of the LIKI TIKI by now but can do little about it. There are no licenses for pleasure craft, though most states have their own registration systems; there are no mandatory inspections, though the Coast Guard may inspect at its discretion, and there are no mandatory tests of competence. Unless the skipper of the boat breaks a law, no one aboard can be penalized. The Coast Guard simply must by law go on rescuing it forever.

The Coast Guard didn't, however. The following day, the *Liki Tiki* died, as she had spent much of her life, at the end of a Coast Guard towline. She went down in 200 fathoms of water.

An obvious question is whether pleasure boating isn't too dangerous to be fun. Of course not, when properly conducted. In fact, with a few precautions and common-sense preparations, it is one of the safest outdoor activities.

Basically, there are five "checks" to accomplish:

1. *Check yourself.* If you are new to the water, take a course in boating and water safety. The Coast Guard Auxiliary, the U.S. Power Squadron, and the Red Cross conduct such courses free.

2. *Check your boat and equipment.* A free courtesy inspection will be made if you request it from the Coast Guard Auxiliary. The inspector can also help in determining what equipment is needed.

3. *Check your fuel.* Compute your needs and, as a minimum, carry enough fuel to expend one-third going out, one-third coming back, and hold one-third for reserve.

4. *Check the weather.* Call or listen to the Weather Bureau, not

the Coast Guard, just before sailing. If the weather is doubtful, come back another day.

5. *Check in with someone ashore.* Tell a reliable person ashore where you are going and when you will be back. If you are not back within a reasonable time, ask him to notify the Coast Guard. They already have their hands full with people who are already overdue; but if your friend calls that you are overdue, you will get full and prompt attention.

With these five basic checks completed, and a good healthy respect for the sea, boating is a safe, relaxing, and pleasurable pastime, and the recreational boatman can stay well clear of the Chamber of Horrors. It is much too crowded already.

11

Lawmen of the Seas

The Revenue Cutter Service, the predecessor of the Coast Guard, was originally created by Alexander Hamilton to enforce the customs laws of the United States and to prevent smuggling. Not for fifty years did rescue work become a significant part of the service's duties. Today, the Coast Guard is not only the world's premiere search-and-rescue organization, but it is also the nation's maritime law-enforcement arm. When the alarm sounds and crews race for their aircraft, or cutters prepare to get underway, they must be prepared to deal with either crime or distress. The 24th of April 1960 was such a day for the flight crews at the Coast Guard's busy air station at Miami, Florida.

On that overcast morning, Captain Angus Boatwright maneuvered his 38-foot charter fishing boat, the *Muriel III*, in closer to the deserted bit of rock 100 miles south of Miami. Elbow Cay, barren of all growth and marked only with a deserted lighthouse, is one of hundreds of small islands lying in the Bahama chain. Since 1959 many of these deserted islands have become rendezvous points for drug and gun smugglers, Cuban escapees, and secretive adventurers. Occasionally, Castro's operatives land there. Boatwright was skeptical as he examined the cay's desolate features and again fixed his binoculars on a boat, aground and broken on the shore of the cay. A short distance up the beach from the wrecked boat, three figures were waving.

Boatwright decided to play it safe and call the Coast Guard. You never knew who you would encounter, with the Cuban mess as unsettled as it was. He picked up the radio telephone and reported the wrecked boat to Coast Guard Radio, Miami. Then he turned his attention to the beach.

Boatwright and Hokenson, his crewman, had left their home port the day before with a charter party of four Pittsburgh area men for marlin fishing. Now, fishing had been forgotten as the *Muriel III* eased in closer to the beach. As they approached the shore, the party could clearly be seen through the glasses. Two were men, the other a pretty red-headed girl, clad in a blouse and shorts. Boatwright stopped the boat and drifted. One of the men removed his shirt, walked down to the water, and swam toward the boat. When he came alongside, Boatwright refused to deal with him. "I've already called the Coast Guard," he said.

The man in the water pleaded to be taken aboard. He and his friends had been shipwrecked three days, he said, and he wanted to place a call to his family through the marine operator. He would be glad to pay.

Boatwright was torn with indecision. He still didn't like the look of things, but to refuse aid in this isolated spot without good cause would violate a sailor's basic obligation to help persons in distress at sea. Reluctantly, the veteran fishing skipper decided to let him use the radio. With help from the others in the party, the swimmer was hauled aboard. It would have been safer had they picked up an angry rattler.

The man was William R. Sees, twenty-four, of Etowah, Florida, and he was no innocent shipwreck victim but a desperado wanted in four states. His career of crime had started a month before in San Antonio, Texas, where he had met Alvin Table, Jr., a twenty-six-year-old former bank clerk, of Bridgeton, N.J. Table had been charged with manslaughter in Ithaca, New York, as a result of a barroom shooting, but the charge had been dismissed. After meeting, the two began a career of bad-check cashing.

In San Antonio, Table met an eighteen-year-old local girl, and several days later, on the spur of the moment, they were married in Laredo, Mexico. The two desperados and the new bride left Texas immediately afterwards in a 1952 Cadillac paid for with a bad check. They then proceeded to Key West to buy a boat, with which they hoped to leave the country. The FBI was trailing them, but the three were keeping ahead of their pursuers.

On Saturday 16 April they negotiated with the owner of a 42-foot cabin cruiser, the *Honiara*, and agreed to buy it. He, however, told them to come back and finish the transaction on Monday. On Saturday, the boat disappeared.

When the three took the *Honiara*, it was no thoughtless act. They stocked and provisioned the boat for an extended trip, following a deliberate and careful plan. Barbara Table later claimed and apparently believed that the boat had been paid for.

Two days later, they ran out of gas and drifted onto the rocks at Elbow Cay. On Thursday, as the boat began to break up, they carried their supplies ashore and set up housekeeping in the abandoned lighthouse.

Table noted in his diary that it was "the fourth anniversary (week) of our marriage. We have been fishing, and caught a cold, but nothing else." The water supply was getting low, and the three were worried.

On Sunday morning, they awoke to see the *Muriel III* off the island. After a hurried consultation, Sees swam out. Tucked in his trousers was a .38-caliber revolver.

See's actions after getting aboard were suspicious. He argued with Boatwright and tried to get him to ease in to shore. He delayed putting in the radio call and stalled for time as he looked over the boat. He didn't, he said, want the Coast Guard to know about the wreck. He took Boatwright's gun off the bulkhead, ejected the cartridge, and went below. Boatwright's fears were confirmed. Here, he now knew, was trouble. As Sees started back up on deck with a pistol in his hand, Boatwright whispered to his mate, "Hand me the gun!" and as Sees came on deck, Boatwright pumped a cartridge into the chamber and tried to raise the gun. Sees was faster. Whipping up his revolver, he fired twice at point-blank range. The first shot hit the skipper in the eye, the second in the chest. As he fell, the rifle went off. Sees covered the others with his revolver, pulled the gun from under the fallen man, and threw it over the side. The other five men were ordered into the stern of the boat.

Now Table swam out. Of the two, he was now the more dangerous. "We can't let them go," he told Sees. "They know us." As the two argued whether or not they should kill everyone, the five men, though covered by Sees's pistol, pleaded with them to call for help for the dying man. The desperados finally relented, and radioed the Coast Guard, reporting that a man on the boat was injured.

At the Coast Guard Air Station at Miami, this message brought immediate action. The duty officer called me at home. Though it was a rainy, overcast day, it appeared to be a routine job. After listening to the steps that had been taken by the duty officer, I concurred with the action, adding before I hung up, "Keep me advised." No one suspected that the first local case of piracy in over 150 years was occurring just 100 miles away. The aircraft crew as they climbed in the plane did not even have side arms.

After making the call for help, Sees and Table had to get away from the island. The mate was kept aboard, but the four fishermen were ordered into the water at gun point. Before jumping in, they buoyed up Boatwright with life jackets, and Sees pushed him over. Two of the party pushed the dying man ahead of them as they swam ashore.

After the four had gone, Kent Hokenson, the mate, saw his chance. He dived overboard and began to swim for shore. The two killers let him go and made no attempt to shoot.

Table soon maneuvered the boat in close, and Sees came ashore to get Barbara Table to go with them, but she refused. After nearly a month of marriage, she at last realized her desperate situation.

"Bring her back anyway," shouted Table.

But as the tearful girl refused, he relented and called to Sees, "Leave her there. I don't want her to get shot."

Leaving the girl and the others marooned, the two men headed south in the *Muriel III* just before the Coast Guard amphibian reached the scene.

Arriving at the island, Lieutenant "Bo" Korenek landed on the water, and Lieutenant (j.g.) Ed Midgette, the copilot, with two crewmen, George Gallagher and Bill Linsley, inflated a rubber raft and rowed ashore. After being told what had happened, they advised Korenek, who broadcast the alarm.

Midgette and his men rowed back to the plane, carrying the dead man and survivors. With everyone aboard, Korenek was anxious to get off and locate the fleeing killers. *Ariadne* was changing course in

Passengers carry the body of the murdered Captain Boatwright down to a waiting rubber raft, followed by Lieutenant Ed Midgette, copilot of the rescue amphibian.

pursuit, and a destroyer and a Navy aircraft from Key West joined the chase. Though the killing had occurred in British territory, piracy had been committed, and pirates can be taken by ships of any nation. It is a crime that has no limitation of jurisdiction on the high seas. While the survivors were being rowed out, the weather had steadily worsened. Six times Korenek attempted to take off, and each time he was forced to abort as the loaded amphibian pounded heavily into the seas. Finally, on the seventh attempt, he pulled the plane into the air and set off after the fleeing men. Other planes had also been dispatched to help.

Darkness was approaching when the boat was sighted by a Navy aircraft, but the weather made it difficult to keep them in sight. As night fell and the boat entered Cuban territorial waters, the chase was called off. Korenek was ordered to proceed to Nassau and land his passengers there. The crime had been committed in British waters, and the Nassau authorities would have jurisdiction in a murder case.

As the plane flew through the stormy afternoon toward Nassau, Barbara Table sat silently in the right rear seat in the cabin. On the deck beside her was the blanket-covered body of Angus Boatwright.

Two days later, the two pirates were captured by a Cuban gunboat and taken to Havana and imprisoned. Fifty miles south of Elbow Cay they had run out of fuel and gone aground. Their reserve tank was full, but again, they hadn't known how to shift tanks!

Shortly thereafter, they were extradited to Nassau to face trial. The Bahamas government could try them for murder and robbery as well as piracy; the U. S. could only try the piracy charge.

Barbara Table was freed on 7 May 1960 by the Bahamian authorities. Her only "crime" seemed to have been one of naivete.

Sees and Table were tried in Nassau in December 1960. By a strange coincidence, several of us involved with the rescue effort on the day of the crime were to see the closing chapter.

On 16 December, we were on a search off the Bahamas when an oil line broke in one engine. After feathering the prop, we limped into Nassau. After dinner at a Nassau hotel, we learned that there was to be a night trial session. Some of the flight crew wanted to see a Crown court in session. Only after entering the court did we learn from spectators that this was the trial of Sees and Table. The jury had just returned after deliberating for an hour and a half and found both men guilty. The two prisoners, gripped tightly by policemen on either side, faced the judge, Mr. Justice Campbell, in his red robe and picturesque wig. He quickly sentenced both men to be hanged. Neither showed a flicker of emotion. We had been in the courtroom less than ten minutes. The condemned men were quickly hustled out through the waiting crowd.

The sentence was appealed to London and the appeal was denied. The hanging warrant was signed. Not since 1790 had a white man been hanged in the Bahamas. In that year, a new royal governor cleaned out the infestation of pirates by hanging over 100 of them.

A double hanging had never occurred. The last hanging in that part of the world for a crime at sea had been by the United States in 1929, when James Alderman was hanged at the Coast Guard Base at Fort Lauderdale, Florida. He had murdered a Coast Guardsman and an alcohol tax agent while resisting a rum-running arrest.

At 0700 10 May 1961, Alvin Table was led out to the gallows at Fox Hill Prison, accompanied by the warden, a chaplain, officials, and guards. He was hanged without making a statement. One hour later, the trap dropped beneath William Sees.

Not all cases are concluded with such finality, for it is difficult to establish a corpus delicti when murder occurs at sea. In many cases, there has been no inkling of foul play until chance evidence turns up. In others, though a crime is suspected, the evidence is concealed by the sea, and there may be no witnesses.

On 28 September 1960, the fishing vessel *Steelhead* broadcast a startling message, "This is Dave on the *Steelhead*. *Coho II* just shot me. This has been a good life, goodby boys!" The message was reported twice and copied by many stations, but no location was given.

The *Steelhead* was a 38-foot commercial fishing vessel owned by E. A. Davison of Oakland, California. He had departed San Francisco twenty-two days before to fish for albacore, and was alone on the boat.

The *Coho II* was a 56-foot fishing boat and had left San Pedro five days before to fish. The owner, Ted Bean, of Bakersfield was the only person aboard.

When the radio message was received, Coast Guard vessels and aircraft were dispatched, and one of the aircraft located the *Coho II* 100 miles southwest of San Francisco. He had not been seen or heard on the radio since the reported shooting. Shortly thereafter, a boarding party from the CGC *Active* went aboard the *Coho II* to search it and question Bean. They took custody of a shotgun, a 30-caliber rifle, and a 22-caliber rifle. An expended shotgun shell and a 30-caliber shell were found on the deck. The weapons had been used, but because of accumulated rust and dirt, it was impossible to determine exactly when they had been fired. Small arms are often carried by commercial fishermen for use against sharks.

Bean, when questioned by the boarding officer, denied any knowledge of the matter. He had not seen the *Steelhead* since passing some mail to him the previous day. He also said that he was hard of hearing and had his radio turned off while fishing. Some hull damage was noted on the *Coho II*, and pictures were taken. No other evidence was found. The *Active* was directed to keep the *Coho II* under surveillance.

Later that day, the fishing vessels *Rogue Ruth* and *Eastern* picked up pieces of debris 12 miles southeast of the *Coho II*'s position. It was identified as coming from the *Steelhead*. Laboratory examination of the debris indicated that the *Steelhead* had been rammed by a vessel on its port quarter with considerable force. A comparison of paint found on the wreckage with that on *Coho II* failed to connect the *Coho II* with the ramming. A later examination of the bow damage on *Coho II* showed it to be an old dent.

The following afternoon, Bean requested clearance to go into Oakland to try and clear his name. He was given permission, but was escorted by the *Active*. As they entered the main ship channel, *Coho II* was observed by the *Active* to be heading out of the channel toward Point Bonita. A boarding party was quickly put aboard, and found the vessel on autopilot at full throttle. There was no one aboard. A cup of warm tea was on the galley table, and a shoe was on the deck near the bow.

Bean had last been seen five hours before by personnel on the escort vessel. The boat had been kept under constant surveillance since that time. The weather was good and the sea was calm.

The boarding party continued checking the vessel. The boat had been cleaned up, and Bean's work clothes were in the cabin. Five bottles of gin that had been in the cabin were missing. There were no notes or any indications of suicide. An intensive sea search later failed to find Bean.

The boat was towed in and an investigation begun by Coast Guard Intelligence personnel and the FBI. Rumors abounded, connecting the *Coho II* with smuggling, narcotics, and complaints about use of aliens as crew members; all were checked out and found to be personal opinions rather than facts. The investigators could find no evidence of past difficulties between the two men. Ted Bean was a quiet person, a sparse drinker, and dedicated to his family. Past habits indicated he did not have a temper that might lead to a spontaneous act of violence. Persons interviewed stated Bean would walk away rather than get involved in an argument.

Davison was well known and active in various organizations and cooperatives aimed at helping the fishing industry. He was not a heavy drinker, but was known to be a little hot-tempered in regard to the plight of the fishermen, caused he believed by the importation of Japanese tuna.

The radio message itself was full of ambiguity. What did Davison mean when he said that "*Coho II* just shot me"? The fishing people often use the expression "shot a bearing" to describe the taking of a radio bearing with their direction finders. Earlier in the day, Bean had "shot a bearing" on the *Steelhead* in order to make the mail rendezvous. Was Davison, sinking rapidly, trying to tell the listeners that Bean had taken a bearing earlier in the day and that it could be used to help locate his position? Or did he mean that Bean had actually fired at him? However the message is interpreted, there is nothing concrete to support the conclusion as to what caused his death.

The investigators concluded that the operator of the *Coho II*, Ted Bean, lost his life due to accidentally falling overboard. From the condition of the vessel, there was every indication that all preparations for entering port had been made and the vessel was "shipshape." In addition to this, Bean had cleaned up and changed into clothing which he normally wore ashore. Prior to arrival he had contacted the fish dock to off-load his fish and also arranged for his wife to meet him there. All of his actions indicated he intended to take the *Coho II* into port and complete his business with the Coast Guard. Bean was very tired, having spent several sleepless nights, and may have fallen over the side while securing the gear. An unlaced dress shoe was found right side up on deck between the wheelhouse and anchor winch. No gear was found between the position of the shoe and the 18-inch raised bulwark. The vessel, between the time Bean was last seen and its deviation on an erratic course toward Point Bonita, was from 4 to 40 miles from the nearest point of land. During the course of the air and surface search for Bean, many sharks were observed in the area. While his wallet, money, and valuables were found in a cupboard on the *Coho II*, it was noted upon the first boarding that these items were stowed in the same place, and apparently it was Bean's practice to store them there while at sea.

Since there was no evidence that the *Coho II* had been involved in a collision with any vessel, the investigators concluded that an unknown vessel had collided with the *Steelhead*. Numerous harbor checks, leads from many sources, and records of the Coast Guard were thoroughly checked and failed to disclose any evidence leading to the identity of the vessel involved.

What happened on the *Steelhead* the morning of 28 September 1960 will probably forever remain another mystery of the sea.

Fortunately, murder constitutes only a small percentage of the crimes committed at sea, but Coast Guard helicopters sometimes assist federal and state law-enforcement officers in apprehending felons ashore.

At Miami, the owner of a hardware store was murdered in a holdup, and the killer escaped. Police got a description of the car and requested help in locating it. Only ten minutes after being launched, our helicopter had found the car on a dirt road on the edge of the Everglades, and tracks led out into the brush. We quickly manned another helicopter, and a lone state trooper climbed aboard. An ordnanceman ran out and handed me a pistol and shoulder holster, and the helicopter crewman a Tommy gun. Over the Everglades, we sighted a shack, and it was in the direction the killer had been heading. We set down 50 yards away, and the trooper jumped out and cautiously approached the house, taking advantage of the brush cover. The Coast Guard does not make arrests ashore when police are present, but a Coast Guardsman has the right to prevent felony, to make a citizen's arrest when a felony is seen, and a duty when requested to support a law officer arresting a felon. These are, of course, also the rights and duty of any citizen. There is also the right of self-defense.

As the trooper approached the shack by himself, it was evident that he might require help. I lifted the helicopter into a hover, and moved to the other side of the building. From there, my crewman covered the building with his Tommy gun, while the trooper eased along the wall, and kicked in the door. The building was empty. For two days we searched the Everglades before the killer was caught. The use of helicopters in several such cases quickly convinced civil authorities of their great usefulness, and most large city police departments now have their own.

Sometimes helicopters have their drawbacks. Lieutenant Commander Bill Sale, flying one out of San Diego with two policemen looking for an escaped killer, came to a hover over a stretch of suspicious bushland. The day was dry, and dust blew in great clouds. Nearby was a large white house. What he didn't know was that it had just been painted, and the wind was carrying the dust clouds down on it. When the helicopter left after checking out the woods, the new layer of paint had on top of it a layer of brown adobe dust. The government later settled the damages out of court.

Law enforcement is a varied job. In Southern California, several adventurers had developed a profitable business of smuggling lobsters from Baja California into the States. It was a violation of Mexican but not United States laws.

We first became aware of this activity when one of the smugglers, flying a single-engine Vultee, was overdue on a flight from lower Baja. Another smuggler, who knew the route usually flown, reported his buddy missing and offered to go along on the search flight to show us the route. After obtaining clearance from the Mexican authorities to enter their air spaces, we searched for eight hours along a 400-mile track. In the towering mountains and parched deserts, there was no sign of the missing Vultee. We started back to San Diego. When 20 miles south of our landing area, the flight engineer started the descent checkoff list. Suddenly I saw a flash of light on a distant mountain and swung over to investigate. It was the missing plane, and the flash had been a brief reflection of sunlight off the torn aluminum. He had hit only 20 feet below the top of the mountain. Had he cleared that, he would have been home free, for the flatlands stretched out ahead. Several natives had climbed the mountain and stood around the wreckage. When our helicopter arrived, the crew found the pilot's body and several hundred dead lobsters. The natives had stripped the pilot's body of all his possessions.

Our smuggler friend who had volunteered to show us the way turned out to be a man of some notoriety. He was badly wanted by the Mexicans as the leader of the lobster smugglers and for reportedly leading a Mexican jailbreak. Several months later he was dead. A Mexican plane intercepted him 200 miles south of the border and pursued him in a twisting chase. Just off the coast, the Mexican pilot closed in on him, and the prop of the chase plane sliced off the smuggler's tail. He plummeted straight down into the Pacific. The Mexican pilot limped in safely. Mexican authorities claimed that it was accidental, but local private pilots were not convinced. They knew how badly he was wanted south of the border.

Bootleggers are cousins of the smugglers, and in some parts of the southern hills are regarded by the locals as industrialists of a sort. The Coast Guard, when requested by the Alcohol Tax people, provided aircraft to hunt down illicit stills. An Alcohol Tax agent was carried as an observer. When a still was spotted, the plane radioed to the agents on the ground, who closed in and captured the still, and sometimes the operators.

On one expedition to the mountains of North Carolina, no bootleggers at all were captured. The small Coast Guard OY (a militarized version of the Cub) landed at a small airport. The agent tapped the pilot on the shoulder and said, "They're here to meet us."

Somehow, the word was already out, and a delegation of local bootleggers had gathered. The atmosphere was fairly cordial as the independent distillers subtly attempted to determine the raiders' plans.

"How do you spot the stills?" asked one Tarheel, offering the pilot a cigar.

"Oh, we've got a new radar," said the pilot, warming up to the game. "We can pick out a still at three miles."

The information caused a flurry of lifted eyebrows, agitated tobacco chewing, and whispered conversation. Actually, the pilot was lying through his teeth. The little plane carried no radar, and even if it had, it could not have detected stills in the woods and mountains. Stills can be spotted from the air if they are in a clearing, but even if they are carefully concealed or buried, the beaten trails leading to them give them away to a trained man. The only way to effectively conceal a trail is to use a different approach each time.

After prolonging the conversation long enough to be polite, the bootleggers departed. For the next few days brewing operations stopped as stills were covered over with brush and concealed as much as possible from the air. The flow of corn liquor dried to a trickle. Though many stills were found and destroyed, no operators were taken. They were hiding from that infernal "radar."

Occasionally, a moonshiner will set up in a place so inaccessible that the agents cannot get in even after the still is spotted. One such still was located deep in the Dismal Swamp of North Carolina. Try as they would, the agents couldn't get through the wilderness. Yet they were convinced that the moonshiner took a load of "white lightning" to Norfolk each week. As he had the choice of when to run it up, attempts to intercept him on the road were futile. The agents became so frustrated that they explored the possibility of bombing the still from the air. They were turned down. There was too much chance of killing someone, and bootlegging is not a capital crime. In desperation, they borrowed an inflatable rubber raft and hacked and cut their way through the swamps, crossing the water areas in the raft. At long last, they reached the still and destroyed it. They never discovered how the enterprising "swamp rat" was moving his products out with such apparent ease.

Some crimes have no lighter side to mitigate their commission. Deliberately false voice distress calls are a very serious matter. In a 1986 case in New England waters, a distress call reported a boat sinking with ten persons aboard and position uncertain. A large-scale search effort was launched. A later call claiming to be from the CGC *Spencer* reported flares. This later proved to be false and malicious. By the time the original distress call was determined to be a hoax, the search costs had risen to $77,000. Working on a number of calls and tips, Coast Guard Intelligence agents and police arrested two men. Charges against them carried maximum penalties of $525,000 and eleven years in prison. In a similar case in New Jersey, the convicted man was sentenced to five years' imprisonment and a $10,000 fine.

Sometimes the results are more serious than a mere economic loss. In 1965, a young boy in no danger on a deserted beach used a flashlight to blink out a false SOS signal. It was sighted by an airline pilot, who reported it to the Coast Guard. A Coast Guard rescue boat was dispatched into the heavy winter seas, and was capsized by the waves. Both crewmen were rescued by a helicopter that fortunately had just arrived on scene. Had it not been there, the two men would have drowned. A day later, the mother of the boy learned what he had done and brought him in to the Coast Guard. Because of his age, he was lectured and placed on probation. The results could have been much grimmer, both for the boy and the Coast Guardsmen he had so needlessly endangered.

A false SOS is a wretched thing, not only because the rescuers

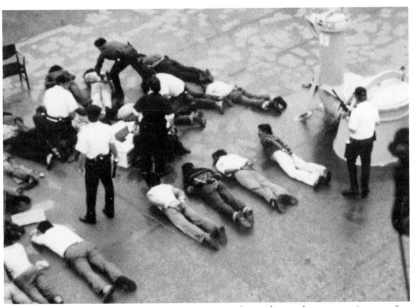

Coast Guard and FBI boarding party personnel stand guard over mutineers after storming the Liberian tanker *Ypapanti*.

cannot delay to check out the source and must risk the dangers attendant on going out in any weather, but also because it may divert help from persons really in trouble. During a recent period, an average of two false alarms a month were turned in. A few years' imprisonment isn't enough for such people, especially when life is imperiled. In a recent cruel "joke" in Oregon, a radio transmission reported a submersible unable to surface on the Columbia River. The call was later evaluated as a hoax, but while searching, the county sheriff's helicopter crashed and one of the two pilots drowned.

Armed boarding parties still deal with crime at sea. In May 1982, crew members of the Liberian tanker *Ypapanti* mutinied and took their officers hostage. After six weeks of stalemated negotiations while anchored in the Indian River, Delaware, the mutineers threatened to blow up the ship. A Coast Guard/FBI SWAT team from the cutter *Alert* stormed the ship, overpowered the crew, and took control of the ship.

In January 1988, a Mayday call was received from the 400-foot containership *Boxer Captain Cook*, reporting that the first mate had murdered the ship's captain and thrown the body overboard. The seventeen-man crew had locked themselves in the wheelhouse, and the armed mate was roaming the deck. An HU-25 Guardian jet was quickly over the ship and soon afterward CGC *Northland* and CGC *Cape York* arrived on scene. With the crew still refusing to leave the safety of the wheelhouse, a boarding was deemed necessary. A lasso was thrown from the bow of the *Cape York* and looped onto a bollard. Lieutenant (j.g.) Clay Wild and Ensign Kevin Mirise climbed aboard, but the other eight members of the boarding party could not get on board because of the pounding of the cutter against the side of the tanker. The *Cape York* backed off, and with the first mate in sight as well as the two boarding officers, directed them by radio around the containers toward the suspect. They quickly confronted, neutralized, and handcuffed him. Entering the captain's cabin, they found a great deal of blood with a trail leading to the boat deck. A large quantity of blood was found on the rail, apparently where the body was thrown over. The first officer was taken to Key West and turned over to civil authorities.

Many serious crimes occurring on the high seas are treated as federal cases because of lack of local jurisdiction. Some lesser acts, if they occur outside local jurisdiction, are not covered in the Federal Code. People having clandestine love affairs seem to have a fascination for conducting such liaisons on boats, perhaps because of the greater privacy, or freedom from local jurisdiction. There is no federal law against this form of recreation, but in SAR operations, the searchers sometime encountered it unavoidably. On several occasions an overdue husband has been located tied up safely at a dock or anchored, sipping a drink contentedly with a girl who could not be assumed to be his wife. The wife had reported him missing. The best course of action seems to be to stick to the facts and advise him to contact his wife. At the same time, the searchers are obligated to report the fact that the boat is safe. Most SAR men then quickly depart the scene.

Off the West Coast, a case proved more difficult. A boat drifted onto the rocks at ten o'clock one night and broke up. Apparently, no one had been operating the boat. We launched a helicopter with a fixed-wing aircraft overhead to drop flares for illumination. After ten minutes of searching, with the help of our helicopter searchlight we sighted a man in the water and after some difficulty, hoisted him out of the water. He was exhausted and nearly gone. Shortly thereafter, a cutter picked up a woman. She was in much better shape, one more instance of woman's greater endurance under stress. The rescue was witnessed by thousands along the shore who had been attracted by the parachute flares and low-flying aircraft. We landed at the air station, and took the man into the sick bay amid the popping of newspaper photographers' flash bulbs. In the sick bay, our victim, now recovering after a shot of brandy, said, "I want you to keep this quiet."

"Well," the hospital corpsman said, "it will be a little hard with five newspapermen outside."

"I'll tell you," he said confidentially, "that girl wasn't my wife."

"Fellow, you have problems," I said, "but we have no authority to keep facts on the rescue from the press. Besides, several thousand people were watching the pickup."

"Just a minute," he said, grabbing my arm, "there is one more reason. Her husband may find out about it."

I started toward the door. Just before I opened it, the doctor said, "John, maybe you should have left him in the water." I opened the door, and the press stood there, with their pads and pencils in hand. I would tell about the rescue. The survivors would have to field the rest.

12

The Drug War

Resuming in 1974 after the end of the Vietnam struggle, the interdiction and suppression of drug smuggling has become an increasingly important part of the Coast Guard's multi-mission load. By 1987, this task required a third of the services's operating budget, half again as much as either SAR or aids to navigation. Such work is not new to the Coast Guard, for the original Revenue Cutter Service was formed in 1790 to prevent smuggling. During the "Rum War" of the 1920s, the Coast Guard was charged with preventing importation by sea of alcohol following the enactment of Prohibition. There are similarities between the "Rum War" of that era and the present "Drug War," but there are also marked differences.

In retrospect, Prohibition was unpopular with the majority of our citizens, and how it came to pass at all is puzzling. Most adults did not deem an occasional drink as inherently evil, and many joined in a national effort to circumvent the law. The courts were often flagrant in their bias for the rum runners who were apprehended, and convictions were difficult. Fortunately, most Americans today seem to regard the widespread use of hard drugs, which reached alarming levels in the sixties and has steadily increased, as an evil that can destroy the very roots of our society, and most support efforts to suppress the traffic. Unfortunately, the efforts of the administration and Congress until recent months seem to have been more posture than action.

In the Rum War, the Coast Guard was provided with greatly increased manpower, 25 destroyers transferred from the Navy, 18 new light cutters, and over 250 new patrol boats. In the present Drug War, there has been little or no increase in personnel and an increase of only 37 new Island-class 110-foot patrol boats capable of 30-knot speeds, and a few aircraft. The 1988 budget year saw a cut of $100 million in Coast Guard operating funds, resulting in an immediate reduction of 50 percent in underway interdiction patrols. Despite this and an increasing number of SAR cases, the fight continued, albeit at a reduced tempo, and the funds were eventually restored.

Though the past five years has seen a steady reduction in the amount of marijuana seized (from 2.5 million pounds in 1984 to only 440,000 pounds in 1988), this has been accompanied by an increase in cocaine seizures, reflecting the shift of smuggling emphasis from the bulky marijuana to the more easily handled, concealed, and profitable cocaine. This was partly caused by heavy Coast Guard pressure against surface smuggling through the Caribbean choke points between islands. Marijuana required a risky ten-day passage by boat through this highly patrolled area, whereas cocaine can be run through in five hours on aircraft at less risk.

Amply funded with their swollen drug revenues, the highly organized drug rings spare no expense in fitting out smuggling craft. This includes hidden compartments, false keels, double hulls, and even containers carried beneath the vessel that can be dropped if boarded. They are also equipped with the latest electronics and detection gear to help evade the patrols.

It is no longer possible to develop an accurate profile of a smuggler. They make use of everything from trawlers to jet aircraft to luxury yachts, often with family members aboard to disguise the boat's purpose.

Even if the seizure rate rises sharply with the introduction of new weapons and tactics, huge floods of drugs will still reach the States. It has been estimated that in 1988, 18,000,000 pounds of marijuana, 300,000 pounds of cocaine, and 13,000 tons of heroin reached this country.

Despite this discouraging outlook, the enforcement effort by the Coast Guard, Customs, Drug Enforcement Administration (DEA), the other four armed forces, and several foreign governments, goes on.

In the fall of 1988, Congress designated the Department of Defense (DOD) as the lead agency in detecting and monitoring the illegal air and sea transport of drugs into the United States. Recognizing the already existing expertise of the Coast Guard in this field, the joint chiefs of staff (JCS) created two joint task forces in the Atlantic and Pacific, headed by Coast Guard admirals, to coordinate the assignment of armed forces' resources to the Coast Guard for operational use. In 1988, DOD lent, procured, or provided $360 million worth of equipment, 28,000 flight hours, and 2,000 ship days to the Drug War. This contribution is likely to increase under the new joint operating setup. Despite this infusion of resources, we must not overlook the fact that overwhelming force may not work well against covert activities, as both we and the Soviets learned in our fights against guerrillas in Vietnam and Afghanistan.

The interdiction of seabourne and aerial drug smugglers has thus been placed in the hands of the Coast Guard and other military services, obviously the most capable and experienced forces for the task. Some of the duplication was also eliminated when certain long-range maritime surveillance facilities were transferred from Customs to the Coast Guard, which has long been charged by law with high seas law enforcement and surveillance.

Interdictions are made far offshore by cutters and naval vessels (with embarked Coast Guard boarding parties). Some seizures are made over a thousand miles from U.S. waters. Another patrol line is maintained at an intermediate distance in the various "choke points," or passages between islands, through which smugglers must pass. A third defense zone lies close to our shores in coastal waters. Unlike the Rum War, where courts consistently freed smugglers caught outside the 12-mile territorial limit, cutters today may board U.S. vessels anywhere on the high seas, as well as foreign vessels, once consent is obtained from the nation of registry. Vessels without proper documentation can be declared "stateless" and seized.

An early seizure under these rules was the 325-foot Panamanian vessel *Don Emilio*, seized in October 1977 by the CGC *Sherman*

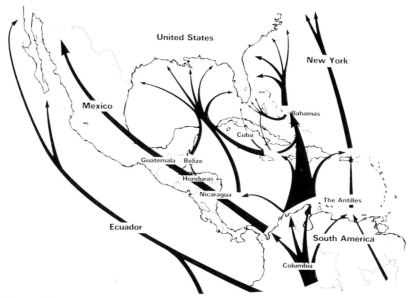

Frequently used drug-smuggling routes. These often change due to interdiction pressures.

Packages of marijuana stowed in the refrigerator of a fishing trawler.

100 miles east of the Crooked Island pass. The *Sherman* trailed her until Panama approved a boarding, then seized the ship and 160 tons of marijuana, the largest drug bust on record at that time.

Though South Florida is the hot spot for drug activity, the smugglers often shift to other areas when surveillance becomes too tight. In July 1982, the CGC *Bibb* seized the 116-foot *Grimurkamban* 270 miles southeast of Cape Cod. It was the largest capture in New England waters up to that time. A short while later, the CGC *Duane* fired on and stopped the freighter *Biscayne Freeze* 400 miles off Cape Cod with 30 tons of marijuana. Off San Clemente Island, California, the 68-foot fishing vessel *Ocean Joy* attempted to flee from the cutter *Point Divide* despite warning shots, and the crew tried to scuttle their boat. Damage-control parties from the cutter and the destroyer USS *Kinkaid* (DD 995) kept the boat afloat, and it was later towed in.

On 2 September 1987, a Coast Guard C-130 sighted a suspected smuggler 105 miles southeast of Bermuda, and the boat was then kept under surveillance for the next three days by Navy and Coast Guard aircraft. The CGC *Gallatin* was detached from a Navy task force conducting exercises and arrived on 5 September. On boarding, 400 bales of marijuana were found. The crew attempted to scuttle the vessel, but the damage was contained and the vessel towed into a U.S. port.

On 19 February 1987, Coast Guard boarding teams from the CGC *Jarvis* and USS *Ouellet* seized the M/V *Christina M.* 700 miles southeast of Hawaii with 24,000 pounds of contraband drugs. In December, a Coast Guard boarding team from the USS *W.S. Sims* seized a 70-foot fishing vessel off the coast of Colombia. Since the boat had no documentation, it was declared stateless and seized under U.S. laws. That same month, the CGC *Cape George* seized the 89-foot yacht *Stella 1* off Tinian in the Mariana Islands.

On 1 July 1988, a long-range reconnaissance aircraft sighted a suspicious 180-foot freighter, flying no flag, 600 miles off the California coast, and apparently heading for the Puget Sound area. It was intercepted by the high-speed CGC *Boutwell* and determined to be Panamanian. After the Panamanian government gave its consent for boarding, the converted oil rig supply ship refused to stop. The *Boutwell* fired 60 rounds of machine-gun projectiles into the ship's rudder and engine room, but only after the cutter swung a five-inch cannon on the smuggler did it heave to. A boarding party arrested the crew of 18 men (of 6 nationalities) after finding 72 tons of pot in 8,000 sealed bales. The loaded vessel was towed into Seattle on July 6th. With a street value of $280 million, it was the largest drug bust ever made on the West Coast. From this small sampling of cases, it is clear that the Drug War is taking place along all our coasts, as well as far out on our ocean approaches, and is one of changing tactics and initiatives. Unfortunately, much of the initiative and choice of routes and landing sites is in the hands of the smugglers.

Because of enforcement pressures in the Caribbean, smugglers have increasingly flown drugs up the west coast of Mexico, where they land and offload, moving the drugs into the U.S. through the porous southwestern land border, patrolled by an overstretched Border Patrol and Custom Service. The drug cartels have also begun routing drugs in seemingly innocent commercial cargo shipments to Europe, whence it is transported, concealed in European cargoes that are under less scrutiny, to the United States. One of the most hardest-to-detect ruses is the shipment of small amounts of cocaine in large cargo containers, concealed among legitimate merchandise. Due to the huge volume of such trade goods, it is estimated that only 1 percent can be given a careful examination. Recent seizures involved cocaine cleverly concealed within the boards of a large lumber shipment, in candy bars, and in canned and frozen foods.

The inspection of such commercial cargoes and protection of our land borders is best done by the Customs Service, aided by the National Guard and law-enforcement agencies. Despite this urgent problem, Customs has devoted much of its effort in recent years trying to develop a long-range air and maritime capability, duplicating already existing capabilities of the far more experienced Coast Guard and other military services. Fortunately, recent actions by the Congress and administration have resolved some of these duplications, and the appointment of an overall drug coordinator in the new administration hopefully will lead to each of the agencies performing in the areas in which they are most qualified.

Other smugglers fly over Cuban air space and drop drug loads to fast boats lying in Cuban territorial waters where U.S. enforcement units cannot go. Still other aerial drops are made to fast boats lying in Bahamian waters, only a short high-speed run into the U.S. To better detect and track these small, fast boats, additional aerostat radars tethered on balloons and with ranges of over 150 miles are being

Crewmen of a seized drug vessel are handcuffed and chained while awaiting transfer to a Coast Guard cutter.

deployed to afford more intelligence information and earlier detection of the smugglers. Despite such high technology, much of the work load is still on the hard-working cutters. Due to the concealment methods now in use, and the shift of drug loads to aircraft, only 200 shipboard seizures are made during the 9,000 yearly boardings. Yet such boardings are essential.

Among the overworked cutters, a "busy bee" award should be given the small CGC *Lipon* that in December 1983 seized a Panamanian craft with marijuana in a concealed compartment. En route in with its prize, the *Lipon* boarded and seized a 60-foot U.S. shrimper with 365 bales of contraband. Continuing toward Guantánamo Bay, the cutter apprehended a stateless vessel with drugs in its cargo hold. Underway again with its growing convoy, the *Lipon* seized a U.S. lobster boat and its six-man crew carrying 40 tons of marijuana and arrested 25 people. Had she been operating under the prize laws of a long-ago era, and had the cargo been sellable at street prices, the entire crew of the cutter could have retired as affluent men.

Boarding and rescue parties from the cutter *Steadfast* work to save the yacht *Corabia II* from foundering. A sea intake hose was found cut when the boat was boarded, with dozens of marijuana bales adrift.

Not all seizures go so smoothly, however. The CGC *Dauntless* had to use machine-gun fire to stop the British vessel *Camray* in the Yucatan Channel off Mexico. After the smuggler failed to heed warning shots and made a direct run at the cutter, the *Dauntless* fired 50 rounds of machine-gun fire into the hull and brought it to a stop. The vessel and 23 tons of marijuana were seized and the crew arrested. Several months later the CGC *Citrus* intercepted the Panamanian freighter *Pacific Star* 825 miles southwest of Los Angeles. After ramming the cutter, the drug crew set their vessel on fire and began scuttling her. Four hundred packages of contraband floated to the surface as the ship sank. The crew were picked up and arrested. In April 1986 the CGC *Cape Fox* approached the vessel *Profiteer*, but the two crew members jumped overboard leaving the vessel cruising at 14 knots. The CGC *Sea Hawk*, a fast surface-effect ship, recovered the two men and gave chase. Nine hours later it caught the runaway 60 miles west of Dry Tortugas. While maneuvering to board the still-racing smuggler, the *Sea Hawk* was rammed, but suffered only minor damage. The *Profiteer* sank. The floating marijuana and the crew were turned over to the Customs Service in Key West.

In another incident, an alert cutter captain noted that a yacht being boarded carried an excessive number of water jugs. Fortunately, the captain was a former chemistry instructor at the Academy and was suspicious. Some of the water was poured into a container and boiled down, leaving only a white residue of cocaine, which had been dissolved in the water.

As the profits on drugs increase, as do the sentences handed out to convicted drug runners, the action becomes grimmer. On 31 March 1988, an aircraft landed on the runway at Spanish Cay, Bahamas, dumped packs of drugs on the runway, and immediately took off. Crews from two fast boats began recovering the contraband, but fled when law-enforcement teams were spotted closing in. An OPBAT* plane chased one boat, while a Coast Guard helo chased the second. When the first boat began jettisoning its cargo, a Customs helicopter opened fire on it, wounding one crewman and causing the drug boat to capsize. The Coast Guard helo then landed on the water, recovered some of the contraband, and seven drug runners, who were arrested. Over 1,200 pounds of cocaine were recovered.

Resistance is not the norm at sea due largely to the overwhelming firepower backing up the boarding parties from Navy and Coast Guard ships. On one seizure by a Navy cruiser off the Bahamas, the drug runners waited on their vessel with hands overhead, and advised the boarding team, "All we have is marajuana!" On another boarding, the smugglers had lined up with suitcases already packed and waited to be handcuffed. But on any boarding, there is always an element of risk until the crew has been searched and neutralized.

Then there are the mystery cases where millions in drugs are found abandoned with no clue as to the owner or operators of the boat. In April 1988, a fishing vessel found a 28-foot boat capsized 30 miles off the Texas coast. Unable to right the boat, the CGC *Point Nowell* towed it to Port Isabel, Texas. Over 2,600 pounds of marijuana were found on board. There were no clues about the operators. An even stranger find occurred on March 30th. A pleasure boat reported a 25-foot fishing boat abandoned and adrift off Key Biscayne, Florida, one

---

* OPBAT—Operation Bahamas, Caicos, and Turks. A special combined anti-drug task group consisting of DEA, Customs, Coast Guard, and Bahamas Defence Force personnel, based in the Bahamas.

of the nation's busiest boating areas. A Coast Guard boarding party found nearly 3,800 pounds of cocaine, with a street value of $250 million dollars. Again, there was no clue as to the operator or his fate.

The U.S. Navy has played an increasing role in a support capacity. On 23 November 1982, the cruiser USS *Mississippi* (CGN 41), carrying a Coast Guard law-enforcement team, became the first Navy ship to engage in an actual seizure of a boat, which carried 30 tons of marijuana. Since that time such seizures have become routine, though the actual boardings and arrests are made by Coast Guard boarding parties attached to the Navy ships. The USS *McCloy* (FF 1038) has had an eventful career in the Drug War. In 1986, operating under Coast Guard operational control, the frigate attempted to board the vessel *Rose Marie* off South America. When the drug runner refused to heave to, the commandant authorized the use of disabling fire, and the fleeing vessel was stopped by gunfire. One smuggler was seriously injured and four bales of marijuana taken as evidence after the crew was arrested. The following year, the *McCloy* attempted to seize the Bahamian lobster boat *Orion I* some 200 miles southwest of Cuba. As the frigate approached, the *Orion I* rammed the warship twice, but after several answering bursts of machine-gun fire, heaved to and surrendered. Two hundred bales of marijuana were discovered.

Making initial contact on vessels transiting a patrol area is a routine maritime surveillance problem in which the Coast Guard and Navy have vast experience. While even marijuana is now routinely carried concealed, cocaine can be so well hidden that a vessel sometimes must be taken apart to locate it.

It is not surprising, therefore, to see a decrease in marijuana traffic and seizures and an increase in cocaine, which is more profitable and easier to conceal and transport. This has resulted in a doubling of the street price of marijuana in a two-year period, while cocaine has become more plentiful and cheaper.

The biggest cocaine bust in history was made in May 1987 when a Coast Guard Auxiliary civilian volunteer, searching for a missing diver off the northwest coast of St. Croix, spotted a boat anchored in a deserted cove. The Auxiliarist approached and offered help, but the skipper of the anchored boat appeared very jittery and said he was having injector problems—obviously impossible with a gasoline en-

An E-2C Hawkeye early-warning radar aircraft. Designed for carrier use, some have been transferred from the Navy to the Coast Guard for use in drug interdiction.

gine! The suspicious Auxiliarist reported the situation to an H-65 helicopter that was also searching for the missing diver, and the alert was passed on. Soon a C-130 aircraft arrived and then the 110-foot patrol boat *Ocracoke*. A boarding party from *Ocracoke*, noting that a fuel tank had been tampered with, found the first cocaine inside. After taking out interior bulkheads and panels, a total of 3,771 pounds of pure cocaine was offloaded, leaving the boat floating a foot higher in the water. The cocaine had an estimated street value of $250,000,000. The crew of five Colombians were arrested and jailed.

Air shipments are harder to intercept than those on the surface. The Coast Guard is now placing in service state-of-the-art equipment such as E2C airborne early-warning aircraft, able to detect other aircraft at ranges over 150 miles; the new HU-25C Nighthawk jets, equipped with night-fighter radar and forward-looking infrared sensors; and more aerostat radars. The Nighthawk interceptors can be vectored to the target by the E2Cs and shore radars and lock on until the smuggler is forced to land, where he can be seized by helicopter-equipped Customs or DEA enforcement teams. Long-range and high-endurance C-130 Hercules aircraft are also being equipped with early-warning detection gear to augment the shorter-range E2C Hawkeyes.

A typical intercept occurred on 7 December 1987. An interceptor picked up a northbound aircraft over Cay Sal Banks in the Bahamas

Interceptor version of the Falcon jet. After a target is picked up by an E-2C, the Nighthawk is vectored in to identify and stay with the suspect aircraft.

and was soon joined by a Bahamas-based Coast Guard helicopter. The drug aircraft dropped bales in the water near Berry Island and then landed on Little Darby Cay. A U.S. Army helicopter, with law-enforcement people embarked, landed behind it, seized the aircraft, and arrested the three crew members. The Coast Guard helicopter retrieved 1,520 pounds of marijuana that had been dropped.

Two weeks later a Coast Guard interceptor latched onto another suspicious aircraft over Great Inagua Island in the Bahamas and was joined soon after by Coast Guard and DEA helicopters. Over Great Sale Cay, the drug craft jettisoned several duffle bags, then headed southeast and ditched near Treasure Cay. Five hundred and fifty pounds of cocaine were recovered, but the aircraft was destroyed and the two crewmen swam ashore and escaped.

So lucrative is the drug trade that smugglers will sometimes buy an aircraft or boat for use on one trip and abandon it on landing. A number of such aircraft have been found on remote Florida roads and landing strips. One did not quite complete a drug run. Attempting to land at night on a hidden strip lit only by the lights of a jeep manned by an accomplice, the drug pilot misjudged his altitude on approach and landed on the jeep! The wrecked jeep, damaged aircraft, and a body were found by law-enforcement personnel.

The battle continues between the amply funded drug smugglers and the inadequately funded drug hunters. In 1987, Coast Guard

A helicopter prepares to take off from a cutter for a night search in the Caribbean.

units interdicted and seized 1.4 million pounds of marijuana, 14,000 pounds of cocaine, and assisted in the seizure of another 11,000 pounds. U.S. Navy units with embarked Coast Guard boarding teams seized 20 vessels during the year, while sightings by long-range Navy patrol planes led to four captures. No one believes that interdiction alone can win the Drug War. Admiral Paul Yost, Commandant of the Coast Guard, made the following frank appraisal:

"In marijuana, I give us about a B+ in our interdiction efforts. We've done a super job the last year, and we ought to take a pat on the back for it. I give us, in cocaine, about a D, and that's not because we're not trying; it's because we don't have the assets to do it."

With the large number of drug runners attracted by huge profits, and able to afford highly sophisticated equipment, it is no surprise that most drug shipments get through. While there is no reliable way to determine the actual volume, Vice Admiral Howard Thorsen, the tough and able former commander of the interdiction forces in the Southeastern U.S. approaches, and now the Atlantic Commander of

the forces fighting smuggling, estimates that between 20 and 50 percent of the more easily spotted marijuana is being seized, but will
not even guess the percentage of cocaine discovered, which he says
"must be very small." Some knowledgeable estimates are as low as 4
percent.

The long-term solution, in the opinion of experts, involves not
just apprehension and punishment of the smugglers and pushers, but
education, treatment, and if necessary, even punishment of the users.
The problem is a major national one requiring a broad consensus
and support of the people. Until that is accomplished, the Drug War
will continue, and we are only holding the line, not winning.

13
The Caribbean Connection

The Drug War is only the latest in a march of events that has required heavy Coast Guard efforts in the Caribbean for over a quarter of a century. Long before the flood of drugs from the south gained momentum, many refugees had been leaving Cuba by sea, usually covertly, and many had to be rescued. This stream of refugees at times reached "flood stage" and finally, in 1980, the proportions of an historic exodus.

The first great rush of refugees came with the new year of 1959 when the Cuban dictator, Batista, abdicated and fled the island. This wave consisted of government and army officials fleeing ahead of Castro's advancing forces. It was a busy day. A boatload of soldiers was picked up off the Keys, armed to the teeth. They were disarmed and towed in. At Miami and Key West, planes loaded with escapees dropped out of the sky. A plane intentionally ditched in the shallow waters off Key Largo, and two of its occupants were picked up by helicopter; two others escaped in the mangrove thickets to hide from the searching helicopters and Immigration officials. At Key West, where several Cuban planes sat on the ramp, one escaping official opened a suitcase packed with ten- and twenty-dollar bills. There was no law against such importation and he was passed through. These

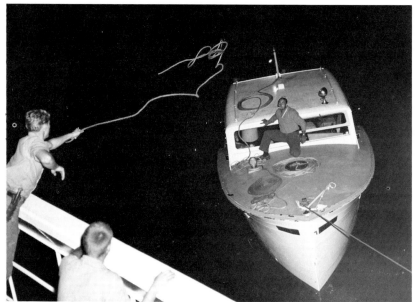

A cutter prepares to tow a Cuban refugee boat in the Florida Straits.

were mostly hot political refugees, men who would have been quickly executed by Castro had they been caught.

As time passed and disillusionment built up in Cuba, the middle- and upper-class citizens began escaping. Some came on commercial airliners, signing away all property rights to get exit visas. Others, doubtful of their ability to get a visa, escaped in boats and came across the 100 miles of water. At first, the boats were fairly substantial. Later, as the better boats were used up, the desperate escapees came across on anything that floated, even inner tubes and poor copies of rafts. Often, a merchant vessel would sight a boat full of refugees drifting helplessly and would radio the Coast Guard. They would then be picked up by a cutter. By 1965, a total of 7,546 Cubans had arrived in Florida in 806 small boats.

For a while, diplomatic relations were maintained with Castro. On 8 February 1960, Castro's private DC-3 was sent to Miami to have work done on its engines. It never arrived. A large search effort was launched. On the second night, I was searching some hundred miles east of Key West when a lookout sighted a flashing light far off to the east. We immediately turned toward it, sure that it was the lost plane crew. Dropping a flare, we discovered instead a boat with seventeen refugees fleeing Cuba. This was reported to a Coast Guard cutter patrolling in the area. Our radio call was intercepted by a Cuban patrol boat, which requested the position, and said he would take them in tow. This placed both the skipper of the cutter and me in a quandary. Already, news of the executions and repression in Cuba were leaking out. There was little doubt that if these people fell into Cuban hands again they would be dealt with severely. Yet we were at peace with Cuba, maintaining diplomatic relations and some commercial intercourse with them. I shifted to a VHF tactical frequency and quickly gave the cutter the position. Only after the refugees were safely aboard the cutter did the Cubans get the position. Sometimes, communications can be very slow.

As early as 1960, Cuban gunboats were using force to deter escapees. We have no record of the escape attempts that failed or were intercepted. Undoubtedly, many escapees were killed by the gunboats, while others drifted out to sea and perished. Some made their way to the Cay Sals, a group of deserted Bahama-owned islands about 50 miles north of Cuba. So many refugees landed on these islands that Coast Guard aircraft began making daily checks of the area. When refugees were sighted, they were taken off by cutters or British frigates. Sometimes, the Coast Guard found them too late. A Coast Guard

An HH-52 helo lands to pick up refugees 70 miles southeast of Key West. Five of the refugees were rowing a crude hand-made boat and were towing a box into which were jammed three men, four women, and a boy.

plane on patrol arrived over Anguilla Cay, a British possession, and saw Cuban soldiers in a Russian-built helicopter ruthlessly kidnap and carry back to Cuba seventeen men and women who had landed there in an escape attempt. It was a flagrant violation of international law, and the world would never have been the wiser but for the arrival of the Coast Guard plane. The photographic evidence was irrefutable.

In September 1965, Castro made the dramatic announcement that any Cubans who wished to leave Cuba would be allowed to do so through the port of Camarioca on the north coast. Friends and relatives already in the States started south to pick up the refugees in anything that would float. The 200-mile round trip across the treacherous Straits of Florida can be a dangerous one in a good boat, and with the many makeshift ones being used, it was almost certain that tragedies would result. The United States government urged them to wait until suitable transportation could be provided, and the Coast Guard tried to slow the voyagers in unsafe craft without the use of actual force. However, when in October, Castro banned men of military age from leaving, desperate relatives in the States renewed their efforts to get their families out before further restrictions were imposed. The Coast Guard beefed up its forces, establishing a barrier of ships, helicopters, and aircraft just off the Cuban coast and another patrol line off the Florida Keys. The patrol forces attempted to discourage boats from entering Cuba, but stood by to help them if they continued in spite of the warning.

Hundreds of people were rescued from sinking boats, and dozens of boats were towed in. In the month of October, over 2,300 persons crossed the straits. Finally, in November 1965 Castro held up further departures of refugees until safe transportation could be provided, and the evacuations by small boat ceased. Over 4,000 people had crossed in six weeks. Weary Coast Guardsmen stepped down with a sigh of relief after weeks of maximum-effort operations and resumed normal area patrols. It was to be only a temporary respite. Many of the cutters were dispatched to Vietnam waters to interdict Viet Cong arms shipments, and ahead lay Mariel, one of the Western Hemisphere's great mass escapes, so that the easing of operations was more relative than significant.

One of the unusual operations in which the Coast Guard became engaged was the cordoning off of Cuba to prevent raids by anti-Castro

Cubans. These exiles were organized into a number of groups, and some operated out of the United States in clandestine raids against the Castro government, and occasionally against vessels of other nations trading with Cuba. After the 1962 missile crisis, when Russian missiles were taken out of Cuba after a U.S. promise to respect Cuba's status quo, the president directed the Coast Guard to suppress the raids by the Cuban exiles. Round-the-clock ship and aircraft patrols were set up, and the raiders were, except for occasional sneak raids, well suppressed. Outside the Coast Guard patrol area, however, violence still erupted at times.

On 13 September 1964 the SS *Thulin* reported that a burning ship had been sighted to the north of Great Inagua Island. It was soon identified by the *Thulin* as the Spanish SS *Sierra Aranzuzu*. They launched a boat to investigate and found it abandoned. It had been badly shot up by cannon and machine-gun fire.

The CGC *Reliance* and aircraft were sent to the scene. The following morning, the *Thulin* located a lifeboat with seventeen survivors and three bodies of the *Aranzuzu*'s crew. The *Thulin* started toward Great Inagua with the survivors. En route, three Cuban torpedo boats stopped them and asked that the survivors be transferred to them. The master of the *Thulin* refused and proceeded to the island, where the survivors were removed by U.S. aircraft. Later in the day, the *Reliance* arrived on the scene and prepared to board the burning vessel to fight the fire. However, a Cuban gunboat and tug had arrived and boarded before the *Reliance* could do so. As the burning vessel was en route to a Cuban port and the owners had arranged for the tug, the Cubans were allowed to take the tow in.

The *Sierra Aranzuzu* survivors reported that they had been attacked without warning the night before by a PT-type vessel. The crew was given no chance to abandon ship, but were ruthlessly machine-gunned. The attackers have never been identified. The Cubans claimed that the attack was by a Cuban exile group. The day following the attack, an exile group announced that they had sunk a Cuban vessel. Later investigation showed that the Cuban vessel claimed sunk was in an entirely different part of the world.

What was later to be known as the Cuban exodus of 1980, or simply as the Mariel exodus, began with the storming of the Peruvian Embassy in Havana by 10,000 desperate Cubans seeking asylum from Cuban Communist oppression. On 11 April, a Miami radio station

broadcast an appeal for Americans to gather with their boats at Key
West, from which point a movement was to be planned to the edge
of Cuban waters to exert moral pressure on Castro to relax emigration
policies. No further action developed due to bad weather.

Ten days later, Havana Radio announced that two small craft had
been allowed to embark refugees from the embassy and that other
small-craft owners would be allowed to enter Cuba to pick up relatives from there. That afternoon a fishing trawler, returning to Key
West with refugees, broke down and was towed in. The exodus had
begun. By the 23rd, large numbers of boats were arriving with hundreds
of refugees. In an urgent marine broadcast the Coast Guard warned
that the transport of aliens into the U.S. was illegal and that violators
faced arrest and seizure of their vessels. Still, the tempo of the evacuation—mainly through the port of Mariel—increased, and the Coast
Guard ordered more cutters and aircraft into the area to respond to
distress calls from the often ill-equipped small boats. Within days,
boats on trailers lined up 50 to 100 deep awaiting launching at Key
West for the 200-mile ocean run to Cuba and return. Many boat
operators had little or no experience in open waters, nor were they
remotely prepared for heavy weather. The more thoughtful ones did
sail in groups of ten–twenty boats for mutual support; nevertheless,
the Coast Guard was soon towing disabled boats around the clock.
On 27 April, an unforecast cold front passed through the area bringing gale-force winds. In just a five-minute period, the Coast Guard
received twenty-two Mayday calls from boats in serious distress! The
action was so hectic that accurate records are still not available; there
wasn't time. The CGC *Ingham* had five boats in tow at one time,
with fourteen persons on board the cutter from four other swamped
boats that had been left adrift. The CGC *Diligence* had six craft in
tow, was escorting two others, and had thirteen people aboard from
still another abandoned vessel.

As soon as the storm abated, the operation was again in full swing.
Hundreds of speculators with boats joined in, attracted by the reputed
price of $1,000 a head for transporting refugees. The Cuban govern-
ment reported more than 1,700 vessels were backed up in Mariel
awaiting the processing of emigrants by the authorities.

Acutely aware of the potential for a catastrophe should a major
storm hit the now huge fleet of unprepared small boats, Rear Admiral
Benedict Stabile, Commander Seventh Coast Guard District, ap-

pealed to the Cubans to provide him with the names of vessels and loadings so that some accountability could be maintained. When the Cubans showed little cooperation, the Joint Chiefs of Staff ordered the USS *Boulder* (LST 1190), which had a complement of small boats, the helicopter-equipped USS *Saipan* (LHA 2), and Navy aircraft from Jacksonville to support the Coast Guard forces already engaged. A task force organization was set up with commander, Coast Guard Group, Key West, responsible for the area within 30 miles of shore; in the *Saipan*, Rear Admiral Warren Hamm, USN, controlled operations in mid-strait, and the commanding officer, CGC *Dallas*, with his force of 4–6 cutters and embarked helicopters, covered the waters off Cuba. All were under the tactical command of Admiral Stabile.

On 5 May, the CGC *Cape Gull* intercepted the tug *Dr. Daniels*, which had been chartered by Cuban-Americans for $70,000 to transport relatives from Cuba. The oceangoing tug had 449 persons on board, but safety gear for only one-third that number. The vessel was seized and impounded by the Coast Guard.

The CGC *Ingham* then learned from a passing yacht that the 150-foot vessel *America* was loading 900 refugees in Mariel, obviously a gross overload. Stabile forcefully brought this to the attention of the Cuban authorities, reminding them of their responsibilities under the treaty for Safety of Life at Sea (SOLAS) to prevent people leaving Cuba in unsafe and crowded vessels.

The Cuban government did little. Between 1,500 and 2,000 U.S. boats were now in Mariel, and up to 100,000 people were awaiting transport there. On 14 May, President Carter implemented a program to bring an end to the chaotic evacuation and provide a safer method of transporting refugees. Vessels with gross safety violations were detained or seized. Others that had transported large numbers of illegal aliens without visas were also detained. Beginning on 10 May, the seizure of a dozen vessels a day was common. An urgent Coast Guard Broadcast to Mariners advised all U.S. vessels to return to U.S. ports, adding that any vessel found in the refugee trade and not under charter to the U.S. government would be seized. Still the traffic continued, though the numbers declined. By 17 May, ninety-one vessels were sighted northbound, but only six southbound, four of which were intercepted.

On that day occurred the *Olo Yumi* tragedy. It is best described by

Commander Alan F. Miller, commanding officer of CGC *Coura-geous* (WMEC 622), whose ship rescued most of the survivors:

It started out with a possible medical evacuation. We launched our helicopter, based on a report of a serious head injury to a passenger on board one of the refugee vessels northbound. We had the ship's helicopter run out on the bearing reported, but the pilot couldn't find the vessel. He was flying a routine reconnaissance of northbound vessels as he came back to the *Courageous*. Then he suddenly said, "Just a minute. I want to take a look at something in the water over here. I'll get right back to you." And the next report was, "There are people in the water; there's a partially submerged boat; I'm going down to assist." Descending, his next report was, "I need assistance. There are many people in the water. I'm going to hoist as many as I can." The helo took eleven. By then, we had already changed course and increased to maximum speed. We were about 2–3 miles away. We passed the situation information to the USCGC *Vigorous* (WMEC 627), which had been working earlier with us, that we needed assistance when we got on the scene.

It was a terrible sight. The bow of the *Olo Yumi* could still be seen; there were people and debris everywhere. There was screaming, shouting, crying—pandemonium. We launched our boats, asked the Coast Guard Group, Key West, to provide aircraft, and alerted the USCGC *Dallas* and the USS *Saipan* (LHA 2). From there, it was just a matter of picking up survivors and bodies, then searching for those still missing. Of the fifty-two who had been on board, thirty-eight were picked up by the cutters, small boats, and the *Courageous* helicopter. We also maneuvered the ship and put the cargo nets—the swimmers' nets—over the side. We put swimmers into the water and assisted people in climbing up the nets. Ten bodies were recovered; four remained unaccounted for.

The *Olo Yumi*'s problem began when the boat lost one of its two engines and had some steering problems. There were 4–5-foot seas running, and it got a little bit in the trough. This was approximately a 35–40-foot boat, and when people pressed aft to see what was happening, they overloaded it in the stern area. The transom went under the water, and from there they took on water and capsized. Most likely, the four missing people were trampled on, knocked overboard unconscious, or left in the boat when it sank. Many of the people that we picked up had lacerations to their arms and legs to indicate the shoving, pushing, and panic that ensued. We saw a lot of debris and gasoline in the water. A lot of people were in shock after spending two or three hours in the water. There were people with broken arms or collar bones that resulted from knocking into each other—shoving, pushing, everything that developed as the boat started to sink. And they either tried to stay with it or go over the side. But just that many people crowded into such a small space caused the vessel to sink. That was the most tragic thing that we saw. It was the largest rescue of its kind during the Cuban exodus.

After mid-May, conditions continued to deteriorate in Mariel and on the sea routes to Florida. Boats leaving Mariel reported a concentration-camp atmosphere, and the master of the fishing vessel *Atlantic* claimed that he was forced at gun point to take on board 354 refugees, though he had only eighty life jackets. Later the badly overloaded boat began taking on water, but was escorted to safety by the CGC *Dallas*. Another boat, after being stopped by the CGC *Point Herron*, was found to have three dead and twenty-seven suffering from

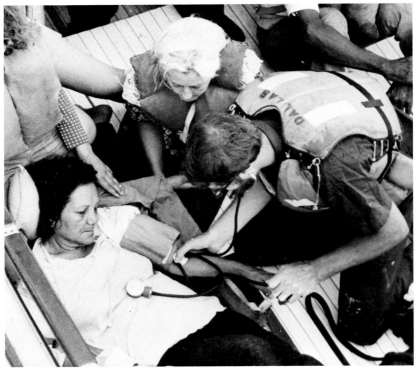

A hospital corpsman boards a refugee boat to check sick passengers.

The vessel *Red Diamond*, packed with Mariel refugees, is intercepted in heavy weather in the Florida Straits. A small boat from the cutter *Dallas* prepares to put a boarding officer on board.

carbon-monoxide poisoning; the operator and crew were above deck and unaffected. Coast Guard officers estimated that 90 percent of vessels returning from Cuba were either overloaded or filled to capacity.

On 2 June, the *Red Diamond*, a 118-foot merchant ship, sailed from Mariel with 731 refugees, including 35 infants, on board! Halfway across she requested urgent medical assistance. The CGC *Dallas* sent a hospital corpsman and a line officer, and the ship's helicopter carried a badly dehydrated mother and her three-day-old infant back to the cutter. The officer and corpsman remained on the freighter to assist another woman in labor.

On 3 June, the president authorized the Coast Guard to call up reservists, and they responded from all over the nation. Their help was sorely needed.

The following day the commodore of the Coast Guard squadron off Cuba reported that over half of all departing vessels required assistance. The Bahamian *Veronica Express*, only 38 feet long, had 222 people on board and was being towed by the cabin cruiser *Once More*, with 69 people on it! Most were removed to the safety of cutters, which then escorted both boats into port.

On 12 June, the 110-foot *God's Mercy*, chartered by a church group, arrived at Key West with 422 refugees. The vessel was seized and the crew arrested for importation of illegal aliens. By mid-June, the exodus had slowed to a trickle. More than 5,000 vessels carried 117,000 people to the United States, and Coast Guard forces and their Navy partners handled 1,300 rescue cases. Only twenty-five lives were lost despite the appalling overloading of often unseaworthy boats and the indifference of the Cuban authorities to even basic safety

A small Cuban boy is passed to another crewman after being picked up by the cutter *Dauntless*.

precautions. The Cuban exodus was the Coast Guard's largest and
most significant prolonged rescue effort since the Normandy invasion
in June 1944. Impressive though the performance was, it left an exhausted service with failing and under-maintained equipment. Its other
missions had suffered due to transfer of forces to the Cuban area, but
none were irreparable. Fortunately, the weather was mostly benign,
and this helped keep down the death rate.

The end of the operation afforded only a temporary respite. The
Drug War resumed its tempo after being relegated to the back burner
during the height of the Cuban evacuation. The following year the
United States and Haiti implemented an agreement to stop the illegal
migration of Haitians from that poverty-stricken country to the United
States.

For many years, Haitians had been infiltrating illegally into the
United States seeking jobs and economic opportunity. Word of the
Cuban Mariel exodus of 1980 quickly spread to the impoverished
villages and back country of Haiti, and thousands of Haitians were
encouraged in their belief that such sanctuary also applied to them.
In the early years after Mariel, thousands of Haitians entered the
United States, many hidden in secret compartments of some 200
Haitian freight boats engaged in trade between Port de Paix, Haiti,
and Miami. These boats made the 700-mile passage from Haiti to
Miami in four to six days over a route called the Haitian Highway,
leading past Great Inagua, up through the Exumas to Nassau, across
the Great Bahama Bank to Bimini, and then across the Gulf Stream
to the mainland. These boats generally had proper papers and were
engaged in mostly legitimate commerce, tainted, of course, by the
smuggling of emigrants. In September 1981, in the aftermath of the
Mariel exodus, the president by executive order suspended entry of
all undocumented aliens from the high seas, and the Coast Guard
was ordered to stop the traffic. In the next two and a half years, over
1,000 persons on seventy vessels were stopped and turned back, but
the traffic was still believed to be moderate. In early April 1983,
however, two boats were apprehended within two days. The first was
a 36-foot sailing vessel, carrying seventy-two Haitians; the second was
a tiny 20-foot sailboat caught off Hollywood Beach, Florida, with
twenty-nine people crammed on board! This new evidence of increased activity hastened the implementation of the Haitian Migrant
Interdiction Operation (HMIO), with greatly increased Coast Guard

forces committed. Soon the use of the easily detected freight boats for immigrant smuggling was largely discontinued, the secret compartments were torn out, and Haitian captains, fearful of legal consequences, became very cooperative in pointing out possible stowage places for aliens.

In their stead came well-organized groups offering to smuggle illegal emigrants to the States for a fee, usually $500–$1,000 per person. The boats used were often 20–40-foot sailing vessels in poor and unseaworthy condition, and nearly always badly overloaded. Passengers were expected to provide their own food and water, which many, to their sorrow, failed to do. Frequently such old boats were sold to a family group or village "consortium" at an exorbitant fee, leaving the inexperienced buyers to load, provision, and sail the boat over the 700 miles of ocean to the Florida coast. The risk to the sellers was minimal, while the buyers and voyagers faced extreme hardship and even death; the former was ever present and the latter a frequent occurrence.

After the implementation of HMIO and intensified patrols in the Windward Passage between Haiti and Cuba, both the Haitian Highway route and that along the Cuban north coast became so risky that those Haitians able to afford it began staging through Bimini, where for an additional $500–$1,500, they would be put aboard a fast boat and run into the States under cover of darkness.

As conditions worsened in Haiti, the pressure to leave increased, and more desperate Haitians were packed into unsafe vessels under conditions that would have made an eighteenth century slaver pale. The early slaver had a profit motive to bring his human cargo in alive and as healthy as possible. The modern migrant smuggler in the Haitian trade collects his money in advance, and has little motive for further concern for his clients except his conscience, a commodity not conspicuous among such entrepreneurs.

With variations, the modus operandi seems to follow a familiar pattern. Agents of the smugglers go among the villages and pass word that a boat will be leaving a spot on the beach at a certain time. Those wishing to go are told to show up with cash in hand. The money is often raised by selling the small farms, cattle, and possessions, together with a life's small savings or occasionally money sent by relatives already in the States. When the emigrants arrive at the beach with their money and rations, they are loaded on the boat after paying. If a large number have shown up, they are generally loaded aboard without regard to the density or lack of habitability. Many must stay below decks as human ballast for the entire passage; too many on deck could capsize the badly overloaded craft. In many cases, the smugglers are satisfied to hand over the boat and leave the emigrants on their own to find their way to the States via the Cuban coast and the Bahamas. At present, none of the three countries will receive the Haitians, and only the U.S. will extend even a helping hand.

At no place in the Western world are people on the water at greater risk than the Haitians trying to reach the U.S. The boats often require constant bailing to stay afloat. Many are decked over, and the people are packed below in stifling heat and filth. The boats have no safety equipment, and many have no qualified sailors on board. Most Haitians cannot swim.

Faced with such conditions, hundreds have been saved from death by the intervention of Coast Guard cutters and aircraft, though such cases are listed by the Coast Guard as law-enforcement activity and not search and rescue. In the four-year period between 1984 and 1988, a total of 15,765 illegal aliens were apprehended at sea, and 14,974 were returned to their starting point. Most were Haitians, and 97 percent of them were returned to Haiti. Only 18 percent of illegal aliens of other nationalities were returned. No Cubans suffered that fate.

A few examples from the hundreds of interdictions may afford some idea of the human suffering involved. Cutters *Ute* and *Chase* intercepted and turned back an 18-foot sailboat with eight Haitians on board. It was the fifth such intercept in three weeks. CGC *Steadfast* caught a 25-foot sailing boat with twenty-one Haitians on board. All were returned to Haiti. Three days later, a Cuban fishing craft with twenty-seven Cubans aboard was intercepted off the Florida Keys. The four crewmen, claiming to be hijacked, elected to return to Cuba, while the other twenty-three who had seized the boat were granted asylum. The CGC *Decisive* intercepted a 30-foot sailboat in the Windward Passage with sixty-nine Haitians on board, an overload indicative of the disregard of safety in the migrant traffic. All were returned to Haiti.

In January 1986, the CGC *Steadfast* boarded two 45-foot sailing vessels. The *Cherché La Vie* had 84 Haitians on board, and the *Sa-*

A boarding party from the cutter *Chase* prepares to transfer a party of Haitian refugees from their overloaded sailboat to the *Chase* for transport back to Haiti.

tela had 104. Both vessels, after their people were removed, were sunk as health and navigation hazards.

On 30 June 1987, the CGC *Spencer* (WMEC 905) stopped the 35-foot Haitian sailing vessel *Parule Peupla 7* and took aboard the fifty-six men and fourteen women for repatriation to Haiti. The vessel was destroyed as a health hazard. The following day CGC *Dauntless* found a 40-foot Haitian sailing vessel near Nassau, Bahamas, with 141 Haitians packed on board. With help from the Bahamas Defense Forces, the cutter took on board the migrants and sank the vessel. Three of the refugees, suffering from diabetic comas, were evacuated to Bahama hospitals.

The blatant disregard for safety and the severe overloading early on resulted in tragedy. On 6 July 1984 in the Windward Passage between Cuba and Haiti, a 28-foot Haitian vessel with over seventy(!) people on board was stopped by the CGC *Hamilton*. A small boat was dispatched to transfer the Haitians to the *Hamilton*. Shortly after the transfer began, people from below deck rushed topside and to the starboard side where the *Hamilton's* boat was approaching for another load. The sudden shift of weight combined with the 20-knot winds to capsize the boat, throwing nearly seventy people into the water. Among them was Chief Warrant Officer Michael Scanlon, who had boarded the sailing craft to oversee the evacuation.

Surrounded by struggling refugees, many unable to swim, Scanlon gave his life jacket to three of them. Although extreme fatigued, Scanlon waved the boat off and continued to direct the rescue of those in the water. For this act of heroism, Chief Warrant Officer Scanlon was later awarded the Coast Guard Medal. Within twenty minutes of the capsizing, sixty-three Haitians were rescued. After an intensive search by Coast Guard and Navy ships and aircraft, the remains of six Haitians were recovered, while at least four others were missing.

One of the "busy beavers" on the Caribbean beat is the 210-foot cutter *Steadfast*, home-ported at St. Petersburg, Florida. On a recent cruise, her helicopter spotted a 65-foot fishing vessel disabled and drifting 45 miles northwest of Great Inagua, Bahamas. Twenty-five minutes later, the *Steadfast* arrived at the scene and put over a boarding party, which quickly discovered that the boat was jam-packed with 339 Haitian refugees. The cutter immediately began taking people off the sinking boat and was soon joined by the Navy frigate *Hancock*, which launched two boats to help. Despite 8-foot seas and 25 knots of wind, all the Haitians were transferred without injury in an eight-hour operation, and taken by the *Steadfast* back to Port-Au-Prince, Haiti. The 339 persons were the most taken off one vessel during the Haitian interdiction operations. Leaving Haiti, the *Steadfast* picked up a 20-foot sailboat packed with forty-two Haitians, eight miles off the coast. Back to Haiti the cutter went. Three days later, the hard-working cutter arrested three people and seized a 50-foot sailboat with 1,160 pounds of cocaine. This vessel, *El Condor*, had been detected on radar by a Coast Guard radar balloon ship in the Windward Passage, and was quickly pounced on by the *Steadfast*. The three prisoners were flown to Miami, and their sailboat sank while under tow. Before the patrol ended, *Steadfast* also conducted six SAR cases, two more Haitian interdictions, sixteen boardings, and launched thirty-five helicopter sorties.

Some of the refugees get heartbreakingly close to their goal before being intercepted. On a June morning in 1986, the sixteen-year-old son of a station keeper at the Hillsboro, Florida, lighthouse sighted what appeared to be a Haitian vessel a quarter mile off the light just before sunrise. When he and his father reached the beach, they saw five of the Haitians in a wooden boat heading for the beach, using a 2×6 piece of wood and a salad bowl to row. A Coast Guard utility boat soon arrived and took the boat and a small wooden mother ship in tow. A total of ninety-six men, thirty-five women, and two children were packed into the dilapidated mother ship. All were sent back to Haiti.

An earlier group of refugees had also reached the coast of the United States, but they were not to fall into the relatively benevolent hands of the Coast Guard or Immigration Service. Instead, there was to be a grisly replay of one of the horrors of the eighteenth century slave trade, where slave-ship masters sometimes disposed of their incriminating cargo after being sighted by a man-of-war by shackling them to an anchor chain and dumping them in 2,000 fathoms of water. On 13 August 1979, two police officers on patrol sighted an unlighted boat moving toward shore near Lantana Beach, Florida. When they illuminated it with a spotlight, the crew of the boat began forcing the passengers into the water at gun point, while throwing children overboard. In the rough seas, the small children had little chance of making it to shore, over a quarter mile away. Officer David Ward and his partner heard a woman screaming.

"They were terrible screams," said Ward. "I guess she was looking for her children."

Five of the children and a young mother were drowned. Ten Haitians survived, and two others were believed to have gotten ashore and hidden themselves. The survivors told police that most of the eighteen migrants were in their teens and early twenties and were trying to get into the States to find jobs because their parents were out of work. They had taken a boat from Haiti to Freeport in the Bahamas, where they met the smugglers. After payment of $500 in advance for each passenger, they left Freeport just before midnight in a 32-foot cabin cruiser owned by John W. Ferguson, thirty-six, of Delray Beach, Florida, and operated by Jeffrey Hastings, twenty-nine, an American, and James Knowles, eighteen, a Bahamas resident. On being sighted by police before dawn, the crew apparently panicked and forced the passengers into the rough seas. Police claimed that both of the Americans had extensive records and had been engaged in migrant smuggling for some time. After their boat was found abandoned on the intracoastal waterway, all three men were arrested and charged with murder. Tom Walker, a Florida Marine Patrol officer, commented: "It takes a tough person to force a two-year-old into high seas."

In the slave-running and piracy days of the late eighteenth century, the hard-bitten captains of warships, far removed and out of communication with their superiors, had godlike powers. With the stench of a captured slaver still in their nostrils, a summary court was often convened on the man-of-war and justice promptly meted out. To the beat of snare drums, the crew of the captured outlaw ship were hoisted one after the other and hanged on the yards. At sunset, the bodies were cut down and thrown to the sharks.

Florida's modern justice system is far more involved and slow moving. After trials for manslaughter, Hastings and Knowles were convicted and sentenced to thirty and fifteen years, respectively. Knowles was paroled in 1981 and deported to the Bahamas; Hastings is still imprisoned. Ferguson, arrested with the others, was not brought to trial due to lack of evidence. Shortly after their trials, however, he was murdered in New Jersey in what police described as a drug-trafficking slaying.

But the mere enumeration of such cases cannot begin to picture human misery too abject for most Americans to comprehend. For a week or more, dozens of people are packed into filthy and hot below-deck spaces, with less than a 3-foot square per person, and only primitive sanitary facilities for both the healthy and sick. Many boats have pregnant women well into their term making the trip in the hope that their child will be born on American soil and entitled to citizenship. In sailing vessels subject to the winds and currents, voyages are often prolonged, and water and food supplies are exhausted. Many boatloads of people are found badly dehydrated, and one load of over 100 people existed for four days on salt water and urine! Coast Guard medical personnel, seeing the wretched condition of women and children and the relatively stable condition of some of the stronger men, believe that the strongest men sometimes take water and food from the weaker females, unless they are from their own group or village, or are protected by other men.

Haiti is not a country with an accurate record system, nor does a covert smuggling activity encourage record keeping. However, on a number of voyages, the count of people picked up did not tally with the number who left Haiti. The missing may have been pushed overboard after fights or disagreements. Determining the facts is difficult, for few servicemen speak Creole, a mixture of French and native tongue that few Frenchmen can understand. Interpreters and officers from the Immigration Service are carried on vessels on the patrol, but conversation between the cutter crewmen and the Haitians is mostly by sign language. People having extensive contact say that the Haitians are docile, hard-working, and quick to obey an order when they comprehend it. Upon being stopped, most are upset to learn that they will be returned to Haiti, but are highly appreciative of any medical treatment by American doctors and hospital corpsmen, in whom the Haitians seem to have unbounded faith. Though many Haitians have never before seen a doctor, they have heard stories from others who have been picked up by cutters. Captain James C. Rahman, the senior medical officer and flight surgeon at the Miami Air Station, has been on scene at many Haitian interdictions, both at sea and on isolated islands where they have landed or been stranded.

On 11 August 1986, a medical team from the air station was alerted to proceed to the CGC *Dependable*, which had intercepted boats with 350 Haitians on board in the Old Bahama Channel. Medical supplies and food for the patients were loaded on board the CGC *Manitou* at Miami, and by late that evening the cutter was speeding south at 28 knots to intercept the *Dependable*. The medical team was transferred to the larger cutter the following morning. Captain Rahman describes the conditions:

> The scene aboard *Dependable* was overwhelming. On the flight deck a canvas had been stretched to cover most of the area. It was supported 3 feet above the deck and under it lay a continuous carpet of black bodies. The smell was indescribable. Women with small children were crowded along the starboard aircastle. On the foredeck were shackled the Haitian troublemakers and the alleged hijackers. The ship's corpsman, Mosher, had been run ragged attending to sick Haitians. Now we brought some relief. I set up the wardroom as a treatment center, and the team began treating the patients.
>
> The patients started pouring in. There were babies with diarrhea and vomiting who had lost so much body fluid that their skin wrinkled. Two women had serious uterine bleeding. One boy had a mas-

sively swollen abscessed jaw. Many women had nausea and vomiting. The mothers nursing infants had their milk drying up. The parade went on until 1830. Most serious were the infants with dehydration. We had fortunately brought plenty of Pediolyte and nursing bottles. Many IVs were given to adults. A special place on the starboard fantail had to be set aside for them. We had treated fifty-two patients. I had seen twenty-two. Considering the limited space and facilities, the language barrier, the heavy rolling of the ship, and general chaos, I was satisfied.

After supper and a brief rest, we again saw the most seriously ill and found all but two showing improvement. These two, a girl of nine and a man of eighteen, had been unable to keep down their medications and had continuing diarrhea. No interpreter was available, and the wardroom was in use. The corridor outside the sick-bay office served as the treatment station/examining room. The man stood up, leaning against the bulkhead while the IV was started. He then sat on the deck. The young girl sat on a stool while a corpsman attempted to start an IV in her arm. She just held it out, but the veins were so small he failed, tearing the vein. I then tried. Bracing myself against the roll of the ship, I knelt in the passageway. A tourniquet was tightened about her upper arm. I demonstrated the "milking action" of the hand to pump up the vein. She caught on and did likewise. A pitifully tiny vein appeared in the fold of the elbow. I timed the roll of the ship and started to insert the needle but as it touched her skin she almost involuntarily twitched her arm. I shook my head and straightened her arm. When the roll paused, I slipped the needle into her skin with a quick jab. This time she held fast. The vein was entered and blood appeared at the hub. Quicker than it takes to tell, the IV tube was connected, the tourniquet removed, and the line opened. It flowed freely. I smiled at her and was answered by a weak smile. A solitary tear leaked from one of her eyes, and she took her place sitting on the floor while the fluid ran into her vein. By 2300 we were through, and when we took the needle out of her arm, she rushed to the bathroom. A very brave little girl, and her kidneys were working.

By the following afternoon, Captain Rahman and his three hospital corpsmen had evaluated 208 patients. Sixty-three were treated by the doctor, twenty-one IVs were administered, seven surgeries performed, and eighty-two medications given. The team had 231 patient encounters.

Not all the refugees are found at sea. On several occasions, large groups have been stranded on deserted and barren cays due to shipwreck or exhaustion. One such group of nearly fifty people was located by patrol aircraft on Cay Lobo, a small deserted island of dubious jurisdiction a few miles north of Cuba. After first dropping food and water from aircraft, a medical team was landed four days later by helicopter. The refugees claimed that their village had been terrorized by an amuck Haitian army unit, many people killed, and the women raped. The survivors had acquired a former ship's lifeboat capable of carrying forty people and sailed for the States. After losing their sail in a storm, they were swept into the surf of Cay Lobo where the boat capsized and was smashed. Twenty people were evacuated by H-3 helicopter to the Bahamas, and a request was made to airlift one man with a fractured gangrenous leg to the States. The request was refused by higher authority unless the doctor on scene certified that death would result in forty-eight hours without such treatment. The doctor promptly affirmed that probability, though his professional opinion was that it would be at least a week before death resulted. The patient was air-evaced.

In nearly every instance, the Haitians are taken by the cutters back to Port-Au-Prince, Haiti, and disembarked. The treaty between the U.S. and Haiti stipulates that such persons will not be punished by Haitian authorities, and thorough checks by U.S. diplomatic personnel in Haiti have uncovered no incidents of such retaliation. Those disembarked are given five dollars by the Haitian Red Cross and told to go home. There is little or no transportation outside the cities, and in any event, most refugees have sold all their earthly possessions to obtain passage money. Their lot is wretched enough without further punishment.

This immunity does not apply to those suspected of crimes. On one interdicted vessel, the three-man crew claimed to have been hijacked and pointed out eight men who they identified as the hijackers, though the other refugees vigorously shook their heads in denial on hearing the accusations. On arrival of the cutter at Port-Au-Prince with the refugees, a Haitian Army squad took custody of the alleged hijackers, loaded them like two layers of cordwood into the back of an army truck, covered all the while by several soldiers with automatic weapons. The officer in charge advised the onlookers on the cutter that they would not be bothered with these people again. One of the men in custody was a young Haitian. He had become popular with the cutter sailors, who now were apprehensive that all the accused men were being taken off to be shot. Several pleaded with the ship's captain to intervene, which he did, and the youngster was led away to another vehicle.

Only rarely does anything humorous emerge from this trail of misery, and it is usually "black humor," such as the boatload of refugees who left the western end of Haiti, only to be buffeted by storm winds for several days. When the weather cleared they sighted several imposing and handsome buildings, which in their naivete they supposed to be Miami. Putting ashore, they were apprehended. The buildings were those of the Cub Med in western Haiti.

Week after week, more unprepared Haitians risk the agony and perils of an ocean smuggling voyage, seeking escape from the grinding poverty of their country. Nearly all are intercepted and turned back, but many try again. One refugee claimed to have been carried back by seven different Coast Guard cutters. A fellow migrant said, "I would rather live in your jails than go back to Haiti and live like an animal."

The frustrations of these repeated failures (only five of the 20,000 Haitians intercepted at sea since 1981 have been brought into this country for asylum hearings) and resentment of the evident discrimination between Haitians and Hispanic refugees has cause increasing tensions. On 25 March 1989, the Coast Guard Cutter *Escape* was en route back to Haiti with 99 refugees that it had captured the previous day only three miles off Ft. Lauderdale, Florida, within sight of the "promised land." Soon after dawn, the cutter sighted another 50-foot Haitian sailboat crowded with over 250 refugees. In contrast with their usual docile behavior, these Haitians refused to leave their horribly overcrowded boat, and threatened to throw babies overboard if boarding parties were used. Additional cutters were sent, and a rope was used to disable the rudder of the refugee craft. During the 30-hour standoff, none of the Haitians had life jackets, and few could swim, and the possibility of a large loss of life should panic or resistance occur caused great concern. When the matter was resolved, the cutter *Steadfast* took the 250 resisters back to Haiti, while the *Escape* did the same with the original 99.

March 1989 has seen more Haitians interdicted at sea than any month since the operation started in 1981. The increased migration pressure and the signs of overt resistance seem to reflect the frustrations felt by many Haitians as Central American refugees pour into the U.S. Gerald Jean-Juste, director of the Haitian Refugee Center in Miami, says, "There will be more violence. Some of those on the boats are army defectors and will do just about anything to keep from going back to Haiti."

Any nation has the right to close its borders to any group, and pragmatism argues that even a wealthy country cannot accept and support an endless stream of illiterate and desperately poor people. Haitians are classified as "economic refugees," which they certainly are. Cubans, on the other hand, are labeled as "political refugees" and thus are entitled to asylum. As a matter of simple honesty, one must question the semantic distinctions between the tyranny of the Duvalier family and their successors in Haiti, and Fidel Castro in Cuba. A more realistic reason for the policy of deliberate bias may lie in the relative wealth and education of the two groups, their color, and the large and politically powerful constituency of Cubans in the United States.

Regardless of such political speculations, the Coast Guard was ordered to stop the migrant traffic and, as good soldiers, to carry out the assignment, distasteful though it was to many. As an offset, satisfaction can be felt in the number of lives saved during the operation, and in the prevention of many other deaths by the seizure and sinking of unseaworthy hulks after the passengers were removed.

Daily the cutters and planes keep up their ceaseless vigil, aided by Navy ships and planes operating in the area. Perhaps the next sighting will be a suspicious boat heading north, which will be boarded to determine if it carries either illegal aliens or dope. A lookout may spot a boat loaded with refugees; if they are Cuban, they will be taken to the U.S.; if Haitians, they will be transported back to Haiti. Suspicious aircraft or those not on a flight plan will be picked up on the powerful radar of an E2C early-warning plane and a Falcon jet vectored in to lock on and stay with it. As the planes approach the coast, helicopters will join in the pursuit, prepared to land with the suspect and search it. Off the Cuban coast, a Russian ship may be sighted and photographed by a patrol plane or vessel. The Caribbean and the southeastern approaches to the States are areas of danger and tension and action. On one mission, the job is SAR. On the next it is law enforcement. Just over the horizon, who knows? Coast Guard people are versatile.

The Changing Picture 14

The rescue of ships and men at sea is a story as long as the over 300-year U.S. history of seagoing. Though ships have been greatly altered in design over the years, rescue methods remained largely unchanged until the beginning of this century, when two events occurred that over the remaining years of the twentieth century would change rescue at sea more than in all of prior recorded history. The first was the invention and use of radio, and the other was the development of aircraft.

In too many cases, however, a distress message is not transmitted or received before the vessel or aircraft goes down. Here the ELTs or EPIRBs have proven to be lifesavers, and with the implementation of the SARSAT/COSPAS satellite system in 1982, detection has been greatly enhanced. If the false-alarm problem can be overcome, and the 406-MHz ELT/EPIRBs should afford such relief, these small emergency radio transmitters may be one of the most significant contributions in years to the safety of life at sea.

Communications between the distressed craft and the rescuers is only part of the picture. A far greater volume of communications involves command and control of the SAR forces, especially in large-scale ocean searches and in events requiring coordination between several nations or services. In addition to conventional radio and landline links, the International Maritime Satellite Organization has a maritime phone system in space that includes six geostationary satellites at altitudes of 22,300 miles, nineteen coast stations in ten countries, and 7,000 ship stations. This network provides instant and reliable weather and safety communications for the commercial and public sectors. Less than a century ago, it was very unlikely that a vessel in distress would at the moment have anyone in visual range with whom to communicate. Today a properly equipped vessel or aircraft should be able to communicate instantly with others similarly equipped over most of the world's surface. This has had a dramatic effect in reducing the death rate at sea.

Looking into the near future, we can expect continued implementation of the Global Maritime Distress and Safety System (GMDSS), a major offshoot of the 1979 Hamburg, Germany, International Convention on Maritime Search and Rescue. This agreement calls for an international effort in SAR featuring state-of-the-art communications, adequate and trained RCCs to conduct SAR operations, and international protocols for providing and conducting SAR. Fortunately, SAR is one area in which nations cooperate regardless of their political philosophies.

More sophisticated detection systems utilizing powerful radars, infrared detection, and television low-light enhancement are being developed and tested to facilitate the detection of small boats and survivors. Unfortunately, such systems are limited by the need to identify the targets, especially in areas of heavy traffic. Attempting to identify numerous small objects detected at radar ranges of 10 miles, when visual "ident range" is only a half-mile, can be quite wasteful of aircraft and ship time unless done systematically.

The eighties have seen a mass replacement of aging aircraft with new models coming off the production lines. The HU-16 and the interim C-131 were replaced by the new Falcon jets, nearly three times as fast, though with shorter legs and endurance. The proven HH-52 helicopters were replaced by the new twin-turbine HH-65 Dolphins, nearly twice as fast and with vastly more sophisticated avionics and navigation capability. In the near future, the capable but aging HH-3F helos will be replaced by the new HH-60, also twin-engined and of similar speed. The updated Hercules remains as the long-range worker.

The contrast in air-search capability over the last fifty years is startling. In June 1937, the CGC *Itasca*, at Howland Island in the Central Pacific, provided radio-beacon service to famed aviatrix Amelia Earhart and her navigator, Fred Noonan, who were attempting a round-the-world flight. Radio contact was established with the plane on the morning of 2 July, but it never arrived at the island. With few clues, the cutter began searching. There were then no long-range aircraft capable of carrying out this type of broad ocean search, and the big carrier USS *Lexington* had to be rushed to the area from San Diego, arriving many days later with her deckload of short-range tactical aircraft. No trace of the missing plane was ever found, and after two weeks the search was abandoned. Today, long-range C-130 Hercules would have been scrambled from Honolulu when trouble was first ascertained, and could have started searching within five hours, perhaps before the lost plane ditched.

Despite the high efficiency level of the SAR forces, it is still better to prevent mishaps than to try and remedy them. Over half of all serious accidents involve collisions, and the primary cause is inattention to the water ahead. Part of this is due to lack of basic safety training, but any solution will also require law enforcement, especially with those who are operating a boat recklessly or while intoxicated. The Coast Guard encourages the various states to take the lead in this, feeling that such enforcement is as much a state as a federal function. To enhance both safety education and law enforcement, many experts feel that operator licensing will inevitably be required. Education will be needed to obtain a license, while unlawful operation will result in loss of the license, as with motor vehicles. Surprisingly, in recent polls a majority of pleasure boaters seem to agree with the need, and an operator-licensing program is already being phased in in Maryland.

A problem that remains to be resolved is the funding for SAR. In 1988, the Coast Guard spent 50 percent more of its budget for law enforcement, primarily against drugs, than it did for SAR. While Coast Guard policy has for many years stated that SAR has priority among its many missions, the dollar outlay says otherwise. Public opinion is now inflamed about the drug problem and demands that steps be taken to more effectively combat it. Yet surveys of these same people show that the saving of a citizen in serious trouble at sea is more important than catching a fleeing smuggler, should the two missions conflict. Whatever the merits, money seems to be available to fight drugs, but SAR is given more lip service than real fiscal support by the administration and Congress. This seems even more surprising when we consider the proven cost effectiveness of SAR. In addition to property, last year Coast Guard forces saved a person from death every seventy-nine minutes, and someone was assisted from a position of peril every four minutes! This can be translated into quantitative economic terms using the well-established legal concept of "the expected life earnings of John Doe," in which expected life earnings after the threatening event are computed. Using in this case a young adult with thirty years of working life remaining, and an average annual income of only $20,000, the projected future life earnings of the 6,638 people saved in 1987 total $3.98 billion dollars. Combining this income preservation with property actually saved shows a preservation of $4.977 billion in national assets in 1987 by an expenditure for SAR of only $409 million. The benefit-to-cost ratio is a resounding 12:1.

Law enforcement does not necessarily have to be sacrificed for SAR, or vice versa. It has been well established that in an emergency-response organization, some jobs can be handled during the waits between more urgent calls, thus reducing nonproductive standby time. This ability to respond to multiple requirements has contributed largely over the years to the Coast Guard's reputation for economy and efficiency.

Many Coast Guard people fear that their long-cherished reputation of excellence in SAR may be overshadowed by their image as policemen of the sea. Whatever the future outcome, travel on and over the high seas is safer today than it has ever been. Day and night, in all weather, dedicated men and women of many nations stand their lonely watches to protect those who encounter trouble at sea or in the air. Whatever their nationality or service, they are members of an elite brotherhood with a common purpose best described by the mottoes of the U.S. Coast Guard and the former Aerospace Rescue and Recovery Service—"Always Ready"—"That Others May Live."

Index

Accamo, Joseph, AD, 138-41
Accident Bulletin, 43
Adler, 183
African Queen, 142
Active Gated Television, 93
Air Stations, Coast Guard, 13
  Argentia, 187
  Astoria, 158, 249
  Barbers Point, 69
  Bermuda, 47, 71
  Cape Cod, 160, 254
  Clearwater, 215
  Elizabeth City, 37, 52-55, 85, 86,
    98, 146, 206, 215, 254
  Kodiak, 37, 39, 96, 156, 164
  Miami, 74, 85, 109, 259
  New York (Brooklyn), 85, 131, 133,
    186, 254, 257
  Port Angeles, 113
  St. Petersburg, 85
  Salem, 16, 26, 83, 85, 129, 240
  San Diego, 104, 113, 119
  San Francisco, 92
  Sitka, 158, 160, 164
Air Traffic Control, 42, 69, 95

Air Transport Command, 133
Alderman, James, 264
Allison, Albert, Cdr., 38
Alva Cape, 221
Ambassador, 183, 185
Ambrose Lightship, 221
America, 295
American Legion, 221
American Trader, 59
Amoco Virginia, 223
Amon Carter Field, 64
Amphialds, 216
Amstelwal, 63
AMVER, 7-9, 12, 23, 39, 69, 88, 190,
    220
Andrea Doria, 220
Applan, 186
Arco Juneau, 224
Argo Merchant, 226
Argos Satellite, 96
ARRS (Aerospace Rescue and Recovery
    Service), 6-8, 38, 129, 130
Athabascan, HMCS, 216
Atlantic, 297
Auto Alarm, 7

Badger State, 217
Baetsen, Ray, Lt., 177
Baker, Carl, 256
Baker, Mark, Lt., 160
Ballantyne, Kent, Capt., 74
Balsa, 182
Bardu, 255
Baune, 222
Bay of Pigs, 35
Bean, Ted, 265
Belize, 33, 34
Belknap, USS, 220
Bellevue Hospital, 186
Bermuda Control, 48, 72
Bermuda Sky Queen, 170
Bethune, 161
Biscayne Freeze, 279
Blades, Jim, 158
Bluebird, 158
Bluehawk, 223
BOAC (British Overseas Aircraft Corporation), 16
Boatwright, Angus, 259-62
Bonitas, 182
Bottcher, Stephen, 256
Bouit, Joseph, 240
Boulder, USS, 295
Bowen, Lt., 172
Boxer Captain Cook, 272
Brant Point CG Station, 212
Braun, Airman 1C, 172
Breithaup, G. B., Lt., 158
Bush, George, President, 160

Calistra III, 234
Campbell, Justice, 264
Camray, 282
Canadian Observor, 185
Canmar Explorer II, 202
Canopus, USS, 252
Cape Disappointment CG Station, 248, 250
Capricorn, 220
Captain George, 182
Carol Deering, 219

Carswell Air Force Base, 64
Cartagena, 183, 185
Castillo Montjuich, 216
Castro, Fidel, 289-92
Cero, USS, 31
Charlotte Lykes, 210
Chatham CG Station, 212
Cherché La Vie, 302
Christina M., 279
CIRM (International Radio Medical Center), 24, 39
Claude Conway, 215
Coast Guard Auxiliary, 5, 257, 284
Cobb, Edward T., Capt., 172-77
Coffin, Gene, Cdr., 170
Coho II, 265
Columbia River Lightship, 248
Comeastarea, Coast Guard, 180
Commandant's Bulletin, 166
Corabia II, 182
Coral Sea, USS, 220
COSPAC, 94
COSPAC/SARSAT, 95
Cupples, Andy, Lt., 126
Curlew, 235
Cutters, Coast Guard, 12
  Active, 265
  Acushnet, 183, 185, 214
  Alert, 272
  Ariadne, 103
  Bering Strait, 196, 223
  Bibb, 78, 170, 279
  Blackthorn, 220
  Boutwell, 164, 165, 279
  Campbell, 134, 178
  Cape Corwin, 62
  Cape Fox, 282
  Cape George, 279
  Cape Gull, 295
  Cape York, 272
  Castle Rock, 216
  Chase, 302
  Chilula, 254
  Citrus, 282
  Cobb, 135

Cook Inlet, 46, 49, 50, 51
Coos Bay, 170, 171-77, 183, 185
Courageous, 296
Cuyahoga, 254
Dallas, 215, 216, 295, 297
Dauntless, 282, 299, 303
Dependable, 307
Diligence, 294
Duane, 279
Eastwind, 212, 220
Escape, 310
Gallatin, 279
Gentian, 225
Half Moon, 178
Hamilton, 136
Hollyhock, 197
Ingham, 182, 294, 295
Itasca, 315
Jarvis, 279
Lipon, 281
Manitou, 307
Matagorda, 187
McCulloch, 187, 212
Mellon, 164, 165
Morgenthau, 223
Northland, 272
Ocracoke, 285
Owasco, 186, 188
Point Divide, 279
Point Herron, 297
Point Newell, 283
Polar Star, 231
Ponchartrain, 170
Reliance, 293
Resolute, 39
Rockaway, 180, 185, 205, 246
Sea Hawk, 282
Sebago, 170, 255
Sherman, 226, 277
Spencer, 179, 270, 303
Steadfast, 302, 304, 310
Tampa, 75
Unimak, 212
Ute, 302
Vigilant, 226

Vigorous, 296
Wachusetts, 178
Woodrush, 164, 165
Yakutat, 178, 212

Dancing Feather, 234
Datum Marker Buoy, 81, 85
Davies, Dave, Cdr., 188
Davison, E. A., 265
Dee Jay, 162
Demon of Hamble, 251
Dibya, 250-52
Dingeman, R. W., 139
Dodson, Dereka, 251
Don Emilio, 277
Dr. Daniels, 295
Dresden, 95
Drug War, 275
Duke of Cornwall's Light Infantry, 34
Durfee, Jim, Lt., 100
Duvalier family, 311
D'Vora, 196
Dynafuel, 142, 143

Eagle, HMS, 12
Earhart, Amelia, 315
Earle, Bill, Cdr., 170
Early, Dave, 69
Eastern, 265
Eastern Airlines, 188
Ebro, 185
Eighth Air Force, 34
El Condor, 304
Elmendorf Air Force Base, 165
ELT (Emergency Location Transmitter), 69, 92-97, 234, 313
Enterprise, USS, 88
EPIRB, 93-97, 235, 313
Erickson, Frank, Capt., 131, 137, 154, 166
Escort Division Forty-Two, 116
Esso Brussels, 221
Evans, Paul, Capt., 171-77
EXCOM, 79

Exxon San Francisco, 251
Exxon Valdez, 227

Fanning Island, 38
FCC, 45
Federal Boat Safety Act, 245
Ferguson, John W., 305
Fernview, 142, 143
Filipowicz, John, Lt., 142, 143
Finmore, 185
Finn Trader, 185
Fisher, Gary, BM3, 249
Fleet Airwing Three, 88
FLIR (forward looking infra-red), 93
Flying Dragon, 215
Folsom, Darrell, Lt., 161, 162
Fort Mercer, 211, 213
Fort Lauderdale CG Station, 264
Fort Pierce CG Station, 205
Fraser, Colin, 251
Frawley, Roger, Lt., 240
Frisia, 183

Galilee, 61, 62
Gallagher, George, 262
Gambler, 248
Garbe, George, Lt., 257
GCA, 54-58
General Colocotronis, 226
Geni, 219
Gibson, 161, 162
Gibson Girl, 61, 93
Giffen, R. C., Capt., 1
Gladstein, Barry, SN, 205
Global Maritime Distress and Safety
    System, 314
Glomar Java Sea, 202
Gloucester CG Station, 197
Gods Mercy, 298
Godstad, 162
Gonzo, 96, 181
Grand Ocean, 223
Grand Zenith, 216
Green Bay, 221
Greene, Walter, 96

Grimurkamban, 279
Group Key West, 295
Grouse, USS, 224
Guillou, Bill, Lt., 33
Gulf Keys, 210
Gunther, Oakley, 256

Haitian Migrant Interdiction Opera-
    tion, 300
Hamilton, Alexander, 259
Hamm, William, RAdm., 295
Hancock, USS, 304
Hancox, Fred, LCdr., 70
Hans Hedtoft, 230
Hanson, Swede, Lt., 69
Harbel Tapper, 9
Harper, Bill, Lt., 159
Hasiguchi, M., RAdm., 1
Hastings, Jeffrey, 305
Havana Control, 34
Helga Bolton, 179, 184, 185
Hemingway, Herb, AO, 100
Hickok, Stephen, Lt., 93
Hinnant, James R., Cdr., 206
Hobson, USS, 200
Hodge, Airman, 172
Hoegh Orchid, 221
Hokenson, Kent, 260
Holcomb, John, AS3, 156, 157
Holman, Charles, Lt., 69
Homestead Air Force Base, 33, 60
Honiara, 261
Horne, Andy, Dr., 37
Hurricanes
    Charles, 205
    Juan, 202, 205
    Kate, 94

Ice Patrol, 230
International Maritime Satellite Orga-
    nization, 314
International Radio Medical Center
    (CIRM), 24
Irenes Challenge, 216
Iri, 216

JATO, 29, 38, 119, 123, 124
Jean-Juste, Gerald, 311
Jenkins, 175, 176
Jinyu Maru, 8
Johannes Kruess, 231
John F. Kennedy, USS, 220
Johnson, Phillip, 140
Jorgensen, Don, HM, 16
Juan, Troy, AM3, 156, 157

Kearney, James A., Lt., 175
Kennaugh, John, 246
Keytrader, 222
Khian Star, 218, 219
Kielland Oil Rig, 203
Kindbom, Larry, Lt., 144
Kindley Air Force Base, 46, 49, 51
Kinkaid, USS, 279
Kirchner, Sig, Lt., 161, 162
Kiyo Maru, 246
Knowles, James, 305
Komsomolets Kirgizii, 160
Korenek, Bo, Lt., 152-54, 262
Kure Maru, 220

Lady D., 243
LaFlamme, Jack, Lt., 143
Lakonia, 222
Lamping, J. J., Lt., 82
Latimer, Jack, Cdr., 170
Laura, 156
Leisy, C. R., Lt., 140
Lewis, David, SKI, 205
Lex, Don, 256
Lexington, USS, 315
Liki Tiki, 256
Linsley, Bill, 262
Lionne, 183
Livingstone, Bob, Lt., 67
Lloyd's, 209, 235
Lombardi, 196
Loran, 167
Lotos, 38
Luinie Bell, 209, 235

Lurline, 190
Lynn, 235

MaCloy, USS, 284
McCulloch, Al, Lt., 99
McLendon, Bob, LCdr., 101
MaMullan, Ira, Cdr., 126
MacDiarmid, D. B., Capt., 113-17
Maffel, Kenneth, 246
Makadonia, 217
Mandoil II, 221
Marconi, 4, 23
Margit, 224
Marie Celeste, 219
Mariel exodus, 293-300
Marine Constructor, 8
Marine Sulphur Queen, 211, 215
Markstaller, Mike, Lt., 158, 159
Massachusetts Humane Society, 2, 3
Mathilde Bolten, 217
MATS, 171, 172
Medico, 24, 28
Mercy Hospital, 242
Mermaid, 248
Merrimack River CG Station, 240
Midgette, Ed, Lt., 262
Miget, 81-83
Military Airlift Command (MAC), 2,
    68, 78
Miller, Alan F., Cdr., 296
Miller, Ray, Cdr., 179, 183, 191
Milne, M. A., AT3, 158
Mirise, Kevin, Ens., 272
Mississippi, USS, 284
Miss Rachel, 162
Mogk, Kelly, ASM3, 158-60
Moly, 255
Monte Carlo, 90, 91
Mormackite, 217
Mormacport, 24
Morris, Geoff, SN, 249
Morro Castle, 222
Mount Baker, USS, 219
Muriel III, 259

Nantucket CG Station, 205
NAPO, 220
NASA, 94
National Airlines, 233
National Motor Lifeboat School, 248
National SAR Manual, 11, 80
National SAR Plan, 6
National SAR School, 12
National Transportation Safety Board (NTSB), 239
Naval Air Force Pacific, 87
Naval Air Station, North Island, 118, 120
Naval Helicopter Association, 158
Naval Ocean Systems Center, 92
New Flame, 255
Newton Ash, 182
New York Overseas Radio, 45, 46
Niagara Falls, USS, 62
Night Sun searchlight, 249
Nolan, Don, AT2, 156, 157
Noonan, Fred, 315
Noronic, 222
Northwest Airlines, 178, 232
Notre Dame, 191
Nova Scotia, 183
NVG (Night vision glasses), 93

Occidental Petroleum's Piper Alpha oil rig, 203
Ocean, 185
Ocean Eagle, 226
Ocean Joy, 279
Ocean Ranger, 201
Ocean Stations
  Bravo, 179, 187
  Charlie, 185
  Delta, 170
  Echo 167, 168, 172-77
  Hotel, 188, 189, 205
  November, 178
Odom, Bonnie, HM, 162
Ogg, Dick, Capt., 170
Olo Yumi, 295
O.M.I. Yukon, 95
Once More, 298

OPBAT Operation, 283
Operation Deep Freeze, 231
Orion I, 284
Osbourne, Edward M., 250
OSC (On Scene Commander), 9, 87
Ouellet, USS, 279

Pacific Arrow, 216
Pacific Star, 282
Pan American, 67
Parule Peupla, 7, 303
Patrick Air Force Base, 59
Patrick Sweeney, 217
Pendleton, 212
Pennsylvania, 83
Penrod Oil rig, 202
Peterson, Bill, LCdr., 158
Petit Bras D'Or, 231
Pfeiffer, Henry J., Lt., 138-41
Pilar, 255
Pt. Adams CG Station, 248
Pollack Rip Light Vessel, 211
Pope, Bob, LCdr., 153
Primevere, 252
Primrose, Angus, 251
Prince, Donald L., LCdr., 141
Princeton, 61
Prinsendam, 163-65
Profiteer, 282
Puerto Rico, 223

Queen of Bermuda, 8

RAF, 66
Rahman, James, Capt., 162, 307, 308
Ranger, USS, 9
RCC (Rescue Coordination Center), 9, 31, 45, 46, 52, 69, 72, 95, 119, 163, 164, 211
Reagan, Ronald, President, 11, 160
Red Diamond, 298
Reese, flight crewman, 159
Reinhart, flight engineer, 101
Rescue Swimmer School, 158
Reunion, 39

Revenue Center Service, 3, 4, 259, 275
Revis, James, AE2, 162
Rhea C., 96
Rice, Jim, AM, 143, 144
Rich Duchess, 246
Roberts, Michael, 59
Rogue Ruth, 265
Romance of the Skies, 231
Rose Marie, 284
Rose S., 216
Roulund, Victor, AD, 138-41
Route de Rhum Race, 96
Royale, 96
Royal National Lifeboat Institution
   (RNLI), 2
Rum War, 275
Russell, Bob, LCdr., 16-20, 151

Sabena Airline, 131
Saci, 9
Saipan, USS, 295, 296
Sale, Bill, LCdr., 268
San Diego County Medical Society, 31
San Jacinto, 215
San Patrick, 228
Santa Cruz II, 220
SARSAT/COSPAC, 12, 94, 97, 234,
   313
Satela, 302
Saufley, USS, 99-102
Saunders, Eileen, 108
Saylor, C. E., AD2, 158
Scandinavian Sea, 223
Scanlon, Michael, CWO, 304
Scheiber, Frederick J., Capt., 231
Seaforth Highlander, 201, 202
Seaman, Elmer, 256
Sea Witch, 221
Sees, William R., 260
Shalom, 221
Shangri La, USS, 87
Shannon, Roger, Ens., 225
Shannon, 225
Sharp Hospital, 29, 30
Sherman, John, AM2, 162
Shook, Paul R., Capt., 102, 103

Shoshi Maru, 95
Side Looking Airborne Radar *(SLAR)*,
   93, 230
Sierra Aronzuzu, 293
Skivvy Waver, 254
Skoiern IV, 96
Smith Voyager, 180, 185, 217
Sno Boy, 250
Sohio Intrepid, 165
Solberg, Harry, LCdr., 47, 126
Southern Districts, 210
Southern Isles, 210, 211
Southern Quest, 231
Sovereign of the Sky, 170
Spanish Fly, 74
Stabile, Benedict, RAdm., 294
Stad Gent, 234
Stations, Coast Guard, 14
Statts, Ralph J., 239
Steelhead, 265
Steel Vendor, 12
Stella 1, 279
Stockholm, 220
Stoldt Dagali, 221
Student Prince, 8
Suggs, Jack W., Lt., 171-77
Sun Quest, 93, 94
SURPIC, 7
Sutton, Vic, Lt., 29, 108
Suwaharu Maru, 220
Swanson, Jim, Lt., 128, 211

Tanguay, Joe, Lt., 37, 142
Tanker and Vessel Safety Act, 227
Taxi Dancer, 94
Taylor, Ray, Lt., 104
Terry, Henry, MD, 31-33
Tetsuho Maru, 228
Texaco Massachusetts, 221
Texas Tower, 16, 199
Thometz, George, LCdr., 138-41
Thorsen, Howard, VAdm., 287
Thu In, 293
Tiros, NOAA, 94
Titanic, 5, 7, 229

Torrey Canyon, 225
Toyama Maru, 196
Trangie, 194
Transoneida, 220
Tunks, Jeff, ASM2, 158
Tuxpan, 95, 216
Typhoon Carmen, 1

U.S. Life-saving Service, 3
U.S. Public Health Service, 39, 63

Vaughn, Bill, Cdr., 171
Veronica Express, 298
Virginia, 182
Viv-Aux, 63
Vukic, John, Lt., 115, 126

Walker, Tom, 306
Walters, Tom, LCdr., 156, 157
Ward, David, 305
Wasp, USS, 200, 220

Weather Bureau, 169
Webbe, Bernard C., BM, 212
Webber, Jim, 151
Weems, Ben, Lt., 60
West, Melvin, 245
West Air Company, 98
Whidden, J. B., LCdr., 158
Wild, Clay, Lt., 272
Williams, John, AD2, 16, 142
Williamsburg, 164, 165
Wilson, Bud, 256
Windfall, 234
W. S. Sims, USS, 279

Yeaton, Russell, PR, 240
Yost, Paul, Adm., Commandant, 228,
    287
Ypapanti, 272

Zhe-Sheng, 224